The Economics of Uncertainty and Information

The Economics of Uncertainty and Information

Jean-Jacques Laffont

translated by
John P. Bonin and Hélène Bonin

The MIT Press
Cambridge, Massachusetts
London, England

Fifth printing, 1995

Published in France under the title
Cours de théorie microeconomique. II. *Économie de l'incertain et de l'information* by
Economica, Paris, 1986
© 1986 Jean-Jacques Laffont

This book was set in Times Roman by Asco Trade Typesetting Ltd., Hong Kong, and
printed and bound in the United States of America.

Library of Congress Cataloging-in-Publication Data

Laffont, Jean-Jacques, 1947–
  [Cours de théorie microéconomique. Economie de l'incertain et de l'information.
English]
  The economics of uncertainty and information/Jean-Jacques Laffont; translated by
John P. Bonin and Hélène Bonin.

  p. cm.
  Translation of: Cours de théorie microéconomique. Vol. 2. Economie de l'incertain
et de l'information.
  Includes index.
  ISBN 0-262-12136-0
  1. Microeconomics. 2. Uncertainty. I. Title.
HB173.L2352513 1989
338.5—dc19   88-13250
                                                                          CIP

Contents

Preface

This book is the second of a series of volumes intended to be used in a year-long course in economic theory designed for advanced undergraduate or graduate students. Each volume can be read independently from the others. In the introduction to the present book, I will review the background that I assume of the reader.

Avoiding whenever possible complicated mathematics, I have sought to make available to the student a treatise in microeconomic theory that takes into account the latest developments. The chapters end with optional (starred) sections that may be skipped in an initial reading and with lists of references and recommended readings that will allow the student to delve more deeply into the topics that have been discussed. These readings will fill in some of the gaps in my presentation and encourage the student to do further research. The volume ends with a series of exercises, which are preceded by a series of worked problems. These problems and exercises will help the student evaluate his or her understanding of the course.

For this volume I have relied on the works of many authors. I am particularly indebted to my teachers, E. Malinvaud and K. Arrow. I have also benefited greatly from discussions with C. Henry, J. Green, R. Guesnerie, R. Kihlstrom, and E. Maskin and from the works of G. Debreu, R. Radner, O. Hart, B. Holmström, S. Grossman, M. Rothschild, and J. Stiglitz. I thank M. Boyer, J. Crémer, G. Dionne, M. Magill, P. Picard, M. Quinzii, and J. Tirole for their comments on some of the chapters.

Mathematical Notation and Definitions

Notation

∃   there exist(s)

∀   for any

∈   belongs to

⊂   is a subset of

⇔   if and only if

Let $x \in \mathbf{R}^n$ and $y \in \mathbf{R}^n$. Then

$$x \cdot y = \sum_{l=1}^{n} x_l y_l$$

denotes the scalar (dot) product.

Definitions

1. A binary relation R^i defined on X^i is

reflexive $\Leftrightarrow \forall x^i \in X^i,\, x^i R^i x^i.$
transitive $\Leftrightarrow \forall x^{i1}, x^{i2}, x^{i3} \in X^i,$
              $x^{i1} R^i x^{i2}$ and $x^{i2} R^i x^{i3} \Rightarrow x^{i1} R^i x^{i3}.$
complete $\Leftrightarrow \forall x^{i1}, x^{i2} \in X^i$
              $x^{i1} R^i x^{i2}$ or $x^{i2} R^i x^{i1}.$

A preordering is a transitive and reflexive binary relation.

2. A set $Y \subset \mathbf{R}^2$ is convex $\Leftrightarrow \forall x \in Y, \forall y \in Y, \forall \lambda \in [0,1], \lambda x + (1-\lambda)y \in Y.$

A function $f(.)$ defined on $\mathbf{R}^L$ is quasi-concave $\Leftrightarrow \forall \lambda \in \mathbf{R},\ \{x : x \in \mathbf{R}^L,\ f(x) \leq \lambda\}$ is convex.

3. A preference relation R^i is convex $\Leftrightarrow \forall x^{i1} \in X^i,\ \forall x^{i2} \in X^i,\ \forall \lambda \in [0,1],$
$x^{i1} R^i x^{i2} \Leftrightarrow (\lambda x^{i1} + (1-\lambda)x^{i2}) R^i x^{i2}.$

A function $f(.)$ defined on $\mathbf{R}^L$ is concave $\Leftrightarrow \forall \lambda \in [0,1], \forall x \in \mathbf{R}^L, \forall y \in \mathbf{R}^L,$
$f(\lambda x + (1-\lambda)y) \geq \lambda f(x) + (1-\lambda)f(y).$

The Economics of Uncertainty and Information

Introduction

Before beginning this book, the reader should be familiar with probability theory and should have a complete understanding of the two fundamental theorems of welfare economics derived from the "basic microeconomic model." These theorems are developed, for example, in the first five chapters of Edmond Malinvaud's *Lectures in Microeconomic Theory*. In this introduction, I review briefly their significance after presenting the notation of the basic model that will be used throughout. I conclude with an outline of the book devoted to the economics of uncertainty and information.

I.1   Notation

The economy consists of L economic goods indexed by $l = 1, \ldots, L$, I consumers indexed by $i = 1, \ldots, I$, and J firms indexed by $j = 1, \ldots, J$. The indices corresponding to economic agents will always be superscripts, and those corresponding to goods will be subscripts.

Let X^i be the consumption set for consumer i; this set is often taken to be the positive orthant $\mathbf{R}_+^L$.[1] The quantity consumed of good l by consumer i is represented by x_l^i, and $x^i = (x_1^i, \ldots, x_L^i) \in X^i$ characterizes the consumption bundle of consumer i. Consumer i's preferences are represented either by a complete preordering (that is, by a complete, reflexive, transitive binary relation)[2] denoted by R^i or by a utility function denoted by $U^i(.)$. Then $x^{i1} R^i x^{i2}$ means: consumer i either prefers the bundle of goods x^{i1} to the bundle of goods x^{i2} or is indifferent between them. Substituting P^i for R^i indicates strict preference. The preordering R^i is represented by a utility function $U^i(.)$ if and only if

$$x^{i1} R^i x^{i2} \Leftrightarrow U^i(x^{i1}) \geqslant U^i(x^{i2}),$$

$$x^{i1} P^i x^{i2} \Leftrightarrow U^i(x^{i1}) > U^i(x^{i2}).$$

Consumer i's initial endowment is denoted by $w^i \in \mathbf{R}_+^L$. Let $y^j = (y_1^j, \ldots, y_L^j)$ be the production vector for producer j. We usually follow the convention that outputs (products) have a positive sign and inputs (factors) a negative sign. Essentially, this convention permits us to write the profit of firm j as the inner (dot) product

---

1. $\mathbf{R}_+^L = \{x: x \in \mathbf{R}^L, x_l \geqslant 0, l = 1, \ldots, L\}$.
2. See the mathematical definitions, p. ix.

$$p \cdot y^j = \sum_{l=1}^{L} p_l y_l^j$$

where $p \in \mathbf{R}_+^L$ specifies the price vector.[3] The technology of firm j is represented either by the production set $Y^j \subset \mathbf{R}^L$ or by the production function $f^j(y^j) = 0$. When the firms are privately owned, θ^{ij} indicates the share of firm j owned by consumer i, $j = 1, \ldots, J$, $i = 1, \ldots, I$.

I.2   The Fundamental Theorems of Welfare Economics

A *private property competitive equilibrium* is characterized by a price vector $p^* \in \mathbf{R}_+^L$ and an allocation $(x^{*1}, \ldots, x^{*I}; y^{*1}, \ldots, y^{*J})$ such that

(i) y^{*j} maximizes profit $p^* \cdot y^j$ in the production set Y^j, that is,

$$p^* \cdot y^{*j} \geqslant p^* \cdot y^j \quad \text{for any } y^j \text{ in } Y^j \qquad j = 1, \ldots, J;$$

(ii) x^{*i} maximizes utility $U^i(x^i)$ in the budget set given by

$$B^i = \left\{ x^i \colon x^i \in X^i \text{ and } p^* \cdot x^i \leqslant p^* \cdot w^i + \sum_{j=1}^{J} \theta^{ij} p^* \cdot y^{*j} \right\} \qquad i = 1, \ldots, I;$$

(iii)   supply equals demand on all markets,

$$\sum_{i=1}^{I} x^{*i} = \sum_{j=1}^{J} y^{*j} + \sum_{i=1}^{I} w^i.$$

The assumption of competitive behavior indicates that each agent takes prices as given: we say that he exhibits parametric behavior with respect to prices. We justify this assumption by modeling the economy with a large number of economic agents so that each agent is "negligible."

An allocation $(x^1, \ldots, x^I; y^1, \ldots, y^J)$ is said to be *feasible* if and only if

(i) $x^i \in X^i$ for $i = 1, \ldots, I$,

(ii) $y^j \in Y^j$ for $j = 1, \ldots, J$,

(iii) $\displaystyle\sum_{i=1}^{I} x^i \leqslant \sum_{j=1}^{J} y^j + \sum_{i=1}^{I} w^i.$

3. When the consumer supplies labor, the labor component of his consumption bundle also has a negative sign. Then the consumption set cannot be characterized by $\mathbf{R}_+^L$.

A *Pareto optimum* is a feasible allocation $(x^{*1}, \ldots, x^{*I}; y^{*1}, \ldots, y^{*J})$ such that there exists no other feasible allocation $(\tilde{x}^1, \ldots, \tilde{x}^I; \tilde{y}^1, \ldots, \tilde{y}^J)$ that would give at least as much utility to all consumers and more utility to at least one consumer, or

$$U^i(\tilde{x}^i) \geqslant U^i(x^{*i}) \qquad i = 1, \ldots, I,$$

and there exist i' such that

$$U^{i'}(\tilde{x}^{i'}) > U^{i'}(x^{*i'}).$$

In this book, we will make strong assumptions on the preferences and on technology in order to facilitate the presentation of problems specific to the economics of uncertainty and information. In this spirit the two fundamental theorems of welfare economics are presented with convenient assumptions.

THEOREM 1   If $U^i(.)$ is strictly increasing with respect to each of its arguments for $i = 1, \ldots, I$, a private property competitive equilibrium (if it exists) is a Pareto optimum.

To be able to prove the existence of a private property competitive equilibrium, we must make much stronger assumptions. However, the Pareto optimality property of the competitive equilibrium (if it exists) is quite general and can be grasped intuitively. Theorem 1 indicates that equilibrium price signals are sufficient to coordinate decentralized economic activities in a satisfactory way according to the Pareto criterion. By his individual maximization behavior, each economic agent responds to prices by equating his marginal rates of substitution (for consumers) and transformation (for firms) to these prices. Since all agents face the same prices, all the marginal rates are equated to each other in the equilibrium. Combined with market equilibria, these equalities characterize Pareto optima in a convex environment.[4]

Although this intuition is useful in interpreting the role of prices, it does not help us understand the optimality of the competitive equilibrium (when it exists) in nonconvex environments. For this purpose, a very simple argument by contradiction will suffice. If the competitive equilibrium is dominated by a feasible allocation (refer to the definition of a Pareto

---

4. By a convex environment, I mean nonincreasing returns for firms and convex preferences for consumers.

optimum), then the value of the consumption bundle for consumer i in this new allocation, at the competitive equilibrium prices, is greater than the value of his endowment (otherwise, he would have chosen this allocation in the competitive equilibrium). For every other consumer, the value of his consumption bundle in the new allocation, at the competitive equilibrium prices, must be at least as large as the value of his endowment. Consequently the new allocation cannot be a feasible allocation.

The second theorem, although just as fundamental, is more difficult to understand intuitively.

THEOREM 2   If $U^i(.)$ is continuous, quasi concave,[5] and strictly increasing on the consumption set $X^i = \mathbf{R}_+^L$ with $w_l^i > 0, l = 1, \ldots, L, i = 1, \ldots, I$, and if Y^j is convex, $j = 1, \ldots, J$, for any given Pareto-optimal allocation $(x^{*1}, \ldots, x^{*I}; y^{*1}, \ldots, y^{*J})$, there exists a price vector $p^* \in \mathbf{R}_+^L$ such that

(i) x^{*i} maximizes $U^i(x^i)$ in the set

$$\{x^i : x^i \in \mathbf{R}_+^L, p^* \cdot x^i \leqslant p^* \cdot x^{*i}\} \qquad i = 1, \ldots, I,$$

(ii) y^{*j} maximizes $p^* \cdot y^j$ in $Y^j, j = 1, \ldots, J$.

Thus, under the convexity assumptions, Pareto-optimal allocations may be decentralized in the following sense. If we give each consumer an income[6] of $R^{*i} = p^* \cdot x^{*i}$ and if we announce to all economic agents the price vector p^*, profit maximization by firm $j, j = 1, \ldots, J$, and utility maximization by consumer i subject to the budget constraint $p^* \cdot x^i \leqslant R^{*i}$, $i = 1, \ldots, I$, lead to consumption and production plans that are compatible and that coincide with the chosen Pareto-optimal allocation. This result is fundamental to understanding decentralized planning and can be interpreted in a private property economy as follows: Pareto optimality of the private property competitive equilibrium is satisfactory with respect to the efficiency criterion, but it may lead to undesirable income distributions. The second theorem states: whichever Pareto optimum we wish to decentralize (therefore whichever Pareto optimum corresponds to the justice criterion taken), it is possible to decentralize this allocation as a competitive equilibrium so long as the incomes of the agents are chosen appropriately, that is, in a private property economy so long as the appropriate lump-sum transfers are made.

5. See the mathematical definitions at the front of the book.
6. R is used to denote an income as well as a preordering.

I.3   The Purpose of This Volume

The introduction of uncertainty into the basic microeconomic model enables us to make decisive progress toward modeling concrete economic problems. However, it raises difficult conceptual issues.

The first part of the book presents the particular form taken by the rationality hypothesis in a stochastic environment and develops a number of technical tools such as the notion of risk aversion, the measure of risk, the notion of certainty equivalent, and the concept of information structure.

The second part formalizes exchange in competitive markets with various market structures and studies the normative properties of these market structures. The roles of a stock market and of insurance companies in the sharing of risks are made precise. This second part in which the information structures of agents are fixed can be defined as the economics of uncertainty.

In the last part information structures are endogenous, and we enter the economics of information. The possibility of personalizing exchanges enables us to make contracts that, directly or indirectly, lead to information exchanges. Moreover some economic variables such as prices create informational externalities—that is, they transmit information for those who observe them carefully. Finally, economic agents can attempt to acquire directly information through the use of experts or by various search activities.

All those phenomena lead us quite far from the elementary Walrasian model, but their analysis may comfort us in the relevance of an open neoclassical approach to economics.

1 Individual Behavior under Uncertainty

Neoclassical theory can be described as a systematic exploration of the implications of rational behavior in economics. Situations of uncertainty sometimes take the neoclassical paradigm of rationality to the limits of acceptability as a description of economic behavior. Nevertheless, if we consider neoclassical theory as an approximation to be tested empirically, it continues to have descriptive power. Indeed, the potential for falsification, which distinguishes neoclassical theory from some quasi-metaphysical theories, is its major asset. The neoclassical paradigm also leads to the construction of a relatively simple normative theory, which provides a mode of thought for political economics.

In this chapter, we present and discuss the fundamentals that we adopt to describe individual behavior in uncertain (stochastic) environments.

1.1 The Expected Utility Hypothesis

Let $(\Omega, \mathcal{O}, \mu)$ be a probability space[1] that represents the space of the states of nature. Ω is the set of the states of nature; $\omega \in \Omega$ is a complete description of the exogenous variables of the model considered; $\mathcal{O}$ is a σ-algebra of events which, in the case where Ω is finite, is simply the set of subsets of Ω. Then an event is a subset E of Ω, and μ is a measure of objective probability over the events of $\mathcal{O}$.

An act $a(.)$ is a mapping of $(\Omega, \mathcal{O}, \mu)$ into a space of consequences C, which will be identified hereafter with $\mathbf{R}$ to represent monetary consequences. Each act induces a probability measure π on $(C = \mathbf{R}, \mathcal{B})$ where $\mathcal{B}$ is the Borelian σ-algebra. We have

$$\forall B \in \mathcal{B}, \quad \pi(B) = \mu[a^{-1}(B)].$$

EXAMPLE An act as a lottery ticket: Consider a ticket that pays \$100 if an odd number is drawn from an urn of 10 equiprobable consequences numbered 1 through 10 (see figure 1.1):

$$\forall \omega \in E \qquad a(\omega) = \$100$$

where E is the set of odd numbers less than 10, and

$$\forall \omega \in \bar{E} \qquad a(\omega) = 0$$

$$\pi(100) = \mu(E) = \tfrac{1}{2}$$

---

1. For an introduction to the calculus of probabilities, see A. Monfort, *Cours de probabilités* (Economica, 1980).

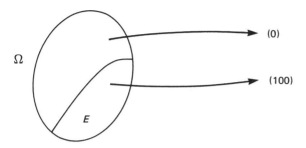

Figure 1.1

where $\bar{E}$ is the complement of E in Ω.

A *lottery* will be defined as the probability distribution on **R** induced by the lottery ticket. In general, we characterize a typical lottery $a = [x, \pi]$ by a vector $[x_1, \ldots, x_S]$ of monetary prizes x_s for each state of nature $s = 1, \ldots, S$ (the support of the distribution) and a vector of probabilities[2]

$$[\pi_1, \ldots, \pi_S], \quad \sum_{s=1}^{S} \pi_s = 1.$$

The problem to be considered is how a rational agent evaluates such a lottery—in other words, how should the value of the lottery ticket be computed? There is a 50 percent chance of winning \$100. Some might suggest that we use the expected value of the monetary consequences, that is, $0.5 \times \$100 + 0.5 \times \$0 = \$50$, or, in general,

$$U(a) = \sum_{s=1}^{S} \pi_s x_s.$$

This approach conjures up the St. Petersburg paradox. Consider a repeated coin toss and the lottery that pays \$2^n if a head appears for the first time on the nth toss:

$$U(a) = \lim_{N \to \infty} \sum_{n=1}^{N} \frac{1}{2^n} \cdot 2^n = +\infty.$$

According to the expected value criterion, this lottery has infinite value, although no one may be willing to pay \$1,000 to play this game. Hence the paradox.

2. We assume that Ω is finite.

Daniel Bernoulli's explanation of this paradox is that agents have decreasing marginal utility for money, and so they evaluate any lottery by the expected utility of its different consequences. For a utility function over the consequences, Bernoulli proposes the logarithmic function

$$U(a) = \lim_{n=1} \sum^{\infty} \frac{1}{2^n} \text{Log } 2^n = \text{Log } 4.$$

This computed amount is more like what you would be willing to pay to play the game.

However, decreasing marginal utility of income is not sufficient to preclude St. Petersburg-type paradoxes. As long as the function $u(.)$ is not bounded above, we can take a sequence x_n such that $u(x_n) = 2^n$. Then, again, we are confronted with the paradox. If lotteries are evaluated according to the expected utility of the consequences, we must assume that this utility is bounded above to avoid such obvious contradictions concerning the behavior of agents whom we have every reason to believe are rational.

The *expected utility hypothesis* represents the rational behavior of an agent under uncertainty by the maximization of

$$\sum_{s=1}^{S} \pi_s u(x_s)$$

for some function $u(.)$ that is nondecreasing and bounded. This hypothesis affords two possible interpretations. The first accepts the above as a working hypothesis and deduces empirically testable implications. If empirical work does not allow us to reject these implications, we conclude that agents behave as if they maximize expected utility. The second, a normative interpretation, consists in demonstrating that a rational agent must maximize his expected utility. Then rationality is defined as the consistency of choices among lotteries characterized by several axioms.[3]

To formalize this second interpretation, we consider the space of lotteries $\mathcal{M}$ over the finite support $[x_1, \ldots, x_S]$. $\mathcal{M}$ is equivalent to the simplex of $\mathbf{R}^S$:

$$a \in \mathcal{M} \Leftrightarrow a = [x_1, \ldots, x_S; \pi_1, \ldots, \pi_S], \quad \sum_{s=1}^{S} \pi_s = 1.$$

3. The methodology here is analogous to that which leads to the definition of rational choice in the absence of uncertainty using the axioms of transitivity, reflexivity, and completeness of a binary relation describing the choices.

First we assume that the choices of a rational agent between lotteries are represented by a preordering $\gtrsim$ that is complete and continuous. In other words, the preference binary relation $\gtrsim$ satisfies the following properties:

(a)   reflexivity $a^1 \gtrsim a^1, \quad \forall a^1 \in \mathcal{M}$,

(b)   transitivity $a^1 \gtrsim a^2$ and $a^2 \gtrsim a^3 \Rightarrow a^1 \gtrsim a^3, \quad \forall a^1, a^2, a^3 \in \mathcal{M}$,

(c)   completeness $\forall a^1, a^2 \in \mathcal{M}$,   either $a^1 \gtrsim a^2$,   or $a^2 \gtrsim a^1$,

(d)   continuity $\forall a^1 \in \mathcal{M}$, $\{a : a \gtrsim a^1\}$,   and $\{a : a^1 \gtrsim a\}$ are closed sets (for the topology of $\mathbf{R}^S)^4$

From utility theory (Debreu 1966), we know that there exists a continuous and nondecreasing function $U(.)$ that is defined up to a monotone increasing transformation that represents $\gtrsim$, that is,

$$a^1 \gtrsim a^2 \Leftrightarrow U(a^1) \geqslant U(a^2),$$

$$a^1 \succ a^2 \Leftrightarrow U(a^1) > U(a^2).$$

As an introduction to their theory of games, von Neumann and Morgenstern (1944) proposed axioms that purport to represent rational choice under uncertainty. From these they deduced that $U(.)$ can be taken to be linear in the probabilities:

$$U(a) = \sum_{s=1}^{S} \pi_s u(x_s)$$

where $u(.)$ is a utility function defined up to an increasing affine transformation. We call $u(.)$ the *von Neumann-Morgenstern utility function*, which we often abbreviate as the VNM utility function.

1.2   The Theory of von Neumann and Morgenstern

An agent's rationality is characterized by three axioms:

AXIOM 1   The agent has a complete preordering on the space $\mathcal{M}$ of lotteries defined over the consequences.

This axiom indicates, in particular, that the agent is indifferent to the way

---

4. For an introduction to topology, see J. Dieudonné, *Eléments d'analyse* (Gauthier-Villars, 1969).

in which the consequences are obtained. By enlarging the space of consequences as needed, it is always possible to model the problem in this
way, sometimes at the cost of increasing the complexity of the space of
consequences.

AXIOM 2   Continuity: $\forall a^1, a^2, a^3 \in \mathcal{M}$ such that $a^1 \gtrsim a^2 \gtrsim a^3$ there exists
$\alpha \in [0, 1]$ such that $\alpha a^1 + (1 - \alpha)a^3 \sim a^2$.

AXIOM 3   Independence:

$\forall a^1, a^2 \in \mathcal{M}$ such that $a^1 \succ a^2$, $\forall \alpha \in \,]0, 1[$, $\forall a \in \mathcal{M}$,

$\quad \alpha a^1 + (1 - \alpha)a \succ \alpha a^2 + (1 - \alpha)a;$

$\forall a^1, a^2 \in \mathcal{M}$ such that $a^1 \sim a^2$, $\forall \alpha \in \,]0, 1[$, $\forall a \in \mathcal{M}$,

$\quad \alpha a^1 + (1 - \alpha)a \sim \alpha a^2 + (1 - \alpha)a.$

We interpret $\alpha a^1 + (1 - \alpha)a^2$ as follows: if

$$a^1 = [x_1, \ldots, x_S; \pi_1^1, \ldots, \pi_S^1], \quad a^2 = [x_1, \ldots, x_S; \pi_1^2, \ldots, \pi_S^2],$$

$$\alpha a^1 + (1 - \alpha)a^2 = [x_1, \ldots, x_S; \alpha\pi_1^1 + (1 - \alpha)\pi_1^2, \ldots, \alpha\pi_S^1 + (1 - \alpha)\pi_S^2].$$

For example, if

$$a^1 = \left[0, 100; \frac{99}{100}, \frac{1}{100}\right], \quad a^2 = \left[0, 100; \frac{97}{100}, \frac{3}{100}\right], \quad \text{and} \quad \alpha = \frac{1}{2},$$

$$a = \frac{1}{2}a^1 + \frac{1}{2}a^2 = \left[0, 100; \frac{98}{100}, \frac{2}{100}\right].$$

Now $\frac{1}{2}a^1 + \frac{1}{2}a^2$ is interpreted as a compound lottery in which we begin
by drawing between lottery tickets a^1 and a^2. In effect,

$\Pr(100) = \Pr(\text{of having ticket } a^1) \times \Pr(100|a^1)$

$\qquad\quad + \Pr(\text{of having ticket } a^2) \times \Pr(100|a^2)$

$\qquad = \alpha\pi_2^1 + (1 - \alpha)\pi_2^2$

$\qquad = \frac{1}{2} \times \frac{1}{100} + \frac{1}{2} \times \frac{3}{100} = \frac{2}{100}.$

Axiom 3 indicates that if ticket a^1 is preferred to a^2, any pair of compound
lotteries $\tilde{a}^1, \tilde{a}^2$ constructed using a^1 and a^2 with the same complement leads

to the preordering $\tilde{a}^1 \succ \tilde{a}^2$. The preordering of $\tilde{a}^1$ and $\tilde{a}^2$ is *independent* of the complement a. Von Neumann and Morgenstern show that these three axioms imply the expected utility hypothesis.

In what follows we sketch a proof of this result in the case where the support is reduced to three points, x_1, x_2, and x_3,[5] such that $x_1 > x_2 > x_3$. Since $u(.)$ is defined only up to an affine transformation, we can normalize $u(.)$ in the following way:

$$u(x_1) = 1,$$

$$u(x_3) = 0.$$

By axiom 2, we know that there exists $\alpha \in [0, 1]$ such that

$$\alpha x_1 + (1 - \alpha)x_3 \sim x_2.$$

Let $u(x_2) = \alpha$. Therefore axiom 2 allows us to construct the function $u(.)$.

It is now sufficient to show that the expected value of $u(.)$ indeed represents the ordering. By definition,

$$U(a) = \sum_{s=1}^{3} \pi_s u(x_s) = \pi_1 + \alpha\pi_2.$$

Since $\sum_{s=1}^{3} \pi_s = 1$, any lottery can be represented by a point in an equilateral triangle of height equal to 1 (see figure 1.2).

If $U(.)$ can be written as above, the indifference curves are straight parallel lines in the coordinate system $x_3 x_1$, $x_3 x_2$ (figure 1.3).

Let N be the point representing the lottery $\alpha x_1 + (1 - \alpha)x_3$. Let M be any lottery; $M \notin Nx_2$. Consider the line parallel to Nx_2 that intersects $x_1 x_3$ at A and $x_1 x_2$ at B. Then we have

$$\frac{Ax_1}{Nx_1} = \frac{Bx_1}{x_1 x_2} = \lambda.$$

From axiom 3 we know that a_A and a_B are equivalent[6] because

$$a_A = \lambda a_N + (1 - \lambda)x_1,$$

$$a_B = \lambda x_2 + (1 - \lambda)x_1,$$

---

5. The outcomes in x_s can be multidimensional (see Malinvaud 1969).
6. a_x is the lottery corresponding to point x in figure 1.3. We denote $x_i, i = 1, 2, 3$, as the lottery that yields x_i with probability 1.

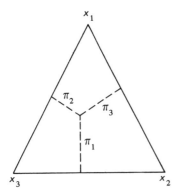

Figure 1.2

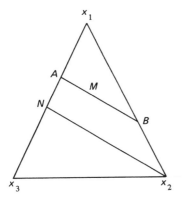

Figure 1.3

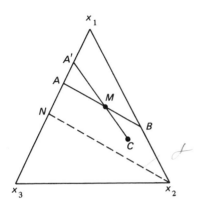

Figure 1.4

and $a_N \sim x_2$ (by construction) implies $a_A \sim a_B$. Any point M on AB is equivalent to A. In effect,

$$a_M = \delta a_A + (1 - \delta)a_B,$$

$$a_A = \delta a_A + (1 - \delta)a_A;$$

then $a_A \sim a_B$ and axiom 3 imply $a_M \sim a_A$. It remains for us to show that there exist no other lotteries in the equivalence class AB.

Assume, on the contrary, that there exists $C \notin AB$ with $a_C \sim a_M$, $M \in AB$. Let A' be the intersection of the line MC with the axis $x_1 x_3$ (see figure 1.4). Then $a_{A'} \sim a_M$. To demonstrate this, let us assume the contrary:

$$a_M = v a_C + (1 - v)a_{A'} \sim v a_M + (1 - v)a_{A'} \qquad \text{(axiom 3)}$$

and

$$a_M = v a_M + (1 - v)a_M.$$

Either $a_{A'} \succ a_M$ or $a_M \succ a_{A'}$ is contradicted by axiom 3. Now we have $a_{A'} \sim a_A$ since $a_A \sim a_M$. However, this leads to a further contradiction:

$$a_{A'} = \theta x_1 + (1 - \theta)a_A,$$

$$a_A = \theta a_A + (1 - \theta)a_A.$$

In this case $x_1 \succ a_A$ implies $a_{A'} \succ a_A$ by axiom 3.[7]

7. See Montbrial (1971), ch. 1, for some extensions.

By generalizing the above arguments, we obtain theorem 1:

THEOREM 1   Given axioms 1 through 3, there exists a nondecreasing continuous utility function defined up to an increasing affine transformation such that

$$a^1 \underset{(>)}{\gtrsim} a^2 \Leftrightarrow \sum_{s=1}^{S} \pi_s^1 u(x_s) \underset{(>)}{\geq} \sum_{s=1}^{S} \pi_s^2 u(x_s).$$

The axiom of rationality that has been debated the most is the axiom of independence. In particular, Allais (1953) questions it on the basis of experimental results (see also Kahneman and Tversky 1981). The following example illustrates Allais's paradox:

$$a^1 = [10,000, 0; 0.1, 0.9] \qquad a^2 = [15,000, 0; 0.09, 0.91]$$

$$a^3 = [10,000, 0; 1, 0] \qquad\quad a^4 = [15,000, 0; 0.9, 0.1].$$

Many of us might prefer a^2 to a^1 and a^3 to a^4. However, if we denote a^0 as the lottery that yields 0 with probability 1,

$$a^1 = \frac{1}{10} a^3 + \frac{9}{10} a^0$$

$$a^2 = \frac{1}{10} a^4 + \frac{9}{10} a^0.$$

Rational behavior in the sense of axiom 3 requires that an agent who prefers a^3 to a^4 should also prefer a^1 to a^2. According to Savage (1954), any individual who is confronted with this inconsistency of his choices will reconsider his decisions. According to others, the criticism is more serious and reflects the impossibility of defining pure lotteries that isolate the phenomena of pleasure from playing the game or potential regret. Here a rational agent can accept the pleasure of greater risk in a^2 than a^1, and yet refuse the risk of loss associated with a^4 compared to the sure prospect of a^3.

1.3   Nonprobabilistic Consequences

In the von Neumann-Morgenstern theory we assume the existence of a measure of objective probability that defines risk unambiguously. Quite often, and in particular in economic problems, such a specification is impossible. Only the space of acts $\mathscr{A}$, which associate consequences in C to the events in a measurable space $(\Omega, \mathcal{O})$ of states of nature, is clearly given.

Savage constructs a theory in which he takes as given a complete choice preordering $\gtrsim$ on $\mathscr{A}$ and in which rational behavior under uncertainty is specified by seven axioms on this preordering. From these seven axioms he deduces the existence of both a subjective probability distribution and a utility function such that the preordering $\gtrsim$ is represented by the expected value of this utility function, the expectation being taken with respect to this subjective probability.

To do this, Savage defines first conditional preferences. Let $E \in \mathcal{O}$ be an event. He defines the preference conditional on E by $\gtrsim|E$, satisfying

$$a \gtrsim_{|E} a' \Leftrightarrow \bar{a} \gtrsim \bar{a}'$$

where

$$\bar{a}(\omega) = a(\omega) \qquad \text{if } \omega \in E$$

$$\bar{a}'(\omega) = a'(\omega) \qquad \text{if } \omega \in E$$

$$\bar{a}(\omega) = \bar{a}'(\omega) \qquad \text{if } \omega \in \bar{E}.$$

Therefore the comparison of a and a' conditional on E is done by using the ordering on the acts, after modifying a and a' so that they coincide on $\bar{E}$, the complement of E. For this definition to be consistent, $\gtrsim_{|E}$ must be independent of the way in which the acts are completed on $\bar{E}$, a condition that can be expressed as the following:

AXIOM 1   Conditional preferences exist.[8]

Like the axiom of independence in the VNM theory, this axiom has been criticized.

Savage continues by defining constant acts. For any $x \in C$, the constant act a_x is defined by

$$a_x(\omega) = x \qquad \forall \omega \in \Omega.$$

AXIOM 2 $\forall x \in C, a_x \in \mathscr{A}$.

This axiom allows the direct construction of a complete preordering $\gtrsim$ on

---

8. Notice the analogy with the assumption of independence of irrelevant alternatives in social choice theory (see Laffont 1988, ch. 4).

the space of consequences according to

$$x \gtrsim x' \Leftrightarrow a_x \gtrsim a_{x'}.$$

This axiom has been criticized because there may exist no acts that guarantee an outcome. Nevertheless, it is sufficient to imagine the existence of these acts.

In order to have a true preference over consequences, the definition must be independent of the feasible states of nature.

AXIOM 3   If $E \neq \emptyset$, $a_x \gtrsim_{|E} a_{x'} \Leftrightarrow x \gtrsim x'$.

Then Savage defines qualitative probabilities. Let $E \in \mathcal{O}$, and $E' \in \mathcal{O}$ be two events, and let x and x' be two consequences such that $x \succ x'$. Construct acts a and a' in the following way:

If $\omega \in E$: $a(\omega) = x$

$\quad \omega \in \bar{E}$: $a(\omega) = x'$.

If $\omega \in E'$: $a'(\omega) = x$

$\quad \omega \in \bar{E}'$: $a'(\omega) = x'$.

If $a \gtrsim a'$, we say that the qualitative probability[9] of E is at least as great as that of E':

$$E \hat{\gtrsim} E'.$$

From this construction we see how it is possible to elicit subjective probabilities from the agent by asking appropriate questions about choices over lotteries. For the relation $\hat{\gtrsim}$ to be well defined, however, it must be independent of the consequences used in the definition. Therefore we need:

AXIOM 4   All the events are comparable in qualitative probability.

Finally there are some technical axioms.

AXIOM 5 $\exists a, a' \in \mathcal{A}$ such that $a \succ a'$ or $a' \succ a$.

AXIOM 6   (continuity axiom, which implies Ω is infinite)   If $a \succ a'$, for any $x \in C$ there exists a finite partition σ of events of Ω such that if a or a' is

---

9. We call this qualitative probability because at this stage we do not yet know if the function that represents $\hat{\gtrsim}$ satisfies the probability axioms.

modified on an event of σ so that x becomes its consequence given this event, the strict preference of a over a' is not changed by this transformation.

AXIOM 7   Let $a \in \mathscr{A}$. Then

$$a' \gtrsim_{|E} a_{a(\omega)} \qquad \forall \omega \in E \text{ implies } a' \gtrsim_{|E} a,$$

$$a_{a(\omega)} \gtrsim_{|E} a' \qquad \forall \omega \in E \text{ implies } a \gtrsim_{|E} a'.$$

Now we can report Savage's result.

THEOREM 2   Given axioms 1 through 7, there exists a unique probability measure μ defined on $(\Omega, \mathcal{O})$ and a continuous, nondecreasing, and bounded function $u(.)$ defined up to an increasing affine transformation such that

$$a \gtrsim a' \Leftrightarrow \int_{\Omega} u(a(\omega))d\mu(\omega) \geq \int_{\Omega} u(a'(\omega))d\mu(\omega),$$

$$\mu(.) \quad \text{is such that} \quad E' \hat{\gtrsim} E \Leftrightarrow \mu(E') \geq \mu(E),$$

and μ is called the *agent's subjective probability*.[10]

One method of proof consists in using axiom 4 to construct a complete preordering over the events. If this preordering is continuous, we can represent it by a continuous function (classical utility theory), and it remains to show that this function satisfies the definitions of a probability measure. Given that $\mu(.)$ is well defined, we are brought back to the von Neumann-Morgenstern problem.

There are many other ways to deal with the nonprobabilistic universe. However, these often correspond to using implicitly the criterion of expected utility with a particular utility function (the maximin criterion; see section 2.3) or with a particular probability measure (the Laplace criterion; all the events are equiprobable).

We could refuse to aggregate the utility functions defined over certain consequences to functions summarizing the valuation of the risky environment. Then we would be faced with a multicriteria-type analysis. Notice how, from the mathematical perspective, the problem of aggregating utilities for the same agent over different states of nature is related to the aggregation of the utility functions of different agents in the construction of a social

10. See Guesnerie and Jaffray (1971) for a detailed explanation of Savage's proof.

welfare function. Utilitarianism is analogous to the Laplace criterion, and the Rawlsian criterion is analogous to the maximin criterion.

Today there are numerous theories that generalize expected utility theory (see Machina 1982). In this book we will only assume either that agents have complete preorderings over their acts or that their preferences can be represented by the expected utility hypothesis.

Suggested Readings

Montbrial, Th. de (1971), ch. 1.   A summary of several extensions of the von Neumann-Morgenstern theory.

Kahneman, D., and A. Tversky (1979).   A collection of experiments contradicting the expected utility hypothesis.

Machina, M. (1982).   A synthesis of the literature and a more general theory than the von Neumann-Morgenstern theory.

References

Allais, M. 1953. "Le Comportement de l'homme rationnel devant le risque. Critique des postulats de l'école américaine." *Econometrica* 21:503–546.

Debreu, G. 1966. *Théorie de la valeur*. Dunod, Paris.

Guesnerie, R. and J. Y. Jaffray. 1971. "Probabilités subjectives et utilité de Von Neumann-Morgenstern." *Bulletin de Mathématiques Economiques*, no. 6. Université Paris 6.

Kahneman, D, and A. Tversky. 1979. "Prospect Theory: An Analysis of Decision under Risk." *Econometrica* 47:263–291.

Laffont, J.-J. 1988. *Fundamentals of Public Economics*. MIT Press, Cambridge.

Machina, M. 1982. "Expected Utility Analysis without the Independence Axiom." *Econometrica* 50:277–323.

Malinvaud, E. 1969. *Leçons de théorie microéconomique*. Dunod, Paris.

Montbrial, T. de. 1971. *Economie théorique*, PUF, Paris.

Neumann, J. von, and O. Morgenstern. (1944). *Theory of Games and Economic Behavior*. Princeton University Press.

Savage, L. 1954. *The Foundations of Statistics*. Wiley, New York.

2 Measuring Risk Aversion and Risk

In this chapter we present and illustrate, as simply as possible, several technical tools that have proved to be useful in the economics of uncertainty. We assume that the VNM utility function $u(.)$ is defined on $\mathbf{R}_+$.[1] Generalizing these concepts to many dimensions is not easy to do. (see section 2.7).

2.1 Measures of Risk Aversion

Let $\tilde{x}$ be a stochastic variable, or a lottery defined by $[x_1,\ldots,x_S;\pi_1,\ldots,\pi_S]$ so that

$$U(\tilde{x}) = \sum_{s=1}^{S} \pi_s u(x_s) = Eu(\tilde{x}).$$

Concavity of $u(.)$ represents risk aversion. For example, concavity implies that

$$\tfrac{1}{2}u(x_1) + \tfrac{1}{2}u(x_2) < u(\tfrac{1}{2}x_1 + \tfrac{1}{2}x_2).$$

On the other hand, risk-loving is represented by the convexity of $u(.)$. Faced with a lottery ticket that yields x_1 with probability 0.5 and x_2 with probability 0.5, the agent prefers to this lottery a certain return equal to the mean of the returns from the ticket (see figure 2.1). We define the certainty equivalent of $\tilde{x}$, $EC_{\tilde{x}}$, as the deterministic return that the agent views as equivalent to the stochastic variable $\tilde{x}$, that is,

$$u(EC_{\tilde{x}}) = Eu(\tilde{x}).$$

Then we can define the risk premium associated with the stochastic variable $\tilde{x}$, denoted $\rho_{\tilde{x}}$ (for example, AB in figure 2.1), by $u(E(\tilde{x}) - \rho_{\tilde{x}}) = Eu(\tilde{x})$.

The risk premium is the maximum amount by which the agent is willing to decrease the expected return from the lottery ticket to have a sure return.

Accepting the VNM axioms, we construct an approximation of the VNM utility function by determining the certainty equivalents for the three following lotteries:

$$\begin{cases} \$1{,}000 & \text{with probability } 1/10 \\ 0 & \text{with probability } 9/10 \end{cases} \quad \text{call it } EC_1,$$

---

1. $u(.)$ can be interpreted either as a direct utility function in a one-good economy or as an indirect utility function for a given system of prices.

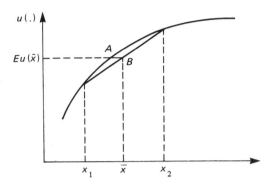

Figure 2.1

$$\begin{cases} \$1,000 & \text{with probability } 1/2 \\ \quad 0 & \text{with probability } 1/2 \end{cases} \quad \text{call it } EC_2,$$

$$\begin{cases} \$1,000 & \text{with probability } 9/10 \\ \quad 0 & \text{with probability } 1/10 \end{cases} \quad \text{call it } EC_3.$$

We normalize $u(.)$ by taking $u(0) = 0$ and $u(1,000) = 1$ since $u(.)$ is defined only up to an affine transformation. Then we have the following relationships:

$$u(EC_1) = \tfrac{1}{10}u(1,000) + \tfrac{9}{10}u(0) = \tfrac{1}{10},$$

$$u(EC_2) = \tfrac{1}{2}u(1,000) + \tfrac{1}{2}u(0) = \tfrac{1}{2},$$

$$u(EC_3) = \tfrac{9}{10}u(1,000) + \tfrac{1}{10}u(0) = \tfrac{9}{10}.$$

From these calculations, we derive three more points to approximate $u(.)$. For example, if $EC_1 = 25$, $EC_2 = 50$, and $EC_3 = 400$, we have figure 2.2.

Risk aversion is related to the concavity of the agent's utility function, but we need some measure of risk aversion. Let $\tilde{x} = \bar{x} + \tilde{\varepsilon}$ be a stochastic variable with mean $\bar{x}$ and variance σ_ε^2 where the higher order moments of $\tilde{x}$ are negligible compared to σ_ε^2 ($\tilde{\varepsilon}$ is small). Furthermore assume that $u(.)$ is twice differentiable, concave, and strictly increasing. The risk premium at the level of wealth $\bar{x}$, $\rho(\bar{x}, \tilde{\varepsilon})$, is the certainty equivalent that the agent finds indifferent to $\tilde{\varepsilon}$, that is,

$$Eu(\tilde{x}) = Eu(\bar{x} + \tilde{\varepsilon}) = u[\bar{x} - \rho(\bar{x}, \tilde{\varepsilon})].$$

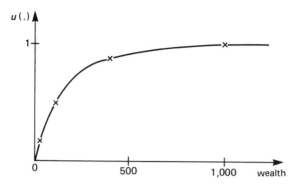

Figure 2.2

For any value ε of $\tilde{\varepsilon}$,

$$u(\bar{x} + \varepsilon) \approx u(\bar{x}) + \varepsilon u'(\bar{x}) + \frac{\varepsilon^2}{2} u''(\bar{x})$$

from which it follows that

$$Eu(\bar{x} + \tilde{\varepsilon}) \approx u(\bar{x}) + \frac{\sigma_\varepsilon^2}{2} u''(\bar{x}).$$

On the other hand,

$$u[\bar{x} - \rho(\bar{x}, \tilde{\varepsilon})] \approx u(\bar{x}) - \rho(\bar{x}, \tilde{\varepsilon}) u'(\bar{x})$$

because $\rho(\bar{x}, \tilde{\varepsilon})$ is small due to $\tilde{\varepsilon}$ being "small." Therefore

$$\rho(\bar{x}, \tilde{\varepsilon}) = -\frac{1}{2} \sigma_\varepsilon^2 \frac{u''(\bar{x})}{u'(\bar{x})}.$$

The *coefficient of absolute risk aversion* at the level of wealth $\bar{x}$, $r_a(\bar{x}) = -u''(\bar{x})/u'(\bar{x})$, is twice the risk premium per unit of variance for small risk. This local measure of risk aversion is better than either the second derivative $u''(.)$ or than the curvature $u''/(1 + u'^2)^{3/2}$ as both of these are affected by increasing affine transformations of $u(.)$. The following important theorem relates this local measure of risk to a global one:

THEOREM 1 (Pratt 1964)   Given two utility functions u^1 and u^2 that are twice differentiable, strictly concave, and increasing, the following conditions are equivalent:

(a) $r_a^1(\bar{x}) \geqslant r_a^2(\bar{x})$,
(b) $\rho^1(\bar{x}, \tilde{\varepsilon}) \geqslant \rho^2(\bar{x}, \tilde{\varepsilon})$ for any small $\tilde{\varepsilon}$,
(c) $u^1 \circ (u^2)^{-1}(.)$ concave, that is, u^1 is more concave than u^2, or $u^1 = g \circ u^2$ with $g' > 0$, $g'' < 0$.

See section 2.4 for a proof.

Taken together, these conditions indicate unambiguously that agent 1 with utility function u^1 is more risk averse than agent 2 with utility function u^2. For example, take

$$u(x) = -e^{-cx} \qquad r_a(x) = c > 0.$$

If $c_1 > c_2$, agent 1 is more risk averse than agent 2.

If, instead of additive risk, we consider proportional risk $\tilde{x} = \bar{x}(1 + \tilde{\varepsilon})$ and a relative risk premium $\hat{\rho}(\bar{x}, \tilde{\varepsilon})$, we have

$$Eu(\bar{x}(1 + \tilde{\varepsilon})) = u(\bar{x}(1 - \hat{\rho}(\bar{x}, \tilde{\varepsilon}))).$$

By definition of ρ,

$$Eu(\bar{x}(1 + \tilde{\varepsilon})) = Eu(\bar{x} + \bar{x}\tilde{\varepsilon}) = u(\bar{x} - \rho(\bar{x}, \bar{x}\tilde{\varepsilon})).$$

Therefore

$$\bar{x}\hat{\rho}(\bar{x}, \tilde{\varepsilon}) = \rho(\bar{x}, \bar{x}\tilde{\varepsilon}) = -\frac{1}{2}\bar{x}^2\sigma_\varepsilon^2\frac{u''(\bar{x})}{u'(\bar{x})},$$

or

$$\hat{\rho}(\bar{x}, \tilde{\varepsilon}) = -\frac{1}{2}\sigma_\varepsilon^2\frac{\bar{x}u''(\bar{x})}{u'(\bar{x})}.$$

The *coefficient of relative risk aversion* at the level of wealth $\bar{x}$, $r_r(\bar{x}) = -\bar{x}u''(\bar{x})/u'(\bar{x})$, is twice the relative risk premium per unit of variance for proportional risk. For example,

$$u(x) = \begin{cases} \text{Log } x & r_r(x) = 1, \\ x^{1-c} & r_r(x) = c < 1. \end{cases}$$

The coefficients of absolute and relative risk aversion have proved useful because they constantly occur in the comparative statics analysis of the economics of uncertainty.

Let W be the wealth of a risk-averse agent where W can be either invested in a risky venture yielding $\tilde{r} = \bar{r} + \tilde{\varepsilon}$ or held (at a certain interest rate equal to zero). Let a be the portion of wealth invested. At the end of the period the agent's wealth is given by

$$x = (W - a) + a(1 + \bar{r} + \tilde{\varepsilon}) = W + a(\bar{r} + \tilde{\varepsilon}).$$

The optimal portfolio is determined by

$$\underset{0 \leqslant a \leqslant W}{\text{Max}} \quad Eu(\tilde{x}),$$

which has as a first-order condition (assuming an interior maximum):

$$E[\tilde{r}u'(W + a\tilde{r})] = 0. \tag{1}$$

How does the amount of wealth invested vary with the initial level of wealth W? Differentiate equation (1), which determines the optimal amount of investment, to derive

$$\frac{da}{dW} = -\frac{E\tilde{r}u''}{E\tilde{r}^2u''}.$$

The sign of this expression depends on $E\tilde{r}u''$.

Assume that absolute risk aversion does not increase with wealth. For any value r of $\tilde{r}$ such that $r > 0$, we have

$$r_a(W) \geqslant r_a(W + ar),$$

that is,

$$u''(W + ar) \geqslant -r_a(W)u'(W + ar)$$

or

$$ru''(W + ar) \geqslant -r_a(W)ru'(W + ar).$$

For any value r of $\tilde{r}$ such that $r < 0$:

$$u''(W + ar) \leqslant -r_a(W)u'(W + ar)$$

or

$$ru''(W + ar) \geqslant -r_a(W)ru'(W + ar).$$

The above inequality holds for all r, from which it follows that

$E\tilde{r}u'' \geqslant -r_a(W)E\tilde{r}u' = 0$

by the first-order condition. Therefore

$$\frac{da}{dW} \geqslant 0.$$

It is of course difficult to obtain sufficient information about an agent's preferences, to know whether his absolute risk aversion increases or decreases (since this requires information about the third derivative of his utility function). However, such a comparative statics result is often used in an inferential way: since we must assume that absolute risk aversion decreases with wealth to obtain results that accord with both intuition and observations of rational behavior (like that of the above agent), we can infer that agents must satisfy this assumption in general. Consequently we may legitimately invoke this assumption when we study comparative statics problems in uncertain environments. (See Arrow 1970, ch. 3, for a classic example of a similar use of the coefficient of relative risk aversion that leads to the conclusion that $r_r(x)$ is close to 1.) A more pessimistic view argues that the microeconomics of uncertainty places few restrictions on agents' behavior.

2.2   Measures of Risk

When can we say that one situation is more risky than another or more precisely, that one stochastic variable is more risky than another from the economic perspective? A comparison of variances proves to be insufficient. In what follows, we develop an appropriate measure of risk for comparing stochastic variables with the same mean.

Without loss of generality, consider a family of stochastic variables indexed by r on the closed unit interval $[0, 1]$. Let $F(x, r)$, $x \in [0, 1]$ be the distribution function for the stochastic variable x_r. $F(., .)$ is assumed to be twice continuously differentiable. Intuitively, we can say that $F(., r_2)$ is more risky that $F(., r_1)$ if the distribution for r_2 is obtained from the distribution for r_1 by displacing weight from the center toward the tails of the distribution while keeping the mean constant (see figure 2.3).

Therefore we say that a distribution $F(., r_2)$ is more risky (MR) than another $F(., r_1)$ if it is obtained from the first by a succession of such

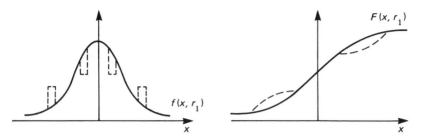

Figure 2.3

displacements or if we wish

$F(.,r_2) \quad \text{MR} \quad F(.,r_1)$

if and only if

(a)   the two distributions have the same mean,

(b) $F(.,r_2)$ is obtained from $F(.,r_1)$ by a succession of displacements of the type illustrated here.

Clearly, (a) and (b) imply (see figure 2.3)

(c) $\int_0^y [F(x,r_2) - F(x,r_1)] \, dx \geq 0 \quad \forall y \in [0,1]$.

On the other hand, Rothschild and Stiglitz (1970) show that (c) and (a) imply (b). Finally, the fact that the x_{r_1} and x_{r_2} have the same mean is equivalent to

$$\int_0^1 [F(x,r_2) - F(x,r_1)] \, dx = 0$$

because

$$\int_0^1 [F(x,r_2) - F(x,r_1)] \, dx = xF(x,r_2)|_0^1 - xF(x,r_1)|_0^1$$

$$- \int_0^1 x dF(x,r_2) + \int_0^1 x dF(x,r_1) = 0.$$

Therefore we are led to the definition using a differential format.

DEFINITION   An increase in r is a mean-preserving increase in risk (or an increase in risk in the Rothschild-Stiglitz sense) if and only if

(i) $\int_0^1 F_r'(x,r)\,dx = 0$,

(ii) $T(y,r) = \int_0^y F_r'(x,r)\,dx \geqslant 0$ $\forall y \in [0,1]$.

Clearly, this definition induces only a partial ordering over distributions with the same mean. Rothschild and Stiglitz show that

$$\tilde{x}_{r_2} \quad \text{MR} \quad \tilde{x}_{r_1}$$

$$\Updownarrow$$

$$Eu(\tilde{x}_{r_2}) \leqslant Eu(\tilde{x}_{r_1}) \qquad \text{for any concave } u(.)$$

$$\Updownarrow$$

$$\tilde{x}_{r_2} = \tilde{x}_{r_1} + \tilde{e}$$

where $\tilde{e}$ is a noise so that $E(\tilde{e}/x_{r_1}) = 0$.

This is a useful economic definition because it implies that if $\tilde{x}_{r_2}$ MR $\tilde{x}_{r_1}$, any risk-averse agent prefers $\tilde{x}_{r_1}$ to $\tilde{x}_{r_2}$.

Remark 1   To demonstrate the inappropriateness of using the variances to measure differential risk, we give an example of two stochastic variables $\tilde{x}_1$ and $\tilde{x}_2$ with the same mean, where $\text{Var } \tilde{x}_1 < \text{Var } \tilde{x}_2$ and $Eu(\tilde{x}_1) < Eu(\tilde{x}_2)$ for a concave function $u(.)$.

EXAMPLE

$\begin{cases} x_1 = 1 & \text{Pr: } 0.80 \\ x_1 = 100 & \text{Pr: } 0.20 \end{cases}$

$\begin{cases} x_2 = 10 & \text{Pr: } 0.99 \\ x_2 = 1090 & \text{Pr: } 0.01 \end{cases}$

$E\tilde{x}_1 = 20.8 \qquad \text{Var } \tilde{x}_1 = 1{,}568.16$

$E\tilde{x}_2 = 20.8 \qquad \text{Var } \tilde{x}_2 = 11{,}547.36$

$E \text{Log } \tilde{x}_1 = 0.92$

$E \text{Log } \tilde{x}_2 = 2.35.$

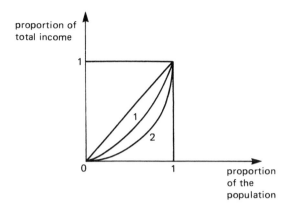

Figure 2.4

Except for particular cases (see problem 5 at the end of the book), there is no reason why the comparison of probability distributions should be limited to a comparison of the first two moments.

Remark 2   The comparison of probability distributions with the same mean is analogous to the comparison of income distributions with the same average income. When the Lorenz curve for distribution 2 is below the Lorenz curve for distribution 1, distribution 2 is more unequal or, analogously, more risky (see figure 2.4).

Assume that income is normalized on $[0, 1]$ and distributed according to the density function $f(x)$. Let

$$F(y) = \int_0^y f(x)\,dx,$$

$$\mu = \int_0^1 xf(x)\,dx$$

be mean income, and

$$\varphi(F(y)) = \frac{1}{\mu}\int_0^y xf(x)\,dx.$$

The Lorenz curve associates to F, which is the proportion of the population ranked in ascending order according to income, the proportion of total income that this segment of the population holds, that is, $\varphi(F)$.

If F_2 is more "risky" than F_1 in the sense discussed earlier,

$$\int_0^y [F_2(x) - F_1(x)]\,dx \geqslant 0 \qquad \forall y \in [0, 1]. \tag{2}$$

Under this condition the Lorenz curve for the distribution F_1 is everywhere above that of distribution F_2. Indeed, at every point where $F_1(y_1) = F_2(y_2)$,

$$\varphi(F_1(y_1)) - \varphi(F_2(y_2)) = \frac{1}{\mu}\left[\int_0^{y_1} xf_1(x)\,dx - \int_0^{y_2} xf_2(x)\,dx\right].$$

Integrating by parts yields

$$= \frac{1}{\mu}\left[\int_0^{y_2} [F_2(x) - F_1(x)]\,dx + \left[\int_{y_1}^{y_2} F_1(x)\,dx - (y_2 - y_1)F_1(y_1)\right]\right] \geqslant 0.$$

Note that the first term is positive because of condition (2) and the second is positive by application of the mean value theorem.

The above definition of more risky situations is more satisfactory than simply comparing variances. It remains to show that it is also manageable and useful.

THEOREM 2   Consider the maximization problem $\text{Max}_a\, Eu(\tilde{x}, a)$ with $u(.)$ three times continuously differentiable, increasing in x and concave in a the control variable. Let $a^*(r)$ be the optimal value of the control variable when the distribution of $\tilde{x}$ is $F(x, r)$. If an increase in r is a mean-preserving increase in risk, we have

$a^*(r)$ increases with r if $u'''_{axx} > 0$,

decreases with r if $u'''_{axx} < 0$.

Proof $a^*(r)$ is defined by the first-order condition

$$\int_0^1 u'_a(x, a)\,dF(x, r) = 0,$$

which yields

$$\frac{da^*}{dr} = -\frac{\int_0^1 u_a' F_{xr}'' \, dx}{\int_0^1 u_{aa}'' F_x' \, dx}.$$

Consequently the sign of da^*/dr equals the sign of $\int_0^1 u_a' F_{xr}'' \, dx$.

Now

$$\int_0^1 u_a' F_{xr}'' \, dx = u_a' F_r' \big|_0^1 - \int_0^1 F_r' u_{ax}'' \, dx = -\int_0^1 F_r' u_{ax}'' \, dx$$

(since $F(0, r) = 0$ for any r and $F(1, r) = 1$ for any r implies that $F_r'(0, r) = 0$ and $F_r'(1, r) = 0$). It follows that the sign of da^*/dr, is the same as the sign of $-\int_0^1 u_{ax}'' d \int_0^x F_r'(y, r) \, dy$. The last expression is equal to

$$-u_{ax}'' \int_0^x F_r'(y, r) \, dy \Big|_0^1 + \int_0^1 \left[\int_0^x F_r'(y, r) \, dy \right] u_{axx}''' \, dx$$

$$= \int_0^1 u_{axx}''' T(x, r) \, dx \quad > 0 \text{ if } u_{axx}''' > 0,$$

$$< 0 \text{ if } u_{axx}''' < 0. \ \blacksquare$$

To illustrate theorem 2, we consider the problem of an agent who consumes during periods 1 and 2 and saves during period 1 when the rate of interest is a stochastic variable $\tilde{x}$. Let

$$u(c_1, c_2) = v(c_1) + \delta v(c_2) \qquad v' > 0, v'' < 0,$$

$$c_1 = (1 - a)W,$$

$$c_2 = a(1 + x)W.$$

The maximization problem can be written as

$$\text{Max}_a \ \{v((1 - a)W) + \delta E v(a(1 + \tilde{x})W)\}$$

$$\Updownarrow$$

$$\text{Max}_a \ Eu(a, \tilde{x}).$$

Here u_{axx}''' is proportional to $2aWv'' + (aW)^2(1 + x)v''' = aW[2v'' + c_2 v''']$.

If we assume that the coefficient of relative risk aversion for the utility function in the second period $v(.)$ is decreasing with consumption and greater than 1, we can show that the rate of savings, a, increases with risk. In effect, $r_r = -c_2 v''/v'$ implies

$$\frac{dr_r}{dc_2} = -\frac{v''}{v'} - \frac{c_2 v'''}{v'} + \frac{c_2 (v'')^2}{v'^2}$$

$$= -\left[\frac{v'''c_2 + (1 + r_r)v''}{v'}\right] < 0.$$

Therefore $2v'' + c_2 v''' > (1 + r_r)v'' + c_2 v''' > 0$.

2.3*   The Maximin Criterion

Consider preferences represented by the following utility function:

$$U(\tilde{x}) = \sum_{s=1}^{S} \frac{1}{|S|} u(x_s)$$

for a stochastic variable that yields x_s with probability $1/|S|$, $s = 1, \ldots, S$. Consider the concave transformation of $u(.)$ given by $-u(.)^{-a}$ where $a > 0$. The agent whose preferences for $\tilde{x}$ are represented by

$$\hat{U}(\tilde{x}) = \sum_{s=1}^{S} \frac{1}{|S|} (-u^{-a}(x_s))$$

is more risk-averse than the first agent (Pratt's theorem).

Furthermore the preferences of this new agent are invariant to an increasing transformation of his utility function $U(.)$ Let

$$V = [-\hat{U}(.)]^{-1/a}$$

$$= \left[\sum_{s=1}^{S} \frac{u^{-a}(x_s)}{|S|}\right]^{-1/a}$$

$$= \left[\operatorname*{Min}_{s'} u(x_{s'})\right]\left[\sum_{s=1}^{S} \frac{1}{|S|}\left[\frac{u(x_s)}{\operatorname*{Min}_{s'} u(x_{s'})}\right]^{-a}\right]^{1/a}.$$

As a tends toward infinity,

$$\left[\sum_{s=1}^{S} \frac{1}{|S|}\left[\frac{u(x_s)}{\operatorname*{Min}_{s'} u(x_{s'})}\right]^{-a}\right]^{1/a}$$

tends toward 1. The coefficient of absolute risk aversion of the utility function $-u^{-a}$ is $a(-u''/u')$. Therefore, when the coefficient of absolute risk aversion tends toward infinity, the expected utility hypothesis converges toward the maximin criterion.

2.4*   Proof of Pratt's Theorem

(i)   c implies b

By definition of the risk premium, we have for any $\bar{x}$ and for any small $\tilde{\varepsilon}$

$$\rho^i(\bar{x}, \tilde{\varepsilon}) = \bar{x} - (u^i)^{-1}(Eu^i(\bar{x} + \tilde{\varepsilon})) \qquad i = 1, 2,$$

which yields

$$\rho^1(\bar{x}, \tilde{\varepsilon}) - \rho^2(\bar{x}, \tilde{\varepsilon}) = (u^2)^{-1}(Eu^2(\bar{x} + \tilde{\varepsilon})) - (u^1)^{-1}(Eu^1(\bar{x} + \tilde{\varepsilon})). \tag{3}$$

If we let $\tilde{t} = u^2(\bar{x} + \tilde{\varepsilon})$, equation (3) can be written as

$$\rho^1(\bar{x}, \tilde{\varepsilon}) - \rho^2(\bar{x}, \tilde{\varepsilon}) = (u^2)^{-1}(E\tilde{t}) - (u^1)^{-1}(E\{u^1((u^2)^{-1}(\tilde{t}))\}).$$

From c, $u^1 \circ (u^2)^{-1}$ is concave; Jensen's inequality implies:

$$Eu^1((u^2)^{-1}(\tilde{t})) \leqslant u^1 \circ (u^2)^{-1}(E\tilde{t}),$$

which yields

$$\rho^1(\bar{x}, \tilde{\varepsilon}) \geqslant \rho^2(\bar{x}, \tilde{\varepsilon}).$$

(ii)   a implies c

We will have established c if we show that the following function is decreasing:

$$\phi(t) = \frac{d}{dt} u^1 \circ (u^2)^{-1}(t)$$

However,

$$\phi(t) = \frac{u^{1\prime}((u^2)^{-1}(t))}{u^{2\prime}((u^2)^{-1}(t))}.$$

Let $(u^2)^{-1}(t) = x(t)$; then x is increasing. Therefore $\phi(t)$ is decreasing in t if and only if $u^{1\prime}(x)/u^{2\prime}(x)$ (and therefore $\text{Log}\, u^{1\prime}(x)/u^{2\prime}(x)$) is decreasing in

x). But

$$\frac{d}{dx} \text{Log}\frac{u^{1'}(x)}{u^{2'}(x)} = \left[-\frac{u^{2''}(x)}{u^{2'}(x)} - \left(-\frac{u^{1''}(x)}{u^{1'}(x)} \right) \right],$$

which is negative if a is true.

(iii) b implies a

By using the same argument and interchanging the roles of 1 and 2, we can show that if a is not true on an interval, then b is not true. ∎

2.5*   Stochastic Dominance

The search for a measure of risk led us to compare probability distributions with the same mean. In order to compare probability distributions more generally, we set forth the notion of stochastic dominance.

Consider a family of stochastic variables indexed by r on the closed interval $[0,1]$. Let $F(x,r)$, $x \in [0,1]$ be the distribution function of the stochastic variable $\tilde{x}_r$. We say that $F(.,r_2)$ dominates in the first-order stochastic sense $F(.,r_1)$ if and only if

$$F(x,r_2) \leqslant F(x,r_1) \qquad \forall x \in [0,1],$$

with strict inequality for a set of values of x with positive probability.

We show that any agent who has a utility function increasing in x prefers $F(.,r_2)$ to $F(.,r_1)$:

$$\int_0^1 u(x)dF(x,r_2) - \int_0^1 u(x)dF(x,r_1)$$

$$= -\int_0^1 (F(x,r_2) - F(x,r_1))u'(x)\,dx > 0.$$

We say that $F(.,r_2)$ dominates in the second-order stochastic sense $F(.,r_1)$ if and only if

$$\int_0^y (F(x,r_2) - F(x,r_1))\,dx \leqslant 0 \qquad \forall y \in [0,1],$$

with strict inequality for a set of values of x with positive probability. We show that any agent who has a utility function increasing and concave in x prefers $F(.,r_2)$ to $F(.,r_1)$:

$$\int_0^1 u(x)dF(x,r_2) - \int_0^1 u(x)dF(x,r_1)$$

$$= -u'(1) \int_0^1 (F(x,r_2) - F(x,r_1))\, dx$$

$$+ \int_0^1 \left(\int_0^x (F(y,r_2) - F(y,r_1))\, dy \right) u''(x)\, dx > 0.$$

Thus the Rothschild-Stiglitz dominance that was examined in section 2.2 corresponds to second-order stochastic dominance if we impose the additional condition of equal means.

The preceding definitions are special cases of the definition of nth-order stochastic dominance, which is written as

$$\int_0^y (-1)^{n-1}(x-y)^{n-1}dF(x,r_2) \leqslant \int_0^y (-1)^{n-1}(x-y)^{n-1}dF(x,r_1)$$

$$\forall y \in [0,1].$$

You can now show that any agent who has a VNM utility function with $u' > 0$, $u'' < 0$, and $u''' > 0$ prefers $F(.,r_2)$, which dominates $F(.,r_1)$ in the third-order stochastic sense.

2.6*   Generalization of the Expected Utility Hypothesis

Machina (1983) proposes a local approach that, under the appropriate differentiability assumptions, generalizes several of the tools developed in this chapter when the expected utility hypothesis is not imposed. Consider again the case of section 1.2, with a support of three states $x_1 > x_2 > x_3$ with probabilities π_1, π_2, π_3, and let $V(\pi)$ denote expected utility when $\pi = (\pi_1, \pi_2, \pi_3)$. The expected utility hypothesis is written

$$V(\pi) = \sum_{i=1}^3 \pi_i u(x_i).$$

An indifference curve is represented by a straight line in figure 2.5, that is,

$$\pi_1 u(x_1) + \pi_2 u(x_2) + \pi_3 u(x_3) = k$$

$$\Leftrightarrow \pi_1 = \frac{u(x_2) - u(x_3)}{u(x_1) - u(x_2)} \pi_3 + k'.$$

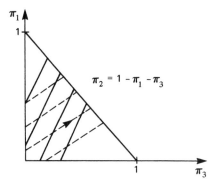

Figure 2.5

The set of lotteries having the same expected value is represented by a dashed line, that is,

$$\pi_1 x_1 + \pi_2 x_2 + \pi_3 x_3 = k$$

$$\Leftrightarrow \pi_1 = \frac{x_2 - x_3}{x_1 - x_2} \pi_3 + k'.$$

A mean-preserving increase in risk is represented by a movement along a dashed line in the northeast direction (effectively the weight in the tails increases). Risk aversion is indicated by the fact that such a movement is unfavorable—that is, the slope of the isoquants is steeper than the slope of the dashed lines, indicating equal mean income as in figure 2.5. Although $V(\pi)$ is not in general linear in π, we can take a Taylor approximation around a point π as follows:

$$V(\pi^*) \approx V(\pi) + \sum_{i=1}^{3} \frac{\partial V}{\partial \pi_i}(\pi)(\pi_i^* - \pi_i).$$

Then the agent will evaluate small changes of the distribution around π as if he satisfied the expected utility hypothesis with

$$u(x_i) = \frac{\partial V}{\partial \pi_i}(\pi) \qquad i = 1, 2, 3$$

(see figure 2.6).

Using this approach, Machina shows how several of the results reported here can be generalized. A necessary and sufficient condition for an agent to be risk averse (that is, utility decreases for a mean-preserving increase

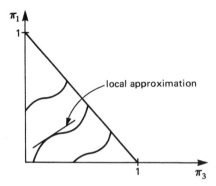

Figure 2.6

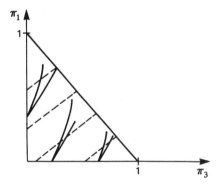

Figure 2.7

in risk) is that his preferences always be locally concave, as in figure 2.7. (Any tangent has a steeper slope than the dashed lines.)

2.7*   Risk Aversion with Many Goods

To extend the measure of risk aversion to many goods, we must either use the indirect utility function for a given system of fixed prices (see Stiglitz 1969) or compare only utility functions that represent the same ordinal preferences. Indeed, when indifference curves differ, choices among lotteries reflect both ordinal preferences and risk aversion. In figure 2.8 we consider the case of two indifference curves and two goods.[2]

2. See also Kihlstrom and Mirman (1981).

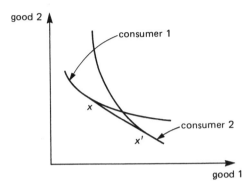

Figure 2.8

Consumer 1 prefers x to x' and also to any lottery including x and x' (as indicated by the chord). On the contrary, consumer 2 prefers x' to x and any lottery including x and x' to x. However, we cannot interpret this as saying that consumer 1 has greater risk aversion than consumer 2. Therefore we restrict ourselves to the case of fixed ordinal preferences, and we consider several VNM functions $u(.)$ defined on $\mathbf{R}^L$ to represent these preferences. We continue to say that $u^1(.)$ exhibits more risk aversion than $u^2(.)$ if and only if $u^1(.)$ is a concave increasing transformation of $u^2(.)$, that is,

$$u^1(.) = f \circ u^2(.) \qquad f' > 0, f'' < 0.$$

Debreu (1976) shows that if there exists one concave continuous representation of preferences $u(.)$, there exists in the set of concave continuous representations for the same preferences on $\mathbf{R}^L$ a function $u^*(.)$ that is the least concave—namely, for any concave increasing $u(.)$, there exists a concave increasing f such that

$$u(.) = f \circ u^*(.).$$

$u^*(.)$ can play the same role as the affine function did in the case where $L = 1$, and we can separate the preferences over the goods as represented by $u^*(.)$ from risk aversion as represented by f.

For example, if the preferences are homothetic, they may be represented by a homogeneous of degree one function so that any other representation is an increasing concave transformation of this function. This homogeneous of degree one representation is the least concave representation u^*. Let $u =$

$f \circ u^*$ with $u^*(\lambda x) = \lambda u^*(x)$ for any $\lambda \geqslant 0$, any $x \in \mathbf{R}^L$, and $f' > 0$. Then f is necessarily concave. Indeed, we have for some x_1 and λ,

$$f(\mu u_1^* + (1 - \mu)u_2^*) = f(\mu u^*(x_1) + (1 - \mu)u^*(\lambda x_1)),$$

where, by definition, $u_1^* = u^*(x_1)$ and $u_2^* = u^*(\lambda x_1)$. From homogeneity of degree one of u^*, we can write the preceding equation as

$$= f(u^*(\mu x_1 + (1 - \mu)\lambda x_1)) = u(\mu x_1 + (1 - \mu)\lambda x_1)$$

$$\geqslant \mu u(x_1) + (1 - \mu)u(\lambda x_1) \text{ from the concavity of } u(.).$$

Rewriting, we have

$$= \mu f(u^*(x_1)) + (1 - \mu)f(u^*(\lambda x_1))$$

$$= \mu f(u_1^*) + (1 - \mu)f(u_2^*).$$

Risk aversion—whether measured by the coefficient of absolute or relative risk aversion and regardless of whether this coefficient is increasing, decreasing, or constant—for the preferences represented by $u(.)$ can be characterized by the coefficients of the function f. Note that here risk aversion coincides with the definitions based on the indirect utility function as a function of income R. Indeed, we have

$$V(p, R) = u(x(p, R)) = f(u^*(x(p, R)))$$

$$= f(u^*(x(p, 1))R) = f(\alpha R)$$

from homogeneity.

Kihlstrom and Mirman (1974) propose a measure of risk aversion using the following concepts. We can define a small risk in the direction of y by $x = \bar{x} + \tilde{\varepsilon}y$, where $\tilde{\varepsilon}$ takes its values in $\mathbf{R}$ and $E(\tilde{\varepsilon}) = 0$, and we obtain the real-valued function

$$V_y(\tilde{\varepsilon}) = u(\bar{x} + \tilde{\varepsilon}y).$$

Thus we are brought back to only one dimension, and we can define risk premia as we did in section 2.1, conditional on the direction y, by $\rho_y(\bar{x}, \tilde{\varepsilon})$.

The following properties can then be shown in the case in which u^1 and u^2 represent the same ordinal preference:

(i)   If u^1 is more risk-averse than u^2,

$$\rho_y^1(\bar{x}, \tilde{\varepsilon}) > \rho_y^2(\bar{x}, \tilde{\varepsilon}) \qquad \forall \bar{x}, \forall y, \forall \tilde{\varepsilon}.$$

(ii)   If there exists a direction y and $\bar{x}$, such that for any $\tilde{\varepsilon}$

$$\rho_y^1(\bar{x}, \tilde{\varepsilon}) > \rho_y^2(\bar{x}, \tilde{\varepsilon}),$$

then u^1 is more risk-averse than u^2.

Therefore to show that u^1 is more risk-averse than u^2, it is necessary and sufficient to demonstrate it in one direction only. Kihlstrom and Mirman propose the following as a measure of risk aversion at the point $x = (x_1, \ldots, x_L)$:

$$\rho(x_1, \ldots, x_L) = \frac{(-1)^L \Delta_L}{((-1)^L \Delta_L^b)^{L/(L+1)}}$$

where Δ_L is the Hessian of $u(.)$ at x and Δ_L^b is the bordered Hessian of $u(.)$ at x. This measure coincides with the coefficient of absolute risk aversion when $L = 1$. It can also be shown that for $L = 2$, u^1 is more risk-averse than u^2 if and only if $\rho^1(x_1, x_2) > \rho^2(x_1, x_2)$ for any x_1 and x_2.

Suggested Readings

Arrow, K. (1970), ch. 3.   A classical reference.

Ross, S. A. (1981).   On measuring risk aversion when initial wealth is stochastic.

Diamond, P., and J. Stiglitz (1974).   A synthesis of risk measures.

Machina, M. (1983).   A remarkable survey of recent developments.

References

Arrow, K. 1970. *Essays in the Theory of Risk Bearing*. North-Holland, Amsterdam.

Debreu, G. 1976. "Least Concave Utility Functions." *Journal of Mathematical Economics* 3:121–129.

Diamond, P., and J. Stiglitz. 1974. "Increases in Risk and in Risk Aversion." *Journal of Economic Theory* 8:337–360.

Kihlstrom, R., and L. Mirman. 1974. "Risk Aversion with Many Commodities." *Journal of Economic Theory* 8:361–368.

Kihlstrom, R., and L. Mirman. 1981. "Constant, Increasing and Decreasing Risk Aversion with Many Commodities." *Review of Economic Studies* 48:271–280.

Machina, M. 1983. "The Economic Theory of Individual Behavior toward Risk: Theory, Evidence and New Directions." *IMSSS*, no. 433. Stanford University.

Pratt, J. 1964. "Risk Aversion in the Small and in the Large." *Econometrica* 32:122–136.

Ross, S. 1981. "Some Stronger Measures of Risk Aversion in the Small and in the Large with Applications." *Econometrica* 49:621–638.

Rothschild, M., and J. Stiglitz. 1970. "Increasing Risk I: A Definition." *Journal of Economic Theory* 2:315–329.

Stiglitz, J. 1969. "Behavior towards Risk with Many Commodities." *Econometrica* 37:660–667.

3 Certainty Equivalence

The solution of maximization problems should satisfy two countervailing conditions: it should be as precise as possible, and it should be easy. The rationale for imposing these conditions is not simply due to a cost–benefit perspective regarding the solution of these problems, but more fundamentally it lends credibility to a theory of rational behavior described by complex maximization problems.

An important objective of economic theory is to explore the world of *bounded rationality*—in particular, to characterize problems for which approximate solutions are easy to obtain. Since it is easier to develop a normative theory for precise solutions, we can claim to obtain a credible descriptive model and at the same time retain the relevancy of an approximate normative theory. In this chapter we survey the theory of certainty equivalence in which the pioneering work was done by Theil and Simon.

3.1 Certainty Equivalence

Theil (1954) developed the first formal model of the intuitive concept of certainty equivalence in the following way. The decision maker has access to a vector of instruments $x \in \mathbf{R}^n$ that generate results described by a vector $y \in \mathbf{R}^m$ according to the following additive model:

$$y = g(x) + e \tag{1}$$

where e is a vector of stochastic variables of dimension m with zero expected value for all x and for which the covariance matrix is finite and independent of x.

The objective function of the decision maker is quadratic and is written as

$$u(x, y) = A(x) + \sum_{i=1}^{m} A_i(x) y_i + \frac{1}{2} \sum_{i=1}^{m} \sum_{j=1}^{m} A_{ij} y_i y_j \tag{2}$$

where A_{ij} is independent of x and y for all (i, j). Then Theil shows that maximizing the expected value of $u(x, y)$ subject to constraint (1) yields the same result as solving the certainty problem in which e has been replaced by its expected value, which is zero here.

THEOREM 1 (Theil 1954) If a solution to the above problem exists, the stochastic problem Max $Eu(x, y)$ subject to $y = g(x)$ can be replaced by the certainty problem:

$\text{Max } u(x, y) \quad \text{subject to} \quad y = g(x).$

Proof

$$Eu(x, g(x) + e) = A(x) + \sum_{i=1}^{m} A_i(x)(g_i(x) + Ee_i)$$

$$+ \frac{1}{2} \sum_{i=1}^{m} \sum_{j=1}^{m} A_{ij}[g_i(x)g_j(x) + g_i(x)Ee_j + g_j(x)Ee_i + Ee_ie_j]$$

$$= u(x, g(x)) + \frac{1}{2} \sum_{i=1}^{m} \sum_{j=1}^{m} A_{ij}Ee_ie_j$$

$$= u(x, g(x)) + C.$$

By assumption, C is independent of x.

The certainty problem $\text{Max } u(x, g(x))$ differs from the stochastic problem only by a constant. Therefore it has the same maximum, and its solutions are identical to the solutions of the certainty problem. ∎

This result generalizes to a dynamic situation in which information accumulates over time in the following way. There are T periods. Uncertainty is represented by a series of T stochastic variables $e_1, \ldots, e_T$. At date 1, all the variables $e_1, \ldots, e_T$ are stochastic from the decision maker's perspective. He chooses his action at date 1 by maximizing the expected value of his future utility. At date 2, he knows the realized value of the stochastic variable e_1, but $e_2, \ldots, e_T$ are still stochastic for him. He chooses his action by maximizing the expected value of his future utility conditional on the value e_1. He continues in this manner over time.

Let $x_t = (x_1(t), \ldots, x_n(t))'$ and $y_t = (y_1(t), \ldots, y_m(t))'$ be the vectors of the instruments and the results at date t:

$$x = \begin{bmatrix} x_1 \\ \vdots \\ x_T \end{bmatrix}, \quad y = \begin{bmatrix} y_1 \\ \vdots \\ y_T \end{bmatrix}, \quad e = \begin{bmatrix} e_1 \\ \vdots \\ e_T \end{bmatrix}.$$

The objective function is quadratic:

$$u(x, y) = y'Ay + x'Bx + y'Cx + K'x + P'y \tag{3}$$

where A, B, C, K, and P are matrices of constants of the appropriate formats. The model is linear:

$$y = Rx + e, \quad Ee = 0, \quad Ee'e = \Sigma, \tag{4}$$

with

$$R = \begin{bmatrix} R_{11} & 0 & \cdots & 0 \\ R_{21} & R_{22} & \cdots & 0 \\ \cdots\cdots\cdots\cdots\cdots\cdots \\ R_{T1} & R_{T2} & \cdots & R_{TT} \end{bmatrix}.$$

Since we assume that the instruments at date t can influence the results at dates t' only with $t' \geqslant t$, the matrix is triangular.

This is a typical stochastic dynamic programming problem for which we will shortly give an example of the solution. Let $\tilde{x}$ be a solution strategy for this problem:

$$\tilde{x} = \begin{bmatrix} x_1 \\ x_2(e_1) \\ \cdots\cdots\cdots\cdots \\ x_T(e_1,\ldots,e_{T-1}) \end{bmatrix}.$$

The description of this strategy indicates that the decision at date T can be based on the knowledge of $e_1, \ldots, e_{T-1}, \ldots$, that at date 2 on the knowledge of e_1. The decision at date 1 must be taken without knowing $e_1,\ldots,e_T$, while at the same time taking into account that more information will become available as future decisions are made.

The solution exhibits *certainty equivalence* if x_1 is equal to the optimal value of the instrument in the first period for the certainty problem where all the stochastic variables $e_1, \ldots, e_T$ have been replaced by their expected values. Since x_1 is the only decision that must be taken at date 1, we have now replaced a complex problem of dynamic programming under uncertainty by a very simple certainty maximization problem.

THEOREM 2 (Theil 1957; Simon 1956)   If a solution to the problem of maximizing the expected value of (3) subject to constraint (4) exists and if information accumulates over time, the certainty equivalence property holds.

The proof is analogous to that of theorem 1, once we notice that optimal future instruments at date t are linear with respect to the stochastic variables at previous dates $t' < t$. By substituting these future instruments (conditional on the values of the previous stochastic variables) into the objective function, we obtain an objective function analogous to that in theorem 1. For this to be valid, the model must now be linear, and not only additive, and the objective function must be quadratic in x, y, and e.

Introducing constraints on the instruments in theorem 1 or on the instruments at date 1 of theorem 2 does not affect these results. Nevertheless, introducing constraints on the future instruments can render the results of theorem 2 invalid as the following example of Sandee's shows. Consider the dynamic maximization problem

$$\text{Max } E[-y_1^2 - y_2^2]$$
$$\scriptstyle (x_1, x_2)$$

subject to

$$y_1 = x_1 + e_1,$$

$$y_2 = x_1 + x_2 + e_1,$$

$$x_2 \geq 0,$$

where e_1 is a stochastic variable that takes the value $(-\varepsilon)$ with probability $2/3$ and the value 2ε with probability $1/3$. Therefore $Ee_1 = 0$ and $\text{Var } e_1 = 2\varepsilon^2$.

The certainty problem with e_1 replaced by 0 has the solution

$$\bar{x}_1 = 0, \quad \bar{x}_2 = 0.$$

To solve a dynamic programming problem, we begin with the solution in the last period. In period 2 the agent knows the value of e_1. If $e_1 = (-\varepsilon)$, then to maximize $(-y_2^2)$, he would choose $x_2 = \text{Max}(0, -x_1 + \varepsilon)$. On the other hand, if $e_1 = 2\varepsilon$, he would choose $x_2 = \text{Max}(0, -x_1 - 2\varepsilon)$. Of course, future decisions depend on the decision taken at date 1. This decision is determined in a second step by substituting the optimal values of x_2 conditional on x_1 and e_1 into the objective function. There are three cases to consider.

Case 1: $x_1 \geq \varepsilon$

Here x_2^* equals zero whether or not e_1 is equal to $(-\varepsilon)$ or to 2ε. The objective function in the first period becomes

$-2E(x_1 + e_1)^2;$

therefore $x_1^* = \varepsilon$ and $U^* = -6\varepsilon^2$.

Case 2: $\varepsilon > x_1 > -2\varepsilon$

Then

$x_2^* = \varepsilon - x_1$ if $e_1 = -\varepsilon$

$x_2^* = 0$ if $e_1 = 2\varepsilon$.

The objective function in the first period becomes

$-E(x_1 + e_1)^2 - \frac{1}{3}(x_1 + 2\varepsilon)^2;$

therefore $x_1^* = -\varepsilon/2$ and $U^* = -3\varepsilon^2$.

Case 3: $x_1 \leqslant -2\varepsilon$

Then

$x_2^* = \varepsilon - x_1$ if $e_1 = -\varepsilon$

$x_2^* = -x_1 - 2\varepsilon$ if $e_1 = 2\varepsilon$.

The objective function in the first period becomes

$-E(x_1 + e_1)^2;$

therefore $x_1^* = -2\varepsilon$ and $U^* = -6\varepsilon^2$. The global optimum occurs where $x_1^* = -\varepsilon/2$ and $x_1^* \neq \bar{x}_1$.

The reason for this divergence is that the constraint $x_2 \geqslant 0$ implies that in certain cases the optimal value of x_2 is no longer a *linear* function of the previous stochastic variables but this property is necessary in order to apply the approach in theorem 1.

3.2   First-Order Certainty Equivalence

Theil (1957) introduces the concept of first-order certainty equivalence in the linear-quadratic case of the preceding section when the parameters are stochastic. Malinvaud (1969a, b) generalizes the notion of first-order certainty equivalence. Laffont (1980) introduces the possibility of the dependence of the stochastic elements on the instruments and also develops a more general notion of first-order certainty equivalence.

Consider the following model

$$y = g(x, e), \quad x \in \mathbf{R}^n, \quad y \in \mathbf{R}^m,$$

where the vector e has a probability density function $f(e, x)$ that can depend on the instruments but $Ee = 0$ for all x. The objective function is

$$u(x, y, e)$$

so that the optimization problem for the decision maker can be written as

$$\operatorname*{Max}_{x} \int_{R^p} u(x, g(x, e), e) f(e, x)\, de. \tag{5}$$

The certainty problem associated[1] with this is written

$$\operatorname*{Max}_{x} u(x, g(x, 0), 0). \tag{6}$$

In order to vary uncertainty in the neighborhood of the certainty problem, we introduce the parameter ε in the following way:

$$\operatorname*{Max}_{x} \int_{R^p} u(x, g(x, \varepsilon e), \varepsilon e) f(e, x)\, de,$$

which is equivalent to (5) if $\varepsilon = 1$ and to (6) if $\varepsilon = 0$. The problem exhibits the first-order certainty equivalence property if the solution to (6) is equal (to the first order in ε) to the solution to (5) in the neighborhood of $\varepsilon = 0$.

THEOREM 3   If $u(x, y, e)$ and $g(x, e)$ are twice differentiable, if $f(e, x)$ is twice differentiable in x, and if a unique optimal solution to the associated certainty problem exists, we will have first-order certainty equivalence if the Hessian matrix of the function $u(x, g(x, 0), 0)$ is nonsingular.

Proof   The optimal solution satisfies the first-order conditions

$$\frac{\partial}{\partial x_i} \int_{R^p} u(x^*, g(x^*, \varepsilon e), \varepsilon e) f(e, x^*)\, de = 0 \qquad i = 1, \ldots, n. \tag{7}$$

1. It is possible to define several types of associated certainty problems (see Malinvaud 1969a).

By differentiating (7), we obtain

$$\sum_{h=1}^{n}\left[\int_{R^P}\left\{\frac{\partial^2 u}{\partial x_i \partial x_h}(x^*, g(x^*, \varepsilon e), \varepsilon e)f(e, x^*)\right.\right.$$

$$+ \frac{\partial u}{\partial x_i}(x^*, g(x^*, \varepsilon e), \varepsilon e)\frac{\partial f}{\partial x_h}(e, x^*) + \frac{\partial u}{\partial x_h}(x^*, g(x^*, \varepsilon e), \varepsilon e)\frac{\partial f}{\partial x_i}(e, x^*)$$

$$+ \left. u(x^*, g(x^*, \varepsilon e), \varepsilon e)\frac{\partial^2 f}{\partial x_i \partial x_h}(e, x^*)\right\} de\left.\right] dx_h^*$$

$$+ \left[\int_{R^P}\left\{\frac{\partial^2 u}{\partial x_i \partial \varepsilon}(x^*, g(x^*, \varepsilon e), \varepsilon e)f(e, x^*)\right.\right.$$

$$+ \left. \frac{\partial u}{\partial \varepsilon}(x^*, g(x^*, \varepsilon e), \varepsilon e)\frac{\partial f}{\partial x_i}(e, x^*)\right\} de\left.\right] d\varepsilon = 0 \qquad i = 1, \ldots, n. \qquad (8)$$

If we evaluate the derivatives in the neighborhood of $\varepsilon = 0$ and $x^*(0) = \bar{x}$, we have the following simplifications:

$$\int_{R^P}\frac{\partial^2 u}{\partial x_i \partial x_h}(x^*, g(x^*, \varepsilon e), \varepsilon e)f(e, x^*)\,de$$

$$= \frac{\partial^2 u}{\partial x_i \partial x_h}(x, g(\bar{x}, 0), 0)\int_{R^P}f(e, x^*)de = \frac{\partial^2 u}{\partial x_i \partial x_h}(\bar{x}, g(\bar{x}, 0), 0)$$

and

$$\int_{R^P}\frac{\partial u}{\partial x_i}(x^*, g(x^*, \varepsilon e), \varepsilon e)\frac{\partial f}{\partial x_h}(e, x^*)\,de$$

$$= \frac{\partial u}{\partial x_i}(\bar{x}, g(\bar{x}, 0), 0)\int_{R^P}\frac{\partial f}{\partial x_h}(e, \bar{x})\,de = 0$$

because

$$\int_{R^P}\frac{\partial f}{\partial x_h}(e, \bar{x})\,de = 0$$

since $\int_{R^P}f(e, \bar{x})\,de = 1$ for all x.

Similarly,

$$\int_{R^p} u(x^*, g(x^*, \varepsilon e), \varepsilon e) \frac{\partial^2 f}{\partial x_i \partial x_h}(e, x^*) \, de = 0,$$

$$\int_{R^p} \frac{\partial u}{\partial \varepsilon}(x^*, g(x^*, \varepsilon e), \varepsilon e) \frac{\partial f}{\partial x_i}(e, x^*) \, de = 0 \qquad \text{at } \varepsilon = 0.$$

Consider now

$$\int_{R^p} \frac{\partial u}{\partial \varepsilon}(x^*, g(x^*, \varepsilon e), \varepsilon e) \frac{\partial f}{\partial x_i}(e, x^*) \, de.$$

It is equal to

$$\sum_{k=1}^{p} \int_{R^p} \left(\sum_{j=1}^{m} u_{2j} \frac{\partial g_j}{\partial \varepsilon e_k} + u_{3k} \right) e_k \frac{\partial f}{\partial x_i}(e, x^*) \, de$$

where

$$u_{2j} = \frac{\partial u}{\partial y_j}(x^*, y^*, \varepsilon e) \qquad j = 1, \ldots, m,$$

$$u_{3k} = \frac{\partial u}{\partial \varepsilon e_k}(x^*, y^*, \varepsilon e) \qquad k = 1, \ldots, p.$$

After we evaluate the derivatives at $\varepsilon = 0$ and $x^* = \bar{x}$, (9) becomes

$$\sum_{k=1}^{p} \left(\sum_{j=1}^{m} u_{2j}^\circ \frac{\partial g_j^\circ}{\partial \varepsilon e_k} + u_{3k}^\circ \right) \int_{R^p} e_k \frac{\partial f}{\partial x_i}(e, \bar{x}) \, de. \tag{10}$$

But since

$$\int_{R^p} e_k f(e, x) \, de = 0 \qquad \text{for any } k$$

and any x,

$$\int_{R^p} e_k \frac{\partial f}{\partial x_i}(e, x) \, de = 0,$$

and (10) is zero. Similarly,

$$\int_{R^p} \frac{\partial^2 u}{\partial x_i \partial \varepsilon}(x^*, g(x^*, \varepsilon e), \varepsilon e) f(e, x^*) \, de = 0.$$

Evaluated at $\varepsilon = 0$, (8) reduces to

$$\sum_{h=1}^{n} \frac{\partial^2 u}{\partial x_i \partial x_h}(x, g(x,0),0)\, dx_h^* = 0 \qquad i = 1, \dots, n.$$

Since, by assumption, the determinant of the matrix

$$\frac{\partial^2 u}{\partial x_i \partial x_h}(\bar{x}, g(\bar{x},0),0)$$

is nonzero, $dx_h^* = 0$, $h = 1, \dots, n$. Therefore to the first order in ε and in a neighborhood of $\varepsilon = 0$, x^* coincides with $\bar{x}$. ∎

The preceding result can be generalized in a dynamic context where we obtain a version of theorem 2 for the first-order certainty equivalence case. Before concluding this section, we attempt to give the intuition of the first-order certainty equivalence result in the simplest case.

Consider the problem

$$\text{Max} \int_{R} u(x, e) f(e)\, de \qquad x \in \mathbf{R}.$$

The first-order condition is

$$\int_{R} \frac{\partial u}{\partial x}(x, e) f(e)\, de = 0.$$

Let $\bar{x}$ by the optimal solution if $e \equiv 0$. If e is a "small" stochastic variable such that

$e = e_1$ with probability $\pi(e_1)$,

$e = e_2$ with probability $\pi(e_2)$,

$Ee = 0$,

a small change in the decision variable (with respect to $\bar{x}$) would be of no avail because

$$dU = \frac{\partial u}{\partial x}(\bar{x}, e_1)\, dx \qquad \text{with probability } \pi(e_1)$$

$$= \frac{\partial u}{\partial x}(\bar{x}, e_2)\, dx \qquad \text{with probability } \pi(e_2).$$

Therefore

$$Edu = \left[\frac{\partial u}{\partial x}(\bar{x}, e_1)p(e_1) + \frac{\partial u}{\partial x}(\bar{x}, e_2)p(e_2) \right] dx.$$

Since e_1 and e_2 are small,

$$\frac{\partial u}{\partial x}(x, e_1) \approx \frac{\partial u}{\partial x}(\bar{x}, 0) + e_1 \frac{\partial^2 u}{\partial x \partial e}(\bar{x}, 0)$$

$$\frac{\partial u}{\partial x}(x, e_2) \approx \frac{\partial u}{\partial x}(\bar{x}, 0) + e_2 \frac{\partial^2 u}{\partial x \partial e}(\bar{x}, 0).$$

Since, by definition of $\bar{x}$,

$$\frac{\partial u}{\partial x}(\bar{x}, 0) = 0,$$

we have

$$Edu = \frac{\partial^2 u}{\partial x \partial e}(x, 0)\, dx [e_1 p(e_1) + e_2 p(e_2)] = 0.$$

The variation dx has as much of a positive effect as it has a negative effect to the first order.

Letting the probability depend on x does not change this intuition. In Edu, we have another term:

$$dx\, u(x, 0) \left[\frac{d\pi(e_1)}{dx} + \frac{d\pi(e_2)}{dx} \right],$$

which is zero because $\pi(e_1) + \pi(e_2) = 1$ for any x. The presence of constraints with the introduction of Lagrangian multipliers is also possible. Nevertheless, if the constraints affect the future values in the dynamic programming problem, we no longer have first-order certainty equivalence, as can be verified by the example of Sandee treated earlier (where x_1^* is in ε and not ε^2).

Irreversibility can be considered as a particular case of a constraint on future instruments. For example, suppose that the timber in a forest at date $t + 1$ is smaller than timber in the forest at date t, $x_{t+1} \leqslant x_t$. For this reason, certainty equivalence and first-order certainty equivalence can not be used in general in these situations (see section 3.4).

Finally, notice that the optimal value of the stochastic problem is equal to that of the certainty problem to the first order. Indeed,

$$\frac{\partial Eu}{\partial \varepsilon}(x^*(\varepsilon), e) = \frac{dx^*}{d\varepsilon} E \frac{\partial u}{\partial x}(x^*(\varepsilon), e) = 0$$

since $dx^*/d\varepsilon = 0$.

3.3   A More General Notion of First-Order Equivalence

Consider the following maximization problem:

$$\text{Max } Eu(x, y, e) \qquad\qquad\qquad\qquad\qquad (11)$$
$$x$$

subject to

$$y = g(x, e)$$

where the stochastic variable e can be written as $e = h(v, w)$ and where h is differentiable, with v and w stochastic variables such that $E(w/v) = 0$. Then the reference problem corresponds to $e = h(v, 0)$, and we can introduce the parameter ε to vary uncertainty in the neighborhood of this reference situation, $e = h(v, \varepsilon w)$.

Under the appropriate differentiability assumptions, we can show that to the first order in ε the solution to problem (11) is identical for small ε to the solution of the *simpler* stochastic problem:

$$\text{Max } \int u(x, g(x, h(v, 0)), h(v, 0)) f(v) \, dv.$$
$$x \in R$$

An interesting application of this result follows. In the neighborhood of no information, the gross value of information is zero to the first order, and if we introduce a cost of information, the net value of information is negative. If the net value of information becomes positive, it must be nonconcave (see Radner and Stiglitz 1984 and figure 3.1).

Consider again the problem

$$\text{Max } \int u(x, e) f(e) \, de$$
$$x \in R$$

where $f(e)$ is interpreted as the prior distribution of the agent over e. This agent can also observe a signal $s \in S$, the probability distribution of which depends on e. Moreover these distributions $\pi(s|e, \varepsilon)$ can be indexed by a parameter ε such that $\varepsilon = 0$ corresponds to an uninformative signal—that

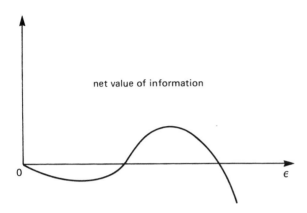

net value of information

Figure 3.1

is, for any $s_1 \in S$,

$$\pi(s = s_1 | e, 0) \qquad \text{is independent of } e.$$

After observing s, the agent maximizes his expected utility by using his posterior distribution over e which, from Bayes's theorem, is equal to

$$f(e|s, \varepsilon) = \frac{\pi(s|e, \varepsilon) f(e)}{\pi(s, \varepsilon)}$$

so that

$$\underset{x \in R}{\text{Max}} \int_R u(x, e) f(e|s, \varepsilon) \, de$$

leads to the optimal response $x(s, \varepsilon)$. The expected utility of this action is given by

$$U(\varepsilon) = \int_S \int_R u(x(s, \varepsilon), e) f(e|s, \varepsilon) \, de \, \pi(s) \, ds.$$

Assume that the stochastic variable s can be written as $s = s_0 + \varepsilon \phi$ where s_0 is a stochastic variable independent from e and ϕ is correlated with e. The case in which $\varepsilon = 0$ corresponds clearly to an absence of information. From the preceding section, we know that

$$\frac{dU}{d\varepsilon}(\varepsilon = 0) = 0.$$

If the cost of information is increasing in ε, the net value of information can be represented by figure 3.1.

3.4*   The Irreversibility Effect

Consider the following dynamic optimization problem

$$\text{Max } E\{u_1(x_1) + u_2(x_2, \omega)\}$$

where $x_1 \in \mathbf{R}$, $x_2 \in \mathbf{R}$, and $\omega \in \Omega$ and where x_2 is constrained by the choice of x_1, for example, $x_2 \leqslant x_1$. Assume that one acquires information at the end of period 1. This information is characterized by a partition S of Ω or by a finer partition S' (see chapter 4). The effect of the stated irreversibility is that the optimal decision with the finer structure of information must constrain the future less than the optimal decision, using the grosser structure of information

$$x_1^*(S') \geqslant x_1^*(S)$$

(see Freixas and Laffont 1984 for a general statement and for sufficient conditions for this property initially put forth by Henry 1974a and Arrow and Fisher 1974).

One must be more "conservative" if one expects to learn more in the future; one must keep open future options. In particular, if we have a problem in which S corresponds to the absence of information ($S \equiv \{\Omega\}$) and if the problem (in the absence of the constraint $x_2 \leqslant x_1$) allows us to use the certainty equivalence result (section 3.1), we may have the following situation: When there is no increase in information, as we go from period 1 to period 2 (that is, $S \equiv \Omega$), we may use the certainty equivalence result (for the linear model with the quadratic objective function, for example). When we take into account the increase in information (S') and if we solve the resulting stochastic dynamic programming problem correctly, we discover the irreversibility effect. In other words, the optimal action must be more conservative than the action associated with certainty equivalence (see Henry 1974b for an example).

This property may be illustrated by recalling the example of section 3.1 and by making several nonsymmetrical assumptions to alleviate the need for changing the numerical values (it would be easy to adapt more completely this example). Add a constant γ to the objective function to represent the available timber in the forest. Then y_t can be interpreted as the amount of timber in the forest that disappears at date t, x_t as the quantity of timber that is harvested (or replanted if $x_t < 0$) at date t and e_t as the amount that is destroyed (or regenerated if $e_t < 0$) by natural phenomena at date t.

We assume that it is possible to plant at date 1, but not at date 2, $x_2 \geqslant 0$. Then the results in this example illustrate the irreversibility effect because $x_1^* = 0$ if there is no future constraint—that is, we do not plant today if the destruction of the forest is not irreversible (or if we use the certainty equivalence result in an inappropriate way). On the contrary, $x_1^* = -\varepsilon/2$—that is, we are more conservative in forest management (and therefore we plant new trees today) if the destruction of the forest is irreversible.

3.5*   The Arrow-Lind Theorem (1970)

Arrow-Lind (1970) propose the notion that in an economy with a large number of agents, we should evaluate public projects for which the risk may be shared among all the agents by their certainty equivalent—that is, we should neglect the risk premium. Consider a risk $\tilde{z}$ in an economy with I identical agents. Each agent has a certain income x and a VNM utility function, u, such that $u' > 0$ and $u'' < 0$. Let $\bar{z}$ be the mean of $\tilde{z}$ and σ^2 be its variance. If the stochastic variable $\tilde{z}$ is shared equally, we can define by ρ^i the risk premium of agent i from the following:

$$Eu\left(x + \frac{\tilde{z}}{I}\right) = u\left(x + \frac{\bar{z}}{I} - \rho^i\right),$$

which, using a reasoning similar to that in section 2.1, yields

$$u\left(x + \frac{\bar{z}}{I}\right) + \frac{\sigma^2}{2I^2} \cdot u''\left(x + \frac{\bar{z}}{I}\right) \approx u\left(x + \frac{\bar{z}}{I}\right) - \rho^i u'\left(x + \frac{\bar{z}}{I}\right),$$

or

$$\rho^i = \frac{\sigma^2}{2I^2}\left(-\frac{u''(x + \bar{z}/I)}{u'(x + \bar{z}/I)}\right),$$

and a global risk premium of

$$\rho = \sum_{i=1}^{I} \rho^i = \frac{1}{I} \cdot \frac{\sigma^2}{2}\left(-\frac{u''(x + \bar{z}/I)}{u'(x + \bar{z}/I)}\right),$$

which goes to zero as I goes to infinity.

Note that if $\bar{z}$ is a function of I or is correlated with a macro-risk, this result can be invalidated.

Suggested Readings

Malinvaud, E. (1969b).   The clearest article on first-order certainty equivalence.

Henry, C. (1974b).   The irreversibility effect.

References

Arrow, K., and R. Lind. 1970. "Uncertainty and the Evaluation of Public Investment Decision." *American Economic Review* 60:364–378.

Arrow, K., and A. C. Fisher. 1974. "Environmental Preservation, Uncertainty and Irreversibility." *Quarterly Journal of Economics* 88:312–319.

Freixas, X., and J.-J. Laffont. 1984. "The Irreversibility Effect." In M. Boyer and R. Kihlstrom eds.), *Bayesian Models in Economic Theory*. North-Holland. Amsterdam.

Henry, C. 1974a. "Option Values in the Economics of Irreplaceable Assets." *Review of Economic Studies Symposium*, 89–104.

Henry, C. 1974b. "Investment Decisions under Uncertainty: The Irreversibility Effect." *American Economic Review* 64:1996–1012.

Laffont, J.-J. 1980. *Essays in the Economics of Uncertainty*. Harvard University Press, Cambridge.

Malinvaud, E. 1969a. "Décisions en face de l'aléatoire et situation certaine approximativement équivalente." *Cahiers du Séminaire de la Société d'Econométrie* 11:37–50.

Malinvaud, E. 1969b. "First Order Certainty Equivalence." *Econometrica* 37:706–718.

Radner, R., and J. Stiglitz. 1984. "A Nonconcavity in the Value of Information." In M. Boyer and R. Kihlstrom (eds.), *Bayesian Models in Economic Theory*. North-Holland, Amsterdam.

Simon, H. 1956. "Dynamic Programming under Uncertainty with a Quadratic Criterion Function." *Econometrica* 24:74–81.

Theil, H. 1954. "Econometric Models and Welfare Maximization." *Weltwirtschaftliches Archiv* 72:60–83.

Theil, H. 1957. "A Note on Certainty Equivalence in Dynamic Planning." *Econometrica* 25:346–349.

4 Information Structures

As we shall see in chapter 5, the economics of information originates with informational asymmetries, which lead to the sharing of information structures either directly or indirectly. As a preparation for this, we propose in this chapter a rigorous formalization of the concept of information. We make explicit the nature of the utility of information to the agents—in particular, that it is indirect and not direct like the utility derived from consuming goods. We compare information structures and show why the value of information is always positive for a Bayesian decision maker. This result will be contrasted with the value of information in an economic game (chapter 5). The demand for information that is contained in expert opinion is then derived in several contexts.

4.1 Prior Information

Let $(\Omega, \mathcal{O})$ be a (measurable) space of states of nature. The prior information of any agent is represented by a probability measure on $(\Omega, \mathcal{O})$ called the *prior distribution* for which the density function is denoted by $\pi(.)$. For example, if Ω has only three elements where $\omega_1 (\omega_2, \omega_3)$ represents good (average or bad, respectively) quality, the seller who knows the product's quality has the following prior distribution:

$$\begin{cases} \Pr(\omega_1) = 1 \\ \Pr(\omega_2) = 0 \\ \Pr(\omega_3) = 0 \end{cases} \quad \text{if the product is good,}$$

$$\begin{cases} \Pr(\omega_1) = 0 \\ \Pr(\omega_2) = 1 \\ \Pr(\omega_3) = 0 \end{cases} \quad \text{if the product is average,}$$

$$\begin{cases} \Pr(\omega_1) = 0 \\ \Pr(\omega_2) = 0 \\ \Pr(\omega_3) = 1 \end{cases} \quad \text{if the product is bad.}$$

On the contrary, based on his experience, the buyer has a prior distribution such that

$$\Pr(\omega_1) = \pi_1$$

$$\Pr(\omega_2) = \pi_2$$

$$\Pr(\omega_3) = \pi_3 \quad \text{with } \pi_1 + \pi_2 + \pi_3 = 1.$$

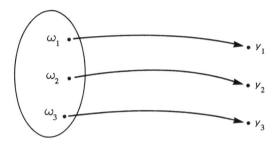

Figure 4.1

4.2   Information Structure without Noise

An *information structure without noise* consists of a space of signals Y and a (measurable) function φ from the space of states of nature to Y. The function defines, in a natural way, a partition of Ω, the elements of which are given by

$$O_i = \varphi^{-1}(y_i) \qquad \text{for } y_i \in Y.$$

Then an informational structure without noise can be identified with a partition of Ω that has the following property: after having received the signal, the agent knows in which element of the partition the true state of nature is located.

We now present an example of an information structure without noise characterized in figure 4.1. In this figure the information structure associates a different signal to each quality. This example corresponds to an expert who never makes a mistake and who provides complete information (we say that the information structure is "perfect"). The partition of Ω associated with this structure is

$$\{\{\omega_1\}, \{\omega_2\}, \{\omega_3\}\}.$$

In figure 4.2 we represent an expert who never makes a mistake but who cannot distinguish good quality from average quality. The partition associated with this structure is $\{\{\omega_1, \omega_2\}, \{\omega_3\}\}$. It must be distinguished from the structure shown in figure 4.3.

The connection that we have made above between an expert and an information structure leads to the following questions: When is one expert more reliable than another? When is one information structure more

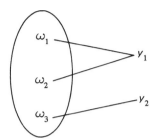

Figure 4.2

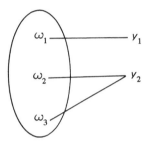

Figure 4.3

valuable than another? To provide some perspective on these questions, we consider a decision-making problem under imperfect information.

A decision maker wishes to maximize his objective function $u(a, \omega)$ with respect to his action $a \in A$ without knowing ω. He has a prior distribution defined by the density function $\pi(\omega)$. As we have seen in chapter 1, he will behave rationally if he maximizes his expected utility, which can be defined by

$$\underset{a \in A}{\text{Max}} \int_{\Omega} u(a, \omega)\pi(\omega)\,d\omega. \tag{1}$$

Let a^{*0} be the solution of problem (1). Let $\mathscr{P}^1 = \{O^1(y), y \in Y^1\}$ be the partition generated by information structure 1. When he receives the signal y, the agent knows that ω is in $O^1(y)$. Then his posterior probability distribution is

$$v(\omega|y) = 0 \qquad \text{if } \omega \notin O^1(y)$$

$$v(\omega|y) = \frac{\pi(\omega)}{\displaystyle\int_{O^1(y)} \pi(\hat{\omega})\, d\hat{\omega}} \qquad \text{otherwise.}$$

He revises his expectations by using Bayes's theorem, that is, $(P(A \cap B) = P(A)P(B|A) = P(B)P(A|B))$

$$\Pr(\omega|y) = \frac{\Pr(\omega, y)}{\Pr(y)} = \frac{\Pr(\omega)}{\Pr(y)} \qquad \text{if } \omega \in \varphi^{-1}(y)$$

$$= 0 \qquad \text{otherwise.}$$

Here

$$\Pr(\omega) = \pi(\omega),$$

$$\Pr(y) = \int_{O^1(y)} \pi(\hat{\omega})\, d\hat{\omega}.$$

For each value of y the agent knows that he will solve the following problem:

$$\underset{a \in A}{\text{Max}} \int_\Omega u(a, \omega)v(\omega|y)\, d\omega = \int_\Omega u(a^{*1}(y), \omega)v(\omega|y)\, d\omega = V(y) \qquad (2)$$

where $a^{*1}(y)$ is the optimal action for the signal y. Before receiving the information contained in y, he can evaluate ex ante the utility of having information structure $\mathscr{P}^1$ by

$$U(\mathscr{P}^1; \pi(.), u(.)) = \int_{Y^1} V(y)\pi(y)\, dy$$

where $\pi(y)$ is the prior probability of the signal y, that is, $\int_{O^1(y)} \pi(\omega)\, d\omega$, or by

$$U(\mathscr{P}^1; \pi(.), u(.)) = \sum_{y \in Y^1} \int_{O^1(y)} u(a^{*1}(y), \omega)\pi(\omega)\, d\omega$$

if there is a finite number of signals.

We say that information structure 1 is better than information structure 2 for the agent if

$$U(\mathscr{P}^1; \pi(.), u(.)) > U(\mathscr{P}^2; \pi(.), u(.))$$

or

$$\sum_{y \in Y^1} \int_{O^1(y)} u(a^{*1}(y), \omega)\pi(\omega)\, d\omega > \sum_{y \in Y^2} \int_{O^2(y)} u(a^{*2}(y), \omega)\pi(\omega)\, d\omega.$$

Clearly, the preceding comparison depends on the agent's preferences and his prior distribution. Is it possible to compare information structures independently from these characteristics?

We say that information structure 1 is *finer* than information structure 2 if the partition generated by structure 1 is finer than the one generated by structure 2, that is,

$$\forall O^2 \in \mathscr{P}^2 \qquad \exists (O_i^1)_{i=1,\dots,k} : \bigcup_{i=1}^{k} O_i^1 = O^2, \, O_i^1 \in \mathscr{P}^1.$$

Then we can state:

THEOREM 1   Information structure 1 is finer than information structure 2 if and only if for any prior probability distribution and for any utility function $u(.)$:

$$U(\mathscr{P}^1; \pi(.), u(.)) \geq U(\mathscr{P}^2; \pi(.), u(.)).$$

Proof   If (1) is finer than (2), this implies that the agent can better adapt his behavior with (1) than with (2). By definition, we have

$$\forall y^2 \in Y^2, \quad \forall O^2 = (\varphi^2)^{-1}(y^2), \quad \exists O_1^1, \dots, O_k^1 : O^2 = \bigcup_{j=1}^{k} O_j^1.$$

Let $a^{*2}(y^2)$ be the best action for the signal y^2. By definition,

$$\forall j \quad \underset{a \in A}{\mathrm{Max}} \int_{O_j^1} u(a, \omega)v(\omega|y_j^1)\, d\omega \geq \int_{O_j^1} u(a^{*2}(y^2), \omega)v(\omega|y_j^1)\, d\omega.$$

Let $a^{*1}(j)$ be the solution to the above problem for $j = 1, \dots, k$. Obviously, we have

$$\sum_{j=1}^{k} \pi(y_j^1) \int_{O_j^1} u(a^{*1}(j), \omega)v(\omega|y_j^1)\, d\omega$$

$$\geq \sum_{j=1}^{k} \pi(y_j^1) \int_{O_j^1} u(a^{*2}(y^2), \omega)v(\omega|y_j^1)\, d\omega.$$

Since the above inequality can be obtained for any signal $y^2 \in Y^2$, we have shown the desired result.

To prove the converse, we must show that for any pair of partitions $(\mathscr{P}^1, \mathscr{P}^2)$ such that $\mathscr{P}^1$ (resp. $\mathscr{P}^2$) is not finer than $\mathscr{P}^2$ (resp. $\mathscr{P}^1$), we can

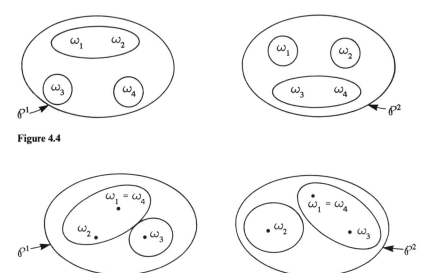

Figure 4.4

Figure 4.5

construct a decision-making problem in which $\mathscr{P}^1$ is preferred to $\mathscr{P}^2$ and another decision-making problem in which $\mathscr{P}^2$ is preferred to $\mathscr{P}^1$. We can always find $\{\omega^1, \omega^2, \omega^3, \omega^4\}$ so that we have either figure 4.4 or figure 4.5.

(a)   Case Shown in Figure 4.4

Assume that the prior distribution is uniform and attributes a probability of $\frac{1}{4}$ to each state of nature. Then it is easy to construct decision-making problems in which either (1) or (2) is preferred. In fact, structure (1) does not distinguish between ω_1 and ω_2, whereas structure (2) does not distinguish between ω_3 and ω_4. It suffices to have, on the one hand, a decision-making problem where the possibility of distinguishing between (1) and (2) is very important and, on the other hand, another problem where the possibility of distinguishing between (3) and (4) is very important.

PROBLEM 1

	ω_1	ω_2	ω_3	ω_4
a_1	1	0	0	0
a_2	0	1	0	0

where the entries represent $u(a_i, \omega_i)$. With structure (1), $U(1) = \frac{1}{4}$ and with structure (2), $U(2) = \frac{1}{2}$.

PROBLEM 2

	ω_1	ω_2	ω_3	ω_4
a_1	0	0	1	0
a_2	0	0	0	1

$U(1) = \frac{1}{2}$ $U(2) = \frac{1}{4}$.

(b) Case Shown in Figure 4.5 (The Same Idea)

Prior information can be identified with an uninformative information structure $\mathscr{P}^0$ where

$$\forall \omega_1, \omega_2 \in \Omega, \; \varphi(\omega_1) = \varphi(\omega_2),$$

and we denote

$$U(\mathscr{P}^0; \pi(.), u(.)) = \underset{a \in A}{\text{Max}} \int_\Omega u(a, \omega)\pi(\omega)\, d\omega.$$

Any information structure is finer than the noninformative structure. From theorem 1 we conclude that an information structure without noise is always valuable to an agent, and we can define the *value* of information structure 1 by

$$V(\mathscr{P}^1; \pi(.), u(.)) = U(\mathscr{P}^1; \pi(.), u(.)) - U(\mathscr{P}^0; \pi(.), u(.)) \geqslant 0.$$

(see problem 4 at the end of the book). Notice that this definition of the value of information has a monetary sense only with reference to a utility function of the following type:

$$u(a, \omega) + x$$

where x is the money that the agent has to spend. Then the value of information is indeed what he is willing to pay, ex ante, to acquire the information structure.

If action a yields monetary consequences, $r(a, \omega)$ in the general case, the utility function is written as $u(r(a, \omega) + x, a, \omega)$ where x has the same meaning as before. The value of information structure 1 can then be defined by the amount x^* such that

$$\sum_{y \in Y^1} \int_{O^1(y)} u(r(a^{*1}(y), \omega) + \bar{x} - x^*, a^{*1}(y), \omega)\pi(\omega)\, d\omega$$

$$= \int_{\Omega} u(r(a^{*0}, \omega) + \bar{x}, a^{*0}, \omega)\pi(\omega)\, d\omega, \tag{3}$$

or by the amount x^{**} such that

$$\sum_{y \in Y^1} \int_{O^1(y)} u(r(a^{*1}(y), \omega) + \bar{x}, a^{*1}(y), \omega)\pi(\omega)\, d\omega$$

$$= \int_{\Omega} u(r(a^{*0}, \omega) + \bar{x} + x^{**}, a^{*0}, \omega)\pi(\omega)\, d\omega \tag{4}$$

where $\bar{x}$ is the agent's initial endowment of money. In (3), x^* represents the compensating variation in income. In (4), x^{**} represents the equivalent variation in income.

4.3   Information Structure with Noise

An *information structure with noise* consists of a (measurable) space of signals and a function from Ω to the space of probability measures over Y. In other words, it is given by a conditional probability function $f(y|\omega)$ over Y which defines the probability that the signal y will be sent for each state of nature $\omega \in \Omega$. The conditional density is the likelihood function of the experiment that supports the information structure.

For example, a draw from a normal distribution with mean ω and variance σ^2 can be interpreted as an information structure, with the following conditional probability distribution:

$$f(y|\omega) = \frac{1}{\sqrt{2\pi}\sigma} e^{-[(y-\omega)/\sigma]^2/2}.$$

Given $f(y|\omega)$, expectations are revised according to Bayes's theorem as follows:

$$v(\omega|y) = \frac{f(y|\omega)\pi(\omega)}{\displaystyle\int_{\Omega} f(y|\hat{\omega})\pi(\hat{\omega})\, d\hat{\omega}},$$

and $v(\omega|y)$ is the posterior distribution.

An information structure without noise is a particular case of an information structure, in which $\forall \omega \in \Omega$, $f(y|\omega)$ is a Dirac function for a given $y(\omega) \in Y$. Returning to the example of a good of unknown quality, an information structure with noise could be likened to an expert who makes mistakes sometimes; for example, if

$y_1 \equiv$ good,

$y_2 \equiv$ average,

$y_3 \equiv$ bad,

the likelihood function,

$$f(y_1|\omega_1) = \tfrac{1}{2} \qquad f(y_1|\omega_2) = \tfrac{1}{8} \qquad f(y_1|\omega_3) = 0,$$

$$f(y_2|\omega_1) = \tfrac{1}{4} \qquad f(y_2|\omega_2) = \tfrac{1}{2} \qquad f(y_2|\omega_3) = \tfrac{1}{4},$$

$$f(y_3|\omega_1) = \tfrac{1}{4} \qquad f(y_3|\omega_2) = \tfrac{3}{8} \qquad f(y_3|\omega_3) = \tfrac{3}{4},$$

characterizes such an imperfect expert where $f(y_j|\omega_i)$ is the probability with which he reports quality y_j when the true quality is ω_i.

The important point to underscore is that the decision maker knows perfectly the function $f(.\,|\,.)$. Therefore he knows with what probability the expert will make a mistake. It is this characteristic that makes an information structure (even with noise) valuable to the decision maker. Indeed, without any information, the decision maker solves

$$\underset{a \in A}{\text{Max}} \int_\Omega u(a, \omega)\pi(\omega)\,d\omega,$$

which yields the optimal decision a^{*0}.

Consider an information structure characterized by $f(y|\omega)$. For any value of y, he solves

$$\underset{a \in A}{\text{Max}} \int_\Omega u(a, \omega)v(\omega|y)\,d\omega,$$

which yields the optimal decision $a^*(y)$. By *definition* of $a^*(y)$, we have

$$\int_\Omega u(a^*(y), \omega)v(\omega|y)\,d\omega \geqslant \int_\Omega u(a^{*0}, \omega)v(\omega|y)\,d\omega,$$

which gives

$$\int_Y \int_\Omega u(a^*(y), \omega) v(\omega|y)\, d\omega\, \pi(y)\, dy \geqslant \int_Y \int_\Omega u(a^{*0}, \omega) v(\omega|y) \pi(y)\, d\omega\, dy$$

$$= \int_Y \int_\Omega u(a^{*0}, \omega) f(y|\omega)\, dy\, \pi(\omega)\, d\omega$$

$$= \int_\Omega u(a^{*0}, \omega) \pi(\omega)\, d\omega.$$

The comparison of two information structures with noise, which is the subject of Blackwell's theorem, is more delicate. Let

$$U[Y, f; \pi(.), u(.)] = \sum_{y \in Y} \pi(y) \int_\Omega u(a^*(y), \omega) v(\omega|y)\, d\omega.$$

We say that information structure $[Y^1, f^1]$ is more valuable than information structure $[Y^2, f^2]$ iff

$$U[Y^1, f^1; \pi(.), u(.)] \geqslant U[Y^2, f^2; \pi(.), u(.)] \qquad \forall u(.), \forall \pi(.).$$

Then we have:

THEOREM 2 (Blackwell 1951)   Information structure $[Y^1, f^1]$ is more valuable than information structure $[Y^2, f^2]$ if and only if there exists nonnegative numbers $\beta_{y_k^2 y_k^1}$ such that[1]

(i) $f^2(y_k^2|\omega) = \sum\limits_{y_{k'}^1 \in Y^1} \beta_{y_k^2 y_{k'}^1} f^1(y_k^1|\omega) \qquad \forall \omega \in \Omega, \forall y_{k'}^2 \in Y^2,$

(ii) $\sum\limits_{y_{k'}^2 \in Y^2} \beta_{y_k^2 y_k^1} = 1 \qquad \forall y_k^1 \in Y^1.$

When Y^1, Y^2, and Ω have a finite number of elements, let

$$F^1 = (f^1(y^1|\omega)) = \begin{bmatrix} f^1(y_1^1|\omega^1) \ldots f^1(y_1^1|\omega^S) \\ \cdots \cdots \cdots \cdots \cdots \cdots \\ f^1(y_{K_1}^1|\omega^1) \ldots f^1(y_{K_1}^1|\omega^S) \end{bmatrix}_{(K_1, S)},$$

$$F^2 = (f^2(y^2|\omega)) = \begin{bmatrix} f^2(y_1^2|\omega^1) \ldots f^2(y_1^2|\omega^S) \\ \cdots \cdots \cdots \cdots \cdots \cdots \\ f^2(y_{K_2}^2|\omega^1) \ldots f^2(y_{K_2}^2|\omega^S) \end{bmatrix}_{(K_2, S)},$$

$$B = (\beta_{y^2 y^1}) = \begin{bmatrix} \beta_{y_1^2 y_1^1} \ldots \beta_{y_1^2 y_{K_1}^1} \\ \cdots \cdots \cdots \cdots \cdots \\ \beta_{y_{K_2}^2 y_1^1} \ldots \beta_{y_{K_2}^2 y_{K_1}^1} \end{bmatrix}_{(K_2, K_1)}.$$

1. Green and Stockey (1978) show that we can redefine the space of the states of nature so that this definition can be expressed as in section 4.2, by stating that one partition is finer than another.

Condition (ii) indicates that B is a Markov probability matrix. Condition (i) may be written as

$$F^2 = BF^1.$$

Condition (i) is a generalization of the following intuitive idea: Consider information structure 1 given by $[Y^1, f^1]$. Each time that a signal y_k^1 is observed, it is garbled by a stochastic mechanism that is independent of the state of nature that generated y_k^1 and it is transformed into a vector of signals in Y^2 by the conditional probability $p(y_k^2 | y_k^1)$. More generally, we would have

$$f^2(y_{k'}^2 | \omega) = \sum_{k=1}^{K_1} p(y_{k'}^2 | y_k^1 \text{ and } \omega) \cdot f^1(y_k^1 | \omega).$$

The garbling condition specifies that the matrix of transitional probabilities $p(.\,|\,.)$ is independent of ω. In theorem 2, $\beta_{y_k^2 y_k^1}$ is not necessarily the conditional probability $p(y_k^2 | y_k^1)$. Therefore we have the following corollary:

COROLLARY   If (Y^2, f^2) is a garbling of (Y^1, f^1), (Y^1, f^1) is more valuable than (Y^2, f^2).

To show this, it is sufficient to take

$$\beta_{y_k^2 y_k^1} = p(y_{k'}^2 | y_k^1 \text{ and } \omega)$$

which is independent of ω by definition.

EXAMPLE   Consider a perfect expert in the example when a commodity of unknown quality has only two characteristics, good and bad. He may be characterized by the following matrix:

$$F^1 = \begin{bmatrix} 1 & 0 \\ 0 & 1 \end{bmatrix},$$

which defines the conditional density $f(y|\omega)$. Consider a Markov matrix B of the following sort:

$$B = \begin{bmatrix} \frac{1}{4} & \frac{1}{2} \\ \frac{3}{4} & \frac{1}{2} \end{bmatrix},$$

Then

$$F^2 = BF^1 = \begin{bmatrix} \frac{1}{4} & \frac{1}{2} \\ \frac{3}{4} & \frac{1}{2} \end{bmatrix}.$$

F_2 represents an expert who is no longer perfect because he errs three out of four times when "good" is the true quality, and one out of two times when "bad" is the true quality. B can be viewed as a noisy communication channel between experts 1 and 2.

4.4   The Demand for Information

In the preceding sections we have defined the (indirect) utility of information for an economic agent. In this section we will continue to identify information with expert advice that can take various forms such as a book or a consultation. The demand for information will be derived from comparing its utility calculated as in section 4.3 with its cost. The economic literature on the cost of information is sparse, however. The costs of information associated with the measure of information used in communication theory—namely, entropy—reflect only a certain portion of these costs. Only rarely have economists tried to use the results of information theory developed by Shannon (1948) and his followers.[2] (See Marschak 1971; Arrow 1970; and Green and Laffont 1986.)

As an example of the demand for information, consider a consumer who purchases a good of unknown quality. He has the utility function $u(x_1, \omega x_2)$ where x_1 is the quantity consumed of a composite good at unitary price and x_2 is the quantity consumed of the good with unknown quality ω at a price p. He has a prior distribution $\pi(\omega)$ over ω, and he can avail himself of expert advice, which is represented by a stochastic variable $\tilde{y}$ that is normally distributed with mean ω the variance of which σ^2/x_3 depends on his actual expenditure on information qx_3.

Let

$$f(y|\omega, \sigma^2/x_3)$$

be the likelihood function of the experiment that summarizes the expert advice, and let

$$v(\omega|y, \sigma^2/x_3) = \left[f(y|\omega, \sigma^2/x_3)\pi(\omega) \right] \Big/ \int_\Omega f(y|\hat{\omega}, \sigma^2/x_3)\pi(\hat{\omega}) \, d\hat{\omega}$$

be the posterior distribution of the consumer who observes y when he

2. See Gallager (1968) for a systematic treatment.

purchases advice, the quality of which is represented by the inverse of the variance σ^2/x_3.

The demand for information is derived in two steps. First the consumer determines his demand for goods 1 and 2, conditional on an observed value of $\tilde{y}$:

$$\text{Max} \int_\Omega u(x_1, \omega x_2) v(\omega | y, \sigma^2/x_3) \, d\omega$$

$$x_1 + px_2 + qx_3 = R.$$

Let $x_1(p, R - qx_3, y)$ and $x_2(p, R - qx_3, y)$ be the solutions to this problem. Then the demand for information is determined by

$$\underset{x_3}{\text{Max}} \int_Y \int_\Omega u(x_1(p, R - qx_3, y), \omega x_2(p, R - qx_3, y)) v(\omega | y, \sigma^2/x_3) \pi(y) \, d\omega \, dy.$$

See Kihlstrom (1974) for an example and some comparative static results.

Often the search for information is sequential by nature, and to derive correctly the demand for information, it is necessary to take into account this dynamic framework. For example, in search theory we acquire information about the true quality or best price of a good by visiting sequentially several sellers.[3] At the individual level, the demand for information becomes stochastic because the decision of whether or not to search further depends on the results of past searches. Instead of determining ex ante the optimal size of a sample, as was implicit in the preceding example of the choice of the variance, the agent chooses a sequential strategy to determine the size of the sample. Often this strategy can be expressed as a reservation price; the agent continues to search until he finds a price lower (if he is a buyer) or higher (if he is a seller) than his reservation price. This could be a possible explanation for frictional unemployment (see Stigler 1961; Kohn and Shavell 1972; and Lippman and McCall 1982).

---

3. Taking search theory seriously leads to the disappearance of the concept of a market. Then exchange must be formalized as if it emerged from more or less haphazard meetings of agents. This viewpoint leads to a fundamental reformalization of economic theory. A major aspect of these models is the externality generated by the decision of one agent to search further because this increases the probability of his encountering all the other agents (see the applications to contract breaking in Diamond and Maskin 1979 and to macroeconomics in Diamond 1982).

4.5*   Proof of Blackwell's Theorem

To prove sufficiency, we consider

$$U[Y^2, f^2; \pi(.), u(.)] = \sum_{y_{k'}^2 \in Y^2} \pi(y_{k'}^2) \sum_{\omega \in \Omega} u(a^{*2}(y_{k'}^2), \omega) v(\omega | y_{k'}^2).$$

By definition of the conditional probabilities,

$$\pi(y_{k'}^2) v^2(\omega | y_{k'}^2) = \pi(\omega) f^2(y_{k'}^2 | \omega)$$

$$= \pi(\omega) \sum_{y_k^1 \in Y^1} \beta_{y_{k'}^2 y_k^1} f^1(y_k^1 | \omega).$$

By the assumptions of the theorem, this expression equals

$$\sum_{y_k^1 \in Y^1} \beta_{y_{k'}^2 y_k^1} v^1(\omega | y_k^1) \pi(y_k^1),$$

which yields

$$U[Y^2, f^2; \pi(.), u(.)] = \sum_{y_k^1 \in Y^1} \pi(y_k^1) \sum_{y_{k'}^2 \in Y^2} \beta_{y_{k'}^2 y_k^1} \sum_{\omega \in \Omega} v^1(\omega | y_k^1) u(a^{*2}(y_{k'}^2), \omega).$$

By definition of a^*, we have

$$\sum_{\omega \in \Omega} v^1(\omega | y_k^1) u(a^{*2}(y_{k'}^2), \omega) \leqslant \sum_{\omega \in \Omega} v^1(\omega | y_k^1) u(a^{*1}(y_k^1), \omega).$$

Using

$$\sum_{y_{k'}^2 \in Y^2} \beta_{y_{k'}^2 y_k^1} = 1 \qquad \forall y_k^1,$$

we have

$$U(Y^2, f^2; \pi(.), u(.)) \leqslant U(Y^1, f^1; \pi(.), u(.)).$$

The proof of necessity is more complicated. It is based on using a separation theorem of a point from a convex set (see Crémer 1982 for a proof).

Suggested Readings

Hayek, F. V. (1945).   The first important treatment of the role of information in economics.

Marschak, J., and R. Radner (1972), ch. 2.   The fundamental approach on which much of this chapter is based.

Crémer, J. (1982).   A simple proof of Blackwell's theorem.

Marschak, J. (1971). An attempt to use the theory of information developed by telecommunication engineers.

References

Arrow, K. 1970. *Essays in the Theory of Risk Bearing.* North-Holland, Amsterdam.

Blackwell, D. 1951. "Comparison of Experiments." In J. Neymann (ed.) *Proceedings of the Second Berkeley Symposium on Mathematical Statistics and Probability.* University of California Press.

Crémer, J. 1982. "A Simple Proof of Blackwell's 'Comparison of Experiments' Theorem." *Journal of Economic Theory* 27:439–443.

Diamond, P. 1982. "Aggregate Demand Management in Search Equilibrium." *Journal of Political Economy* 90:881–894.

Diamond, P., and E. Maskin. 1979. "An Equilibrium Analysis of Search and Breach of Contracts, I: Steady States." *Bell Journal of Economics* 10:232–316.

Gallager, R. 1968. *Information Theory and Reliable Communication.* J. Wiley and Sons, New York.

Green, J., and J.-J. Laffont. 1986. "Incentive Theory with Data Compression." In W. Heller, R. Starr, and D. Starrett, (eds.), *Essays in Honor of K. Arrow,* Vol. 3. Cambridge University Press.

Green, J., and Stockey, N. 1978. "Two Representations of Information Structures and Their Comparisons" IMSSS, Stanford University.

Hayek, F. A. von. 1945. "The Use of Knowledge in Society." *American Economic Review* 35:519–530.

Kohn, M., and S. Shavell. 1974. "The Theory of Search." *Journal of Economic Theory* 9:93–123.

Lippman, S., and J. McCall. 1982. "The Economics of Uncertainty. Selected Topics and Probabilistics Methods." In K. Arrow and M. Intrilligator (eds.), *Handbook of Mathematical Economics,* ch. 6.

Marschak, J. 1971. "Economics of Information Systems." In *Economic Information, Decision and Prediction.* D. Reidel Publishing Co., 1974, pp. 270–334.

Marschak, J., and R. Radner 1972. *Economic Theory of Teams.* Yale University Press, New Haven.

Shannon, C. 1948. "A Mathematical Theory of Communication." *Bell System Technical Journal* 27:379–423, 623–656.

Stigler, G. 1961. "The Economics of Information." *Journal of Political Economy* 69:213–225.

5 The Theory of Contingent Markets

How should exchange be organized in an economy with uncertainty? The neoclassical methodology consists in associating to each physical good as many *contingent* goods as there are states of nature. Such an extension of the commodity space along with the appropriate multiplication of the number of competitive markets leads to a formal structure that is isomorphic to the basic microeconomic model. This chapter is devoted to an explanation of this methodology and leaves to subsequent chapters the task of specifying its relevancy and its limitations in helping us understand the uncertain economic world.

5.1 A New Interpretation of the Edgeworth Box

Consider an economy consisting of two consumers and one good, wheat. The endowments of the agents in wheat depend on the weather. If the weather is nice, agent 1 (2) has an endowment of w_1^1 (w_1^2); if the weather is inclement, agent 1 (2) has an endowment of w_2^1 (w_2^2). Let us pursue the analysis as if there were two types of wheat that we treat as different goods: good 1 is wheat when the weather is nice; good 2 is wheat when the weather is inclement.

A vector of quantities (x_1^i, x_2^i) for consumer i represents a contingent consumption *plan* in which he consumes a quantity x_1^i of wheat in the state of nature corresponding to "nice weather" and a quantity x_2^i of wheat in the state of nature corresponding to "inclement weather." Consumer i has preferences over the contingent consumption plans which we assume can be represented by a utility function $U^i(x_1^i, x_2^i)$. Moreover, if we use the expected utility hypothesis, $U^i(x_1^i, x_2^i) = \pi_1^i u^i(x_1^i) + \pi_2^i u^i(x_2^i)$, where (π_1^i, π_2^i) is the vector of subjective probabilities of consumer i over the events (nice weather, inclement weather) and $u^i(.)$ is his VNM utility function.

The expected utility hypothesis places an additional restriction on the drawing of indifference curves in the Edgeworth box. Indeed, the marginal rate of substitution of agent i is

$$\frac{\partial U^i/\partial x_2^i}{\partial U^i/\partial x_1^i} = \frac{\pi_2^i}{\pi_1^i} \frac{du^i/dx_2^i(x_2^i)}{du^i/dx_1^i(x_1^i)}.$$

If, as we have assumed until now, the VNM function is independent of the states of nature, the marginal rate of substitution is constant along the diagonal where $x_1^i = x_2^i$, and we have (see also figure 5.1):

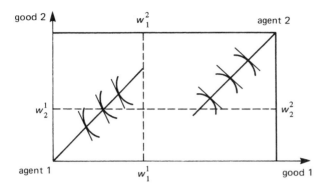

Figure 5.1

$$\frac{\partial U^i/\partial x_2^i}{\partial U^i/\partial x_1^i} = \frac{\pi_2^i}{\pi_1^i}.$$

By analogy with the classical theory of exchange, we can organize a market for good 1 (wheat in nice weather) and a market for good 2 (wheat in inclement weather) and assume that the agents behave competitively in these markets. Under the assumption of risk aversion, which implies convexity of preferences, a competitive equilibrium as represented in figure 5.2 exists. In the exchange associated with the competitive equilibrium of figure 5.2, agent 1 supplies wheat to agent 2 if the weather is nice and receives wheat from agent 2 if the weather is inclement. This allows him to bring his vector of consumption closer to the diagonal, that is, to have less variability in consumption than he has in his initial endowments.

In what follows, we consider several particular cases. Assume that the aggregate quantity of wheat is invariant to the weather, that is, $w_1^1 + w_1^2 = w_2^1 + w_2^2$. In other words, there is no macroeconomic risk. Assume also that the two consumers have the same subjective probabilities (figure 5.3).

The only equilibrium corresponds to an allocation on the diagonal in which the agents' consumption is independent of the weather. Both consumers are totally insured. When the weather is nice, the agent who is relatively well endowed provides wheat to the other agent who is, in turn, relatively well endowed when the weather is inclement so that he then reciprocates. The price ratio is equal to the ratio of subjective probabilities. On the other hand, if $w_1^1 + w_1^2 > w_2^1 + w_2^2$ and if the subjective probabilities

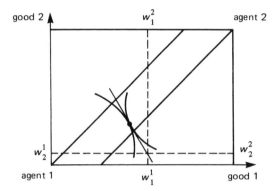

Figure 5.2

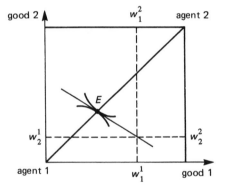

Figure 5.3

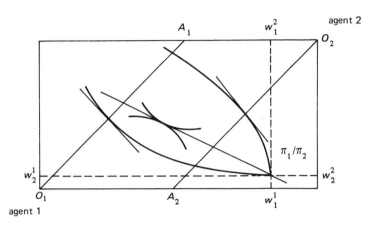

Figure 5.4

remain identical, we can validate our intuition that $p_1/p_2 < \pi_1/\pi_2$ (figure 5.4).

Consider a price ratio such that $p_1/p_2 > \pi_1/\pi_2$. Since the slope of the indifference curves of agent 2 is π_1/π_2 along $O_2 A_2$, convexity of preferences implies that the point of tangency between the budget constraint given the price ratio $p_1/p_2 > \pi_1/\pi_2$ and the indifference curves of agent 2 is located to the right of $O_2 A_2$. Symmetrically, the point of tangency of the same budget constraint with the indifference curves of agent 1 falls to the left of $O_1 A_1$. Therefore this price ratio cannot support a competitive equilibrium.

Consider a final case in which agent 1 is not risk-averse and the two agents have the same subjective probabilities. The absence of risk aversion for agent 1 implies that his indifference curves are parallel lines and that the equilibrium prices reflect the subjective probabilities $p_1/p_2 = \pi_1/\pi_2$ (see figure 5.5). Agent 1 plays the role of an insurer with respect to agent 2 and allows him to have a sure income.

In all the examples, we have assumed that the agents behave competitively (implicitly there are a large number of agents of each type). It would be easy to analyze the consequences of monopolistic behavior on the part of some agents, for example, agent 1. Then we would have the situation depicted in figure 5.6. Agent 1 chooses allocation E on the reaction function of agent 2 (the dashed curve in figure 5.6). The allocation obtained is not Pareto optimal, and agent 2 is not totally insured—in contrast with the competitive case which corresponds to an "actuary fair" price for insurance.

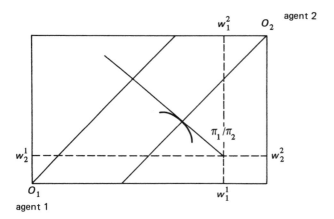

Figure 5.5

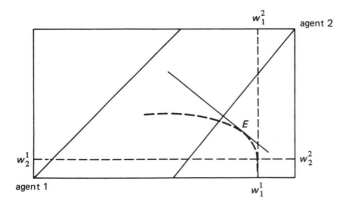

Figure 5.6

These particular cases are designed to give the reader some intuition into the problem. But, in general, prices depend on preferences and initial endowments just as in the classical theory of exchange. Here the dependence on preferences can be analyzed as a dependence partially on subjective probabilities and partially on the VNM utility function (in particular, its risk aversion). The isomorphism with the theory of exchange is now clear. The existence of markets for contingent commodities allows agents to attain a Pareto-optimal allocation before the state of nature is revealed in the sense of ex ante preferences—that is, in the sense of expected utilities, given that we are employing the expected utility hypothesis.[1]

5.2 Generalization

Consider a one-period exchange economy with I consumers, L physical goods, and S events observable by all the consumers. Let w_{ls}^i be the endowments of good l in state s for agent i, $i = 1, \ldots, I$, $l = 1, \ldots, L$, and $s = 1, \ldots, S$. A consumption bundle, x_{ls}^i, $l = 1, \ldots, L$, $s = 1, \ldots, S$ for agent i is here a *consumption strategy* (or an act) that specifies a consumption vector for each state of nature:

$$\Omega \xrightarrow{\quad x^i \quad} \mathbf{R}^L.$$

We assume that the preferences of each consumer are representable by a convex, continuous preordering over his consumption set $X^i = \mathbf{R}_+^{LS}$. Moreover we assume that w^i is in the interior of $\mathbf{R}^{LS}$, that is, $w_{ls}^i > 0$, for any l and any s.

If we set up LS (contingent) markets—that is, a complete system of Arrow-Debreu markets in which all the consumers behave competitively—a competitive equilibrium exists under the preceding assumptions. Furthermore the competitive equilibrium is an ex ante Pareto optimum, and to any ex ante Pareto optimum we can associate prices and incomes so that the corresponding competitive equilibrium coincides with this Pareto optimum (refer to the introduction).

Remark The convexity assumption on the preordering (which implies quasi concavity of the VNM utility function under the expected utility hypothesis) does not imply risk aversion of the sort that we have defined

1. See G. Debreu (1966) for a historical note concerning the theory of contingent markets.

in chapter 2. Surely, if the VNM utility functions are concave (risk aversion), the preference preordering is convex.

Let $U^i(.)$ be the utility function that represents the preference preordering over consumption strategies. The consumer's optimization problem is written as

Max $U^i(x^i)$

$$\sum_{l=1}^{L} \sum_{s=1}^{S} p_{ls} x_{ls}^i \leqslant \sum_{l=1}^{L} \sum_{s=1}^{S} p_{ls} w_{ls}^i \qquad x_{ls}^i \geqslant 0, l = 1, \ldots, L, s = 1, \ldots, S.$$

Notice that the price per unit of good 1, p_{ls} (if state s is realized), is paid before we know what state will be realized. If state s is realized, the consumer receives x_{ls}^i units of good l; if state s is not realized, he receives nothing from this contract.

All transactions are contracted for at date 0; each agent maximizes his utility in contingent purchases and sales subject to his budget constraint. Then, if state of nature s is realized, the transactions contracted for in state s are undertaken. A contingent contract is an exchange of numéraire against the promise of delivering a given quantity of a good if an event occurs. Each agent faces only a single budget constraint, and contingent markets allow him to transfer his purchasing power from one state to the other. In particular, he can insure his consumption relative to his mean income in states where his endowments are very low.

We call $\bar{p}_l = \sum_{s=1}^{S} p_{ls}$ the sure price of good l. To obtain one unit of good l with certainty, it is necessary to buy one unit of good l on each contingent market for this good. These prices must be differentiated from conditional prices that the buyer must pay only if an event is realized.

Let q_{ls} be the conditional price for good l—that is, expressed in units of the numéraire (good 1) if state s is realized. To be able to pay q_{ls} when state s is realized, one must purchase today q_{ls} units of "income if state s is realized" for which the price is p_{1s}, so that the expenditure would be $p_{1s} q_{ls}$. Arbitrage between the contingent market for good l in state s and this transaction requires that $p_{ls} = q_{ls} \cdot p_{1s}$.

The introduction of production into the theory of contingent markets poses no problem. Since the payments corresponding to all contracts are made before the state of nature is known, profits are certain. Therefore the criterion of profit maximization creates no new difficulty. The production set Y of the typical entrepreneur can be imagined as a subset of $\mathbf{R}^{LS}$ that specifies the technically feasible production vectors for each $s = 1, \ldots, S$.

To supply the outputs in state s, the enterprise purchases inputs deliverable in state s. Therefore goods corresponding to different states are treated just like different goods, and the enterprise's profit is written as

$$\sum_{l=1}^{L} \sum_{s=1}^{S} p_{ls} y_{ls}$$

where $(y_{11}, \ldots, y_{L1}, \ldots, y_{1S}, \ldots, y_{LS}) \in Y \subset \mathbf{R}^{LS}$.

This theoretical construction generalizes in a formal manner the basic microeconomic model. It defines the system of ideal markets that allow a competitive equilibrium to achieve an ex ante Pareto-optimal allocation. Two major weaknesses are contained in this extension, the essential merit of which is its provision of the ideal normative framework to study exchange and production under uncertainty. First, the number of markets required is exorbitant even if we accept the representation of uncertainty by a finite number of states of nature. The millions of necessary markets would surely be encumbered with various transactions costs, which our theory has ignored to this point. Subsequently, we will study several systems of incomplete markets and compare their results with those from the Arrow-Debreu model. The second weakness of this approach lies in the assumption of a common information structure for all agents. We will examine next several consequences of dropping this assumption.

5.3   Different Information Structures

Consider the following example of two agents and four states of nature. Four types of weather are possible: ω_1 of a little rain and a little sun, ω_2 of a little rain and much sun, ω_3 of a lot of rain and a little sun, and ω_4 of a lot of rain and much sun; that is,

$$\Omega = \{\omega_1, \omega_2, \omega_3, \omega_4\}.$$

Agent 1 has a rain gauge so that he can distinguish the event "a little rain"—namely, $E_1 = \{\omega_1, \omega_2\}$—from the event "a lot of rain"—namely, $E_2 = \{\omega_3, \omega_4\}$. On the contrary, he cannot observe the amount of sunshine. His information structure is characterized by the partition of Ω shown in figure 5.7.

Agent 2 does not have a rain gauge, but he can distinguish between a little sunshine—namely, $E_3 = \{\omega_1, \omega_3\}$—and much sunshine—namely, $E_4 = \{\omega_2, \omega_4\}$, which generates the partition of Ω shown in figure 5.8.

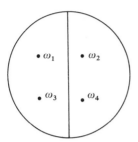

Figure 5.7

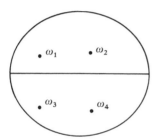

Figure 5.8

Obviously, it is impossible to have contingent markets for events that are not observable by the two agents. For example, it is not possible to have a system of markets for the finest partition of Ω—that is, four markets. Indeed, assume that agent 2 has received a payment from agent 1 so that he must deliver z_1 units of a good in state ω_1 and z_2 units of a good in state ω_2 where $z_1 \neq z_2$. If such a contract is signed, for example, with $z_1 > z_2$, agent 2 will always pretend that state ω_1 is realized, which affirms a fact that the information structure of agent 1 does not allow him to contradict. Understanding this situation, agent 1 will never sign such a contract. Only contracts verifiable by the finest commonly known information structure are possible. Since in the above example only Ω is commonly observed, no contract is possible.[2]

Radner (1968) extends the theory of the preceding section by considering all the contracts with respect to all events observable by the parties to the

2. See, nevertheless, chapter 10 where the concept of a contract is extended.

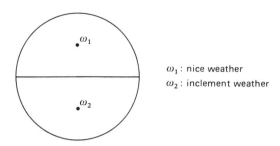

ω_1 : nice weather
ω_2 : inclement weather

Figure 5.9

exchange. Ex ante optimality of the obtained competitive equilibrium is conditional on a given information structure. On the one hand, the preceding example shows that this constraint may be so strong that the optimality of this equilibrium is devoid of meaning. On the other hand, the concept of equilibrium thus obtained is very weak because differences in agents' information structures are the foundation of multiple activities that will change the equilibrium.

In particular, informational asymmetries allow us to imagine exchanges of information between agents that render endogenous the information structures when the theory presented above considers them fixed. Furthermore observable variables, like prices and quantities, will reflect the information of the most informed agents and lead the others to modify their information structures. All these activities—which originate from recognizing the endogenous character of information structures—make up the economics of information.

5.4   The Value of Information

We return to the example of section 5.1 (figure 5.3) where the two agents have the same information structure in the absence of macroeconomic risk (figure 5.9). In chapter 4 we saw that an improvement in information is always beneficial for a Bayesian statistician. This is not necessarily the case in an economic game.

Assume that the government knows the weather before time t_0, whereas exchange takes place when the state of nature is revealed at time $t_0 + \Delta t$. Should the government reveal this information? If the government reveals the information at time t_0, there is no longer any exchange between the

two agents. The agent who is in "his good state of nature" benefits while
the other suffers. We now evaluate the welfare of agent 1 if the government
commits itself to reveal the information. Since no exchange will be possible,
his utility will be

$$\pi_1 u(w_1^1) + \pi_2 u(w_2^1).$$

In the absence of government intervention, the competitive equilibrium
(see figure 5.3) leads to a level of utility equal to

$$u(\pi_1 w_1^1 + \pi_2 w_2^1).$$

Indeed, the budget constraint of the agent is

$$\pi_1 x_1^1 + \pi_2 x_2^1 = \pi_1 w_1^1 + \pi_2 w_2^1$$

since (π_1, π_2) is the vector of prices. In equilibrium, the agent has a certain
consumption given by

$$x_1^1 = x_2^1 = \pi_1 w_1^1 + \pi_2 w_2^1.$$

Concavity of $u(.)$ implies that the agent is less well off ex ante when the
government makes the information public. This example due to Hirschleifer
(1971) shows the subtle interaction between systems of markets and information structures. In the absence of information the feasible market
system allows the agents to insure each other. The public announcement
of information renders this type of insurance impossible. Finally, notice
that the agents could agree to meet before the government announces the
state of nature so that they might attain the mutually beneficial insurance
solution.

The ill-fated nature of public information is associated with a private
incentive to obtain that information. Indeed, suppose that agent 1 knows
that state 1 will be realized. His preferences are represented by indifference
curves parallel to the good 2 axis, leading to a corner solution represented
in figure 5.10.

Agent 1 profits from his information by selling all his wheat in state 2
and attains a consumption level of wheat in state 1 that is larger than what
he would obtain in the absence of information. The "immoral" character
of this behavior is nevertheless counteracted by a subtle phenomenon. By
his demand in the market for good 1, he induces an increase in the price of
good 1 relative to good 2. This change in prices can be interpreted by agent
2, who knows all the other characteristics of the economy, as evidence that

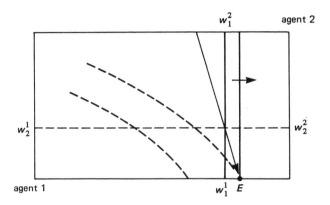

Figure 5.10

agent 1 knows that state 1 will be realized. He in turn alters his own behavior by demanding only good 1, which renders exchange impossible. However, if there is no exchange at equilibrium, how can agent 2 acquire agent 1's information? We shall reconsider these difficulties and these paradoxes in the chapter devoted to the transmission of information by prices (chapter 9).

Suggested Readings

Malinvaud, E. (1969), ch. 9.   The best summary treatment of the introduction of uncertainty into the microeconomic model.

Debreu, G. (1966), ch. 7.   The fundamental isomorphism between the basic model and the model with contingent commodities.

Radner, S. (1968).   The extension to different information structures.

References

Arrow, K. 1953. "Le Role des valeurs boursières pour la répartition la meilleure des risques." *Cahiers du Seminaire d'Econométrie*. CNRS, Paris.

Debreu, G. 1966. *La Théorie de la valeur*. Dunod, Paris.

Hirshleifer, J. 1971. "The Private and Social Value of Information and the Reward to Inventive Activity." *American Economic Review* 61:561–574.

Malinvaud, E. 1969. *Leçons de théorie microéconomique*. Dunod, Paris.

Radner, R. 1968. "Competitive Equilibrium under Uncertainty." *Econometrica* 36:31–58.

6 Equilibria with Perfect Foresight in Incomplete Markets

The formal extension of the basic microeconomic model to include uncertainty, using an Arrow-Debreu market structure, is burdened with a formidable number of necessary markets. In this chapter we model an economy with a system of incomplete markets, and we study the normative properties of this type of economy.

6.1 Back to the Arrow-Debreu Equilibrium

Consider an exchange economy with I agents and L goods. We distinguish two dates, date 0 called ex ante, and date 1 called ex post. At date 0, the future is uncertain. The space of states of nature consists of S states. At date 1, each agent observes the realized state of nature and consumes accordingly.

Let x_{ls}^i be the quantity of good l consumed in state s by agent i, $i = 1,$ $\dots, I, l = 1, \dots, L$, and $s = 1, \dots, S$. Let $x^i = (x_{11}^i, \dots, x_{LS}^i)$ be a contingent consumption plan. Consumer i has preferences over the feasible consumption plans—that is, those that belong to the consumption set $X^i \subset \mathbf{R}^{LS}$ (X^i is convex, closed and bounded from below).

The ex ante preferences of consumer i over contingent consumption plans are representable by a utility function $U^i(.)$ defined on X^i to be strictly increasing, quasi-concave, and differentiable.[1] Finally, let $w_{ls}^i > 0$ be the initial endowment of good l for agent i in state s. If a market for each good l and each state s is created at date 0, we have a system of complete Arrow-Debreu markets.

Let p_{ls} be the system of prices for $l = 1, \dots, L$ and $s = 1, \dots, S$. Agent i solves the following problem:

$$\text{Max } U^i(x^i)$$

$$\sum_{s=1}^{S} \sum_{l=1}^{L} p_{ls} x_{ls}^i \leqslant \sum_{s=1}^{S} \sum_{l=1}^{L} p_{ls} w_{ls}^i \tag{1}$$

$$x^i \in X^i.$$

An *Arrow-Debreu equilibrium* is a system of prices $p^* \in \mathbf{R}_+^{LS}$ and an allocation $(x^{*1}, \dots, x^{*I})$ such that

(i) x^{*i} is a solution to (1) for the system of prices p^* for any $i = 1, \dots, I,$

---

1. Therefore agents do not consume at date 0.

(ii) $\sum_{i=1}^{I} x^{*i} = \sum_{i=1}^{I} w^i$.

Under the preceding assumptions, an Arrow-Debreu equilibrium exists and the two fundamental welfare theorems hold if Pareto optimality is understood in the ex ante sense—that is, according to preferences over contingent consumption plans and with respect to the commonly known structure of information at date 0.

Assume, moreover, that each consumer satisfies the Savage axioms so that $U^i(.)$ can be written as

$$U^i(x^i) = \sum_{s=1}^{S} \pi_s^i u^i(x_s^i).$$

Then we call an allocation $(x^{*1}, \ldots, x^{*I})$ ex post Pareto optimal if there exists no state s and no allocation (x_s^i) such that $u^i(x_s^i) \geqslant u^i(x_s^{*i})$ for all i with at least one strict inequality.

Clearly, ex ante optimality implies ex post optimality. In essence, we have from the ex ante Pareto-optimal condition for each value of s:

$$\frac{\pi_s^i(\partial u^i/\partial x_{ls}^i)}{\pi_s^i(\partial u^i/\partial x_{ks}^i)} = \frac{\pi_s^j(\partial u^j/\partial x_{ls}^j)}{\pi_s^j(\partial u^j/\partial x_{ks}^j)}$$

$$= \frac{p_{ls}^*}{p_{ks}^*} \qquad \forall i, j, l \tag{2}$$

$$\sum_{i=1}^{I} x_{ls}^i = \sum_{i=1}^{I} w_{ls}^i \qquad l = 1, \ldots, L,$$

or simplifying by eliminating the probabilities,

$$\frac{\partial u^i/\partial x_{ls}^i}{\partial u^i/\partial x_{ks}^i} = \frac{\partial u^j/\partial x_{ls}^j}{\partial u^j/\partial x_{ks}^j} \qquad \forall i, j, l$$

$$\sum_{i=1}^{I} x_{ls}^i = \sum_{i=1}^{I} w_{ls}^i \qquad l = 1, \ldots, L,$$

which are conditions characterizing Pareto optimality for the utility functions $u^i(.)$, that is the ex post utility functions.

To be sure, the converse is not true. An allocation can be Pareto optimal in each state s without realizing the transfers between states of nature (insurance) that would make it an ex ante Pareto-optimal allocation.

Given an ex ante Pareto optimum, reopening the markets after the realization of the state of nature s would not lead to any trade because the allocation is ex post Pareto optimal as well. Notice that if at date 0, the agents know that markets will be opened at date 1, and they anticipate (correctly) that the prices will then be determined by (2), the equilibrium allocation is not affected.[2] The following section helps us to understand this remark.

6.2 The Equilibrium with Perfect Foresight

If we assume that only a limited number of markets are open at date 0, it becomes useful to open markets for goods at date 1, called "spot markets." We now specify precisely this sequence of markets.

Assume that at date 0, markets for K securities are opened. A security, a^k, is a vector in $\mathbf{R}^{LS}$ represented below in matrix form that specifies the delivery of goods in the different states of nature at date 1:

$$a^k = \begin{bmatrix} a^k_{11} \dots a^k_{1S} \\ \cdots\cdots\cdots \\ a^k_{L1} \dots a^k_{LS} \end{bmatrix} = [a^k_1, \dots a^k_S]$$

and $\tilde{a} = \text{Vec}\,[a^k_1, \dots, a^k_S]$ where a^k_{ls} is the quantity (positive or negative) of good l delivered in state s.[3]

Notice that a contingent good is a particular case of a security; for example, the contingent good (l, s) is characterized by the matrix

$$l \begin{matrix} & s & \\ \begin{bmatrix} 0 & \dots & 0 \\ \vdots & 1 & \\ 0 & \dots & 0 \end{bmatrix} \end{matrix}.$$

The unconditional delivery of one unit of good l (in the futures market) is characterized by the matrix

$$l \begin{bmatrix} 0 & 0 & & 0 \\ \cdots\cdots\cdots\cdots \\ 1 & 1 & \dots & 1 \\ \cdots\cdots\cdots\cdots \\ 0 & 0 & & 0 \end{bmatrix}.$$

Let z^{ik} be the amount of security k purchased by agent i if z^{ik} is positive, and the amount sold if z^{ik} is negative for all $k = 1, \dots, K$. Securities are

---

2. Svensson (1981) points out that if agents do not have perfect foresight about market prices at date 1, this reintroduces uncertainty and can change the allocation.
3. Let $x \in \mathbf{R}^L$, then $\text{Vec}\,x = (x_1, \dots, x_L)'$.

exchanged at date 0 on competitive markets at prices $q = (q_1, \ldots, q_K)$. Owning a vector of securities $(z^{i1}, \ldots, z^{iK})$ gives agent i in state s an endowment of goods equal to

$$v_s^i = \sum_{k=1}^{K} z^{ik} a_s^k.$$

This amount must be added to his initial endowment w_s^i to determine the aggregate resources of agent i when markets for goods at prices p_s open at date 1 after the realization of the state of nature s.

A date 0, when the agents determine their optimal portfolio of securities, they must form expectations about the prices of goods that will be established at date 1. In the Radner equilibrium, price expectations are assumed to be exact for all agents. The agents do not necessarily agree on the probabilities of different states of nature, but they expect the same prices. The reader may be surprised by this assumption of perfect foresight. It should be viewed as a necessary methodological step. We must first understand how the economy performs with incomplete markets in the best case where expectations are correct. Note that this assumption is very demanding when there are multiple spot market equilibria at date 1. Agents must coordinate on the same equilibrium.

A *Radner equilibrium* is a system of prices for the securities $q^* \in \mathbf{R}_+^K$, price expectations in each state of nature $p_s^* \in \mathbf{R}_+^L$ for $s = 1, \ldots, S$ and an allocation—that is, portfolios of securities $(z^{*1}, \ldots, z^{*I})$ and consumption plans $(x^{*1}, \ldots, x^{*I})$ such that

(a)   for any $i = 1, \ldots, I, (z^{*i}, x^{*i})$ maximizes $U^i(x^i)$ subject to the following constraints:

(1) $q^* z^{*i} \leqslant 0$,
(2) $p_s^* x_s^i \leqslant p_s^* (\sum_{k=1}^{K} a_s^k z^{ik} + w_s^i)$ $s = 1, \ldots, S$,

(b) $\sum_{i=1}^{I} z^{*i} = 0$,

(c) $\sum_{i=1}^{I} x_s^{*i} = \sum_{i=1}^{I} w_s^i$ $s = 1, \ldots, S$.

Condition (a) expresses the optimization behavior of agent i when he is faced with a sequence of markets. Condition (a1) expresses his budget constraint when he purchases and sells securities at date 0. Condition (a2) is the date 1 budget constraint in each state s. The essential difference from the Arrow-Debreu equilibrium is that the agent can reallocate his resources among different states of nature only in a limited way by using the securities markets. In the Arrow-Debreu equilibrium, (a1) is replaced by the budget constraint of problem (1) (with $q^* = p^*$ and $z^{*i} = x^{*i} - w^i$), and as we explained, (a2) is redundant inasmuch as the agents have exact expectations. Therefore reopening these markets is unnecessary.

In a simple example we show how consumption is constrained by the absence of a set of complete markets. Assume that we have only one good at date 1 ($L = 1$), three states of nature and two assets characterized by the following matrices:

$$a^1 = [1 + r, 1 + r, 1 + r],$$

$$a^2 = [\quad 0, \qquad 0, \qquad 1 \quad].$$

Security 1 is a bond which returns $1 + r$ in each state of nature. Security 2 is the contingent good in state 3. Then consumption is constrained by

$$x_1^i - w_1^i = (1 + r)z^{i1},$$

$$x_2^i - w_2^i = (1 + r)z^{i1},$$

$$x_3^i - w_3^i = (1 + r)z^{i1} + z^{i2}.$$

Whatever the prices of the assets, the excess demands must belong to a subspace defined by the two basic vectors a^1 and a^2 represented by the arrows in figure 6.1. Therefore it is obvious that we cannot achieve an ex

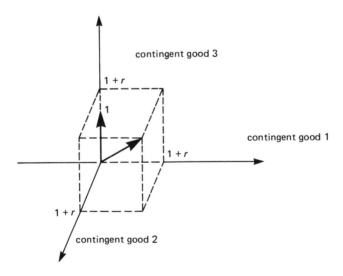

Figure 6.1

ante Pareto optimum in general. Moreover notice that here this subspace is independent of the ex post prices since there is only one price and all ex post prices are normalized to be 1. As soon as there are several goods, this subspace is a function of ex post prices, and this will be the origin of the inefficiency of the Radner equilibrium conditional on existing markets.

The concept of equilibrium defined here and developed in all its generality by Radner (1972) has been used by Arrow (1953) to show how, under the strong assumption of perfect foresight, we can organize the economy with $S + L$ markets rather than $S \times L$ contingent markets.

Suppose that we have an economy in which there are S markets for "contingent money" (good 1) at date 0 and L markets for goods at date 1. First, consider the vector of Arrow-Debreu prices (p_s^*). In state s the agent's net expenditure (with respect to his endowment) is given by

$$m_s^i = p_s^*(x_s^{*i} - w_s^i).$$

His budget constraint can be written as

$$\sum_{s=1}^{S} m_s^i = 0.$$

To represent the equilibrium in the form of a perfect foresight equilibrium, we can take

$$q_s = 1,$$

$$z^{is} = m_s^i,$$

$$p_s = p_s^* \qquad s = 1, \ldots, S,$$

$$a^s = \begin{bmatrix} & & \dfrac{1}{p_{1s}^*} & & \\ & \vdots & & \vdots & \\ 0 & \cdots & 0 & \cdots & 0 \\ & \vdots & & \vdots & \\ & & 0 & & \end{bmatrix}.$$

Notice, nevertheless, that strictly speaking, we do not have here a Radner equilibrium because the matrix a^s depends on prices. This approach is used when financial assets are considered and the returns are specified in units of account (Cass 1984; Werner 1985; and Duffie 1987). Identification with the Arrow-Debreu equilibrium requires that prices $q_s = 1$ for all $s = 1, \ldots,$ S. If these prices are allowed to vary, we should expect to obtain a set of equilibria of quite large dimensionality, actually the number of possible normalizations minus 1, $S - 1$.

Alternatively, we can normalize the prices at date 1 so that the price of a good, good 1, will always be 1. Therefore

$$q_s = p^*_{1s},$$

$$z^{is} = \frac{1}{p^*_{1s}} m^i_s,$$

$$p_s = \frac{p^*_s}{p^*_{1s}},$$

$$a^s = \begin{bmatrix} 0 \ldots 1 \ldots 0 \\ 0 \ldots 0 \ldots 0 \\ 0 \ldots 0 \ldots 0 \end{bmatrix}.$$

At date 0 the agent acquires several contingent monies which he needs to make the transfers of resources between different states. Since the relative prices of goods are anticipated correctly, this is the only important decision that must be taken before the realization of the state of nature, because the choice of the specific quantities to be consumed can be left for the second period.

Therefore the possibility of recontracting limits the number of markets to a significant degree.[4] However, notice again the necessity of exact expectations. Moreover other non-Pareto-optimal Radner equilibria can exist (Hart 1975). Nevertheless, this last phenomenon is nongeneric when the number of assets is equal to the number of states of nature (see Magill and Shafer 1985).

6.3   The Normative Analysis of Equilibria with Perfect Foresight

We consider now the case where $K < S$. Clearly, when the available securities do not allow consumers to reallocate their resources among the different states of nature as they wish, the equilibrium, if it exists, is not an ex ante

---

4. See also Kreps (1982) and section 6.4.

Pareto optimum (even though it is an ex post Pareto optimum for each realization of s since all the agents face ex post the same vector of prices). For a qualitative understanding of the normative properties of these equilibria, we will define a concept of constrained optimality that allows us to reformulate the fundamental welfare theorems of economics.

An allocation $(z^{*1}, \ldots, z^{*I}, x^{*1}, \ldots, x^{*I})$ is a *Nash social optimum* (NSO) with respect to the system of markets if

(a)   it is feasible, that is,

$$\sum_{i=1}^{I} z^{*i} = 0,$$

$$\sum_{i=1}^{I} x^{*i} \leq \sum_{i=1}^{I} w^i;$$

(b)   there exists no feasible reallocation of securities $\tilde{z}^1, \ldots, \tilde{z}^I$ such that

$$U^i\left(x^{*i} + \sum_{k=1}^{K} (\tilde{z}^{ik} - z^{*ik})\tilde{a}^k\right) > U^i(x^{*i}) \qquad i = 1, \ldots, I;$$

(c)   for any $s = 1, \ldots, S$, there exists no feasible reallocation of goods in state s, $(\tilde{x}_s^1, \ldots, \tilde{x}_s^I)$, that is,

$$\sum_{i=1}^{I} \tilde{x}_s^i \leq \sum_{i=1}^{I} w_s^i,$$

for which

$$U^i(\tilde{x}_s^i, x_{-s}^{*i}) > U^i(x^{*i}) \qquad i = 1, \ldots, I,$$

where

$$x_{-s}^i = (x_1^i, \ldots, x_{s-1}^i, x_{s+1}^i, \ldots, x_S^i)$$

and

$$(x_s^i, x_{-s}^i) = x^i.$$

This weak notion of optimality indicates that it is not possible to increase the agents' welfare by reallocations limited either to the securities or to the goods in any given state $s, s = 1, \ldots, S$. It is as if $S + 1$ uncoordinated central planners tried to improve social welfare independently. An NSO state is a Nash equilibrium of their decentralized allocative actions. The two following theorems assure us that we have the appropriate concept of optimality for our purpose:

THEOREM 1 (Grossman 1977)   A Radner equilibrium is a Nash social optimum.

Proof   Assume the contrary. If condition (b) in the definition of the NSO is violated, there exists $\tilde{z}^1, \ldots, \tilde{z}^I$ such that

$$\sum_{i=1}^{I} \tilde{z}^i = 0$$

and

$$U^i\left(x^{*i} + \sum_{k=1}^{K} (\tilde{z}^{ik} - z^{*ik})\tilde{a}^k\right) > U^i(x^{*i}) \qquad \text{for } i = 1, \ldots, I.$$

Since $\sum_{i=1}^{I} \tilde{z}^i = 0$, there exists i such that $q^*\tilde{z}^i \leq 0$.

This would mean that the allocation of the securities $\tilde{z}^i$ is both feasible for agent i and preferred, which would contradict condition (1) in the definition of an equilibrium.

If condition (c) in the definition of NSO is violated, there exists s and $\tilde{x}_s^1, \ldots, \tilde{x}_s^I$ such that

$$\sum_{i=1}^{I} \tilde{x}_s^i \leq \sum_{i=1}^{I} w_s^i$$

$$U^i(\tilde{x}_s^i, x_{-s}^{*i}) > U^i(x^{*i}) \qquad i = 1, \ldots, I.$$

Strict monotonicity of preferences then implies that

$$p_s^* \tilde{x}_s^i > p_s^* x_s^{*i} \qquad i = 1, \ldots, I,$$

which yields

$$p_s^* \sum_{i=1}^{I} \tilde{x}_s^i > p_s^* \sum_{i=1}^{I} x_s^{*i} = p_s^* \sum_{i=1}^{I} w_s^i,$$

which contradicts the feasibility of $(\tilde{x}_s^1, \ldots, \tilde{x}_s^I)$. ∎

THEOREM 2 (Grossman 1977)   If the allocation $(z^{*1}, \ldots, z^{*I}, x^{*1}, \ldots, x^{*I})$ is a Nash social optimum, then there exists a system of prices $(q^*, p_1^*, \ldots, p_S^*)$ and a distribution of initial endowments such that this system of prices and this allocation constitute a Radner equilibrium.

The proof consists of repeated applications of a separation theorem for convex sets in order to obtain $q^*, p_1^*, \ldots, p_S^*$ successively.

The property of Nash social optimality is very weak. Hart (1975) gives some examples in which one Radner equilibrium is dominated in a Paretian sense by another Radner equilibrium.[5] Moreover, establishing some supplementary markets without reaching complete markets does not guarantee a Pareto improvement. These results are analogous to some found in the theory of the second best.[6] Indeed, incomplete markets can be analyzed as a second best constraint in the Arrow-Debreu model.

Since the notion of Nash social optimality is quite insufficient, we may wonder if some meaningful restrictions do not lead to a stronger notion of optimality. We continue the normative analysis by querying when it is impossible to realize an improvement in the Pareto sense by redistributing only the portfolios (z^{ik}) and by letting the prices in the different states of nature (p_s) adjust to equate supply and demand. We say that an allocation is *Pareto optimal in the Diamond sense* if such a redistribution is not possible. We also refer to this notion as *optimality conditional on existing markets*.

Assume that each consumer has a VNM function and denote the indirect utility functions specific to each state s by $V^i(p_s, R_s^i)$[7] for $i = 1, \ldots, I$ and $s = 1, \ldots, S$. The ex ante utility of agent i can be written as

$$\sum_{s=1}^{S} \pi_s^i V^i(p_s, R_s^i),$$

with

$$R_s^i = p_s \left(\sum_{k=1}^{K} a_s^k z^{ik} + w_s^i \right) \equiv p_s e_s^i.$$

Consumer i chooses his portfolio (z^{ik}) by correctly anticipating the prices (p_s), and therefore his contingent income (R_s^i), and by solving the following problem:

$$\underset{(z^i, R_s^i)}{\text{Max}} \sum_{s=1}^{S} \pi_s^i V^i(p_s, R_s^i)$$

subject to

5. Hart's examples are in the case $L = S$, but this phenomenon is clearly general.
6. See Laffont (1988), ch. 7.
7. That is, $V^i(p_s, R_s^i) = \text{Max}_{x_s^i} \{U^i(x_s^i); p_s x_s^i \leqslant R_s^i\}$.

$$qz^i = 0, \tag{2}$$

$$R_s^i = p_s \left(\sum_{k=1}^{K} a_s^k z^{ik} + w_s^i \right) \qquad s = 1, \ldots, S, \tag{3}$$

or, by substituting (3) in the objective function,

$$\underset{(z^i)}{\text{Max}} \sum_{s=1}^{S} \pi_s^i V^i \left(p_s, p_s \left(\sum_{k=1}^{K} a_s^k z^{ik} + w_s^i \right) \right)$$

subject to

$$\sum_{k=1}^{K} q_k z^{ik} = 0.$$

The first-order conditions are

$$\frac{\sum_{s=1}^{S} \pi_s^i (\partial V^i / \partial R_s^i) p_s a_s^k}{\sum_{s=1}^{S} \pi_s^i (\partial V^i / \partial R_s^i) p_s a_s^{k'}} = \frac{q_k}{q_{k'}} \qquad \forall k \neq k', \forall i. \tag{4}$$

Ex ante, the agents equate their marginal rates of substitution between the assets k and k' (that is, the ratios of expected marginal utility from an increase of one unit of asset k and the expected marginal utility from an increase of one unit of asset k') to the ratio of the prices of these assets. In incomplete markets the agents cannot completely insure themselves—that is, they cannot equate their marginal rates of substitution between incomes in different states of nature, given by

$$\frac{\pi_s^i (\partial V^i / \partial R_s^i)}{\pi_{s'}^i (\partial V^i / \partial R_{s'}^i)}.$$

Since he behaves competitively, each consumer takes the prices (p_s) as given. We now examine the conditions under which a planner who understands the impact of the allocations of assets on prices can improve welfare.

Consider a planner who attempts to allocate the *existing* assets so as to maximize expected social welfare. He would solve the following problem:

$$\underset{(z^i)}{\text{Max}} \sum_{i=1}^{I} \lambda^i \left(\sum_{s=1}^{S} \pi_s^i V^i \left(p_s, p_s \left(\sum_{k=1}^{K} a_s^k z^{ik} + w_s^i \right) \right) \right) \qquad \lambda^i \geqslant 0$$

subject to

$$\sum_{i=1}^{I} z^{ik} = 0 \qquad k = 1, \ldots, K$$

where the prices p_s adjust to equate demand and supply ex post. The first-order conditions for this problem are written as

$$\frac{\lambda^i \sum_{s=1}^{S} \pi_s^i (\partial V^i/\partial R_s^i)(p_s a_s^k) + \sum_{j=1}^{J} \lambda^j (\sum_{s=1}^{S} \pi_s^j \sum_{l=1}^{L} (\partial p_{ls}/\partial z^{ik})(\partial V^j/\partial p_{ls} + e_{ls}^j(\partial V^j/\partial R_s^j)))}{\lambda^i \sum_{s=1}^{S} \pi_s^i (\partial V^i/\partial R_s^i)(p_s a_s^{k'}) + \sum_{j=1}^{J} \lambda^j (\sum_{s=1}^{S} \pi_s^j \sum_{l=1}^{L} (\partial p_{ls}/\partial z^{ik'})(\partial V^j/\partial p_{ls} + e_{ls}^j(\partial V^j/\partial R_s^j)))} = \frac{\mu_k}{\mu_{k'}}$$

$$\forall k \neq k', \forall i. \qquad (5)$$

A necessary and sufficient condition for constrained optimality is that (4) = (5). By generalizing the method of Geanakoplos and Polemarchakis (1986), it can be shown that these conditions are never satisfied generically when $L \geqslant 2$.

We now examine several cases where these conditions are verified. A sufficient condition for Diamond optimality is that the second terms of the numerator and of the denominator in the expression on the right-hand side of (5) be zero. For example, if there is only one good, there can be no change in relative prices within each state of nature and $\partial p_{ls}/\partial z^{ik} = 0$ for all s, i, k, and $l = 1$. This is the case examined by Diamond (1967) in a richer context with firms, and it will be the subject of our analysis in the next chapter.

Similarly, any conditions on preferences that make the prices (p_s) in each state of nature independent from the incomes of consumers lead to $\partial p_{ls}/\partial z^{ik} = 0$ and therefore to Diamond optimality. As examples of such a condition, let all agents have quasi-linear VNM utility functions or identical VNM utility functions that are homothetic. We will also have Diamond optimality if there is no possibility for trade in any state of nature. By Roy's identity, we have

$$\frac{\partial V^j}{\partial p_{ls}} + e_{ls}^j \frac{\partial V^j}{\partial R_s^j} = \frac{\partial V^j}{\partial R_s^j}(-x_{ls}^j + e_{ls}^j). \qquad (6)$$

Therefore, if $x_{ls}^j = e_{ls}^j$ for any j, l, and s, the appropriate terms cancel.

We also verify that if we have a complete system of markets, Diamond optimality is satisfied. In such a case, we have equality of the social marginal utilities of contingent goods for the weights (λ^j) corresponding to the equilibrium considered, that is,

$$\lambda^j \pi_s^j \frac{\partial V^j}{\partial R_s^j} = \lambda^{j'} \pi_s^{j'} \frac{\partial V^{j'}}{\partial R_s^{j'}} \qquad \forall j \neq j', \qquad (7)$$

which yields from (6)

$$\sum_{j=1}^{I} \lambda^j \left(\sum_{s=1}^{S} \pi_s^j \sum_{l=1}^{L} \frac{\partial p_{ls}}{\partial z^{ik}} \cdot \frac{\partial V^j}{\partial R_s^{\,j}} (e_{ls}^j - x_{ls}^j) \right)$$

$$= \sum_{s=1}^{S} \sum_{l=1}^{L} \frac{\partial p_{ls}}{\partial z^{ik}} \left(\lambda^1 \pi_s^1 \frac{\partial V^1}{\partial R_s^1} \left(\sum_{j=1}^{I} (e_{ls}^j - x_{ls}^j) \right) \right) = 0$$

since by market equilibrium it follows that

$$\sum_{j=1}^{I} e_{ls}^j = \sum_{j=1}^{I} x_{ls}^j \qquad \forall l, \forall s.$$

To sum up, we have seen that when the structure of assets is incomplete and does not span the space of states of nature, the Radner equilibrium is not even, in general, locally optimal conditionally on the existing markets. Competitive agents do not internalize the pecuniary externality consisting of the effect on prices in the second period of their choice of portfolios, though these prices define the achievable subspaces of the space of contingent goods. By taxing the assets, the government can improve social welfare because by influencing the distribution of prices (p_s) in the different states of nature, it improves the insurance properties provided by a given asset structure.

6.4   Existence of Equilibrium

In the Radner equilibrium we assume that each agent can sell securities short in unlimited quantities. The absence of a lower bound to short sales creates a problem of nonexistence of equilibrium. This was noticed by Radner who imposed limits on short sales, for example, $-z^{ik} \leqslant L^k$ for $k = 1, \ldots, K$. However, the equilibrium thus obtained depends crucially on these artificial limits, a rather unsatisfactory situation. Hart (1975) constructs an example of the nonexistence of a Radner equilibrium. Nonexistence is due to the fact that the budget correspondence cannot be continuous. This point is illustrated in the following way:

Consider two securities in the case where $S = 2$, and let $r_s^k = p_s \cdot a_s^k$ for $s = 1$ and 2 be the monetary return from security k in state s for $k = 1$ and 2 (see figure 6.2).

The budget constraints in period 1 are written as

$$p_1(x_1 - w_1) = z^1 r_1^1 + z^2 r_1^2 \qquad \text{in state 1,}$$

$$p_2(x_2 - w_2) = z^1 r_2^1 + z^2 r_2^2 \qquad \text{in state 2.}$$

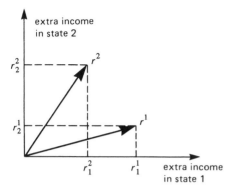

Figure 6.2

Then consider a sequence of prices (p_{1n}, p_{2n}) converging to $\bar{p}_1$ and $\bar{p}_2$ so that the vectors of monetary returns $r_n^1 = (r_{1n}^1, r_{2n}^1)$ and $r_n^2 = (r_{1n}^2, r_{2n}^2)$ are linearly independent for all n and colinear in the limit when n approaches infinity. For all n, it is possible to generate any vector in $\mathbf{R}^2$ from r_n^1 and r_n^2 by an appropriate choice of z^1 and z^2. On the other hand, in the limit it is possible to generate only the subspace of dimensionality 1 defined by

$$\mathrm{Lim}\ r_n^1 = \mathrm{Lim}\ r_n^2.$$
$$\quad n \qquad\quad n$$

The ratio of the excess values of consumption in the two states is necessarily fixed. The set of feasible consumption points is not upper semicontinuous, which can lead to discontinuous demand functions and therefore to the possibility of the nonexistence of equilibrium (see problem 6 at the end of the book).

The preceding argument shows that the difficulty stems from the dependence of the monetary returns from the assets on prices in the second period. Two types of restrictions on the nature of traded assets allow us to eliminate this dependence and the possibility of the nonexistence of equilibrium as well. If, in each state of nature, the assets deliver only the good chosen as the numéraire in that particular state (Arrow 1953; Geanakoplos and Polemarchakis 1986), or alternatively units of account that are independent of prices (Cass 1984; Werner 1985),[8] then the monetary returns are independent of prices by construction and the existence of equilibrium can be demonstrated, given the traditional assumptions. Moreover, in the

8. This second construction does not lead strictly to a Radner equilibrium.

general case, recent work shows that Hart's example mentioned earlier is an exception and that the existence of the Radner equilibrium is assured generically (when $L = S$, see Magill and Shafer 1985, and even when $L < S$, see Duffie and Shafer 1986; Hirsch, Magill and Mas-Colell 1987).

6.5   On the Incompleteness of Markets

To discuss incomplete markets in a concrete way, it is necessary to introduce the temporal dimension of economic activities, a facet that we have ignored intentionally in this book which is devoted essentially to static aspects of uncertainty and information. Such an extension forces us to grapple with many new problems, and here we discuss these issues in a limited way. In the following chapters we will analyze the basic institutions for sharing risk, namely, the stock market and insurance. However, there are several other institutions for sharing risk, and we turn to these briefly.

First, we have options' markets. An option is a security whose returns depend on the returns of some other security. Consider a security that yields x_s in terms of the numéraire in state s or $x = [x_1, x_2, \ldots, x_S]$ where the states of nature have been ordered so that x_s is increasing in s. An option to buy the security at a price a after the state of nature has been revealed is a security derived from the fundamental security x and can be written as

$$c(x, a) = \text{Max}\,[x_s - a, 0]$$

because if $x_s < a$ the security will not be purchased. For example, in the case where $|S| = 3$ and the fundamental security is given by $x = [1, 2, 3]$, we can construct two options:

$$c(x, 1) = [0, 1, 2] \quad \text{and} \quad c(x, 2) = [0, 0, 1].$$

Then we notice that the three securities x, $c(x, 1)$ and $c(x, 2)$ generate $\mathbf{R}^3$—that is, the securities are equivalent to a system of complete markets. The interest in options as a tool for generating an important subspace of $\mathbf{R}^S$ comes from the belief that the transaction costs associated with organizing these markets are lower than the analogous costs of creating new contingent markets (see Ross 1976).

In a dynamic context, an important possibility emerges from repeated exchanges over time as uncertainty unfolds. The relationship between the speed at which we can recontract and the speed at which information arrives plays a crucial role in evaluating the efficiency of a system of markets organized in this manner. This idea can be explained simply as follows. Consider two dates, date 0 and date 1, and two goods. At date 1, two states of nature are possible. At date 0, consider a consumer who is interested in consuming at date 1 only. Consider first complete contingent markets. Since there are two goods, there are four contingent goods at date 0 with no need to reopen markets at date 1. The budget constraint of the consumer is written as

$$p_{11}x_{11} + p_{21}x_{21} + p_{12}x_{12} + p_{22}x_{22}$$

$$= p_{11}w_{11} + p_{21}w_{21} + p_{12}w_{12} + p_{22}w_{22}$$

where p_{ls} is the price of good l in state s and w_{ls} is his endowment of good l in state s at date 1.

Now assume that we have only spot markets and futures markets. At date 0, the consumer buys no goods on spot markets (because he does not want to consume anything at date 0), but he buys goods 1 and 2 on futures markets at prices q_1 and q_2 for unconditional delivery at date 1 subject to the following budget constraint:

$$q_1 z_1 + q_2 z_2 = 0. \tag{8}$$

At date 1, there are only spot markets on which prices (p_1^1, p_2^1) prevail in state 1, and prices (p_1^2, p_2^2) prevail in state 2. The respective budget constraints are

$$p_1^1 x_{11} + p_2^1 x_{21} = p_1^1 z_1 + p_2^1 z_2 + p_1^1 w_{11} + p_2^1 w_{21}, \tag{9}$$

$$p_1^2 x_{12} + p_2^2 x_{22} = p_1^2 z_1 + p_2^2 z_2 + p_1^2 w_{12} + p_2^2 w_{22}. \tag{10}$$

In the Radner equilibrium for this system of markets, arbitrage is precluded only if

$$\frac{\pi_1 p_2^1 + \pi_2 p_2^2}{q_2} = \frac{\pi_1 p_1^1 + \pi_2 p_1^2}{q_1} \equiv 1 + r$$

Multiplying (9) by $\pi_1/(1 + r)$ and (10) by $\pi_2/(1 + r)$ and adding to (8), we obtain

$$\frac{p_1^1 \pi_1}{1 + r} x_{11} + \frac{p_2^1 \pi_1}{1 + r} x_{21} + \frac{p_1^2 \pi_2}{1 + r} x_{12} + \frac{p_2^2 \pi_2}{1 + r} x_{22}$$

$$= \frac{p_1^1 \pi_1}{1 + r} w_{11} + \frac{p_2^1 \pi_1}{1 + r} w_{21} + \frac{p_1^2 \pi_2}{1 + r} w_{12} + \frac{p_2^2 \pi_2}{1 + r} w_{22}.$$

We can establish the following correspondence between Arrow-Debreu prices and the prices in sequential markets:

$$p_{11} = \frac{p_1^1 \pi_1}{1 + r},$$

$$p_{21} = \frac{p_2^1 \pi_1}{1 + r},$$

$$p_{12} = \frac{p_1^2 \pi_2}{1 + r},$$

$$p_{22} = \frac{p_2^2 \pi_2}{1 + r},$$

with

$$(1 + r) = \frac{\pi_1 p_1^1 + \pi_2 p_1^2}{q_1} = \frac{\pi_1 p_2^1 + \pi_2 p_2^2}{q_2}.$$

However, for the consumers to have the same budget sets in the two systems of markets with this correspondence of prices, it is necessary that the price vectors at date 1 be independent—that is, there is no $\lambda \neq 0$ such that

$$(p_1^1, p_2^1) = \lambda(p_1^2, p_2^2).$$

Indeed, if such were the case, by denoting the excess demand for good l in state s as $\xi_{ls} = x_{ls} - w_{ls}$, we would have an additional constraint in spot and futures markets obtained from (9) and (10), written as

$$\frac{\xi_{11} - \xi_{12}}{\xi_{22} - \xi_{21}} = \frac{p_2^2}{p_1^2}.$$

Since we have two goods and two states of nature, when prices at date 1 are independent, transactions on futures markets alone allow the agent to transfer purchasing power between states of nature, as he would do with contingent goods. More generally, to be able to associate to any Arrow-Debreu equilibrium a Radner equilibrium with only futures prices and spot prices, it is necessary to have at each date at least as many goods as there are states of nature at the following date and also that the prices at the following date be linearly independent across the states of nature (see Kreps 1982; Magill and Shafer 1985).

In the theory of finance the situation often arises in which repeated transactions of assets without contingent markets generate the Arrow-Debreu equilibrium (see Duffie and Huang 1985). Therefore introducing options into such a situation cannot enlarge the space of markets as it did in the case just examined. The motivation given for introducing options is then based only on economizing transactions costs. The option can achieve directly a result that would require multiple transactions in spot and futures markets. Since the asset prices prior to the introduction of options generate Arrow-Debreu prices, it is not surprising that we can derive formulae for evaluating options as a function of the rate of interest and the price of a fundamental asset (the formula of Cox-Ross-Rubinstein in discrete time, and of Black and Scholes in continuous time; see Cox and Rubinstein 1985).

6.6*   Law and Economics

A large part of the law and economics literature is devoted to studying the performance of certain legal rules designed to adjudicate conflicts stemming from unforeseen contractual circumstances. Transactions costs prevent the specification of contracts determining the nature of the exchange in each state of nature. Therefore efficiency properties, risk-sharing, and the cost of implementing different regulations are analyzed. When there is a breach of contract, one could imagine reimbursing the victim an amount equal to the benefit that he could legitimately expect from the execution of the contract, an amount which brings him back to his initial pre-contract situation, or an amount equal to the benefits that he has provided to the party who broke the contract, and so on. Therefore these legal regulations appear as institutional instruments that allow the management of the consequences from using noncontingent contracts. These rules are applicable in competitive situations like those in this chapter but also in any other market structure (see Polinsky 1983, for an introduction to this rapidly expanding field).

6.7*   Sunspot Equilibria

A sunspot is a random variable that is not relevant for defining the data of an economy with a complete or incomplete system of markets. Sometimes a sunspot is referred to as extrinsic uncertainty to distinguish it from

intrinsic uncertainty which is the usual uncertainty concerning endowments, preferences, and technology.

Two main questions are raised by sunspots. Does the mere existence of
sunspots affect economic variables? Does the creation of markets contingent on the values of sunspots affect the economy?

Consider the Arrow-Debreu equilibrium of section 1 where intrinsic
uncertainty has been eliminated to simplify notations. We then have:

THEOREM 3 (Cass and Shell 1983)   If the VNM utility functions are strictly
concave, any competitive equilibrium of a system of markets extended to
include markets conditional on the values of sunspots coincide with an
Arrow-Debreu competitive equilibrium.

Proof   Suppose the contrary, and consider for simplicity a single sunspot
variable $\tilde{\theta}$ that takes the values $\theta_1, \ldots, \theta_K$ with probabilities $\pi_1, \ldots, \pi_K$. Let
$p^*(\theta), x^{*1}(\theta), \ldots, x^{*I}(\theta)$, $\theta \in \{\theta_1, \ldots, \theta_K\}$ be a competitive equilibrium of the
extended market system. From chapter 5 the contingent consumption
plans $x^{*1}(.), \ldots, x^{*I}(.)$ are ex ante Pareto optimal.

For every θ we have, by feasibility,

$$\sum_{i=1}^{I} x^{*i}(\theta) = \sum_{i=1}^{I} w^i.$$

Consider the average allocation $Ex^i = \sum_{k=1}^{K} \pi_k x^{*i}(\theta_k)$. It is a feasible
allocation, and from Jensen's inequality, we have for any i,

$$u^i(Ex^i) \geqslant \sum_{k=1}^{K} \pi_k u^i[x^{*i}(\theta_k)],$$

with strict inequality for at least one i contradicting the ex ante Pareto
optimality of $x^{*1}(.), \ldots, x^{*I}(.)$. ∎

In the preceding case extrinsic uncertainty does not affect the economy.
However, if the VNM utility functions are not concave, the competitive
equilibrium (if it exists) is not necessarily ex ante Pareto optimal—that
is, Pareto optimal in the class of stochastic allocations. The creation of
markets conditional on sunspots can give rise to an improvement in the
Pareto sense.

More generally, any source of inefficiency such as incomplete markets,
externalities, and imperfect competition makes possible, by virtue of a
general second-best principle, Pareto improvements by stochastic alloca-

tions. This in turn makes often possible the emergence of equilibria affected by sunspots.

The role and relevance of sunspots is not completely elucidated. We can distinguish at least among four types of channels through which sunspots have an effect on economic variables: different prior distributions (see section 5.1), wealth effects between agents who are sufficiently different, coordination across multiple equilibria, and infinite horizon (see, for example, Shell 1987, Cass and Shell 1983, Guesnerie and Laffont 1987, for an introduction to this topic).

Suggested Readings

Radner, R. (1972). The concept of an equilibrium with perfect foresight.

Hart, O. (1975). The difficulties posed by incomplete markets.

Grossman, S. (1977). The concept of Nash social optimality.

Cox, J., and M. Rubinstein (1985). Theory and applications of options.

References

Arrow, K. 1953. "Le Rôle des valeurs boursières pour la répartition la meilleure des risques." *Cahiers du Séminaire d'Econométrie*, CNRS, Paris.

Cass, D., and K. Shell. 1983. "Do Sunspots Matter." *Journal of Political Economy* 91: 193–227.

Cass, D. 1984. "Complete Equilibrium with Incomplete Financial Markets." CARESS Discussion Paper. University of Pennsylvania.

Cox, J., and M. Rubinstein. 1985. *Options Markets*. Prentice-Hall, Englewood Cliffs, NJ.

Diamond, P. 1967. "The Role of a Stock Market in a General Equilibrium Model with Technological Uncertainty." *American Economic Review* 57: 759–776.

Duffie, D. 1987. "Stochastic Equilibria With Incomplete Financial Markets." *Journal of Economic Theory* 41: 405–416.

Duffie, D., and Chi-Fu-Huang. 1985. "Implementing Arrow-Debreu Equilibria by Continuous Trading of Few Long-Lived Securities." *Econometrica* 53: 1337–1356.

Duffie, D., and W. Shafer. 1986. "Equilibrium in Incomplete Markets II: Generic Existence in Stochastic Economies." *Journal of Mathematical Economics* 15: 199–216.

Geanakoplos, J., and H. Polemarchakis. 1986. "Existence, Regularity, and Constrained Suboptimality of Competitive Allocations when the Asset Market Is Incomplete." In W. Heller, R. Starr, and D. Starrett (eds.), *Uncertainty, Information and Communication, Essays in Honor of K. S. Arrow*. Vol. 3, ch. 3.

Grossman, S. 1977. "A Characterization of the Optimality of Equilibrium in Incomplete Markets." *Journal of Economic Theory* 15: 1–15.

Guesnerie, R., and J. J. Laffont. 1987. "Sunspots in Finite Horizon Models." *Volume in Honor of E. Malinvaud*, forthcoming.

Hart, O. 1975. "On the Optimality of Equilibrium When Markets are Incomplete." *Journal of Economic Theory* 11:418–443.

Hirsch, M. D., Magill, M., and A. Mas-Colell. 1987. "A Geometric Approach to a Class of Equilibrium Existence Theorems." *Journal of Mathematical Economics*, forthcoming.

Kreps, D. 1982. "Multiperiod Securities and the Efficient Allocation of Risk: A Comment on the Black-Scholes Option Pricing Model." In J. M. Call (ed.), *The Economics of Information and Uncertainty*. NBER, Chicago.

Magill, J. P., and W. Shafer. 1985. "Equilibrium and Efficiency in a Canonical Asset Market Model." *Journal of Mathematical Economics*, forthcoming.

Polinsky, M. 1983. *An Introduction to Law and Economics*. Little, Brown, Boston.

Radner, R. 1972. "Existence of Equilibrium of Plans, Prices and Price Expectations in a Sequence of Markets." *Econometrica* 40:289–303.

Ross, S. 1976. "Options and Efficiency." *Quarterly Journal of Economics* 90:75–89.

Shell, K. 1987. "Sunspot Equilibrium." In *The New Palgrave*. Mcmillan, New York.

Svensson, L. 1981. "Efficiency and Speculation in a Model with Price-Contingent Contracts." *Econometrica* 49:131–151.

Werner, J. 1985. "Equilibrium in Economies with Incomplete Financial Markets." *Journal of Economic Theory* 36:110–119.

7 The Stock Market

In the preceding chapter we could easily have introduced initial endowments of securities without changing the analysis so long as we would allow short sales in these securities. The bonds and equity shares issued by firms are particularly important examples of such securities. In an imperfect way they facilitate risk sharing when the firms face technological uncertainty. Initial endowments in securities could consist of ownership shares of these firms.

The introduction of firms leads to two important economic questions: To what extent does the availability of a stock market, that is, an incomplete substitute for a system of contingent markets, affect the production decisions of firms? What are the properties of a production economy equipped with a stock market? In the first section we show how the model in chapter 6 can be extended to construct a competitive theory of the stock market. The second section is devoted to a discussion of the literature from the perspective of this model. Finally, the third section presents the Modigliani-Miller theorem.

7.1 Competitive Equilibrium in the Stock Market

We distinguish two dates; at date 0, the J firms finance their inputs y_0^j (negative numbers) for $j = 1, \ldots, J$ by issuing bonds at a rate of interest r.[1] To simplify the notation, we assume that there is only a single good at date 0 that serves as an input for all the firms, and we set its price equal to 1. Let B^j be the quantity of bonds necessary to finance y_0^j so that $B^j = -y_0^j$.

The consumers are endowed with initial amounts of this good given by $w_0^i > 0$ that they do not consume at date 0. Therefore, in equilibrium, firms will have to "invest" an amount equal to

$$\sum_{j=1}^{J} B^j = \sum_{i=1}^{I} w_0^i.$$

At date 1, firm j produces outputs y_s^j, depending on the state of nature $s = 1, \ldots, S$, and sells them at price $p_s \in \mathbf{R}^L$ prevailing in state s. The firm repays its debt, that is, $(1 + r)B^j$, and distributes as dividends to its shareholders, its profits, that is, $p_s y_s^j - (1 + r)B^j$ in state s. Here profit is expressed in the numéraire of date 1 which we take equal to good 1.

---

1. The rate of interest is equal for all firms because we exclude the possibility of bankruptcy. See section 7.3 for a consideration of alternative methods of financing.

At date 0, a market for shares exists in which holding an equity share equal to 1 in firm j corresponds to owning all of firm j and is a claim at date 1 to an $L \times S$ matrix a^j of the following form:

$$\begin{bmatrix} p_1 y_1^j - (1+r)B^j, \, p_2 y_2^j - (1+r)B^j, \ldots, \, p_S y_S^j - (1+r)B^j \\ 0 \qquad\qquad\qquad 0 \qquad\qquad\qquad 0 \\ \vdots \qquad\qquad\qquad \vdots \qquad\qquad\qquad \vdots \\ 0 \qquad\qquad\qquad 0 \qquad\qquad\qquad 0 \end{bmatrix}$$

Analogously, holding a quantity of bonds equal to 1 is a claim to an $L \times S$ matrix given by

$$\begin{bmatrix} (1+r) & (1+r)\ldots(1+r) \\ 0 & 0 \qquad 0 \\ \vdots & \vdots \qquad \vdots \\ 0 & 0 \qquad 0 \end{bmatrix}$$

These $J + 1$ securities will play the same role as the securities considered in chapter 6.

Initially, upon arrival at the equity market, consumer i is endowed with a fraction θ_0^{ij} of firm $j(\sum_{i=1}^{I} \theta_0^{ij} = 1)$, and we denote by θ^{ij} the fraction that he retains after trade. The number of bonds that he obtains is denoted b^i. Therefore the date 0 budget constraint of consumer i is

$$\sum_{j=1}^{J} \theta^{ij} v^j + b^j \leqslant w_0^i + \sum_{j=1}^{J} \theta_0^{ij} v^j$$

where v^j indicates the value (that is, the price) of firm j on the equity market. At date 1, in state s we have

$$p_s x_s^i \leqslant b^i(1+r) + \sum_{j=1}^{J} \theta^{ij}(p_s y_s^j + (1+r)y_0^j) + p_s w_s^i.$$

Let π_s^i be the subjective probability of consumer i concerning state s and $u^i(.)$ be his von Neumann-Morgenstern utility function.[2] His maximization problem is

2. As in the preceding chapter, to make the presentation less burdensome, we assume that the consumer obtains no utility from consumption in period 0. The extension to intertemporal utility functions is necessary if we wish to determine the equilibrium rate of interest in some way other than by a certain exogenous technology.

$$\text{Max} \sum_{s=1}^{S} \pi_s^i u^i(x_s^i) \tag{1}$$

subject to

$$\sum_{j=1}^{J} \theta^{ij} v^j + b^i \leqslant w_0^i + \sum_{j=1}^{J} \theta_0^{ij} v^j, \tag{2}$$

$$p_s x_s^i \leqslant b^i(1 + r) + \sum_{j=1}^{J} \theta^{ij}(p_s y_s^j + (1 + r)y_0^j) + p_s w_s^i$$

$$x_s^i \geqslant 0 \qquad s = 1, \ldots, S. \tag{3}$$

As in the preceding chapter we assume that at date 0 the consumers have perfect foresight about date 1 prices.

Given the production vectors of the J firms, we could appeal to the analysis of chapter 6 and consider the Radner-type competitive equilibria with perfect foresight for the $J + 1$ securities mentioned earlier. In particular, if the space generated by these $J + 1$ securities is of dimension S, the equilibria coincide with the equilibria of a system of complete Arrow-Debreu markets. The purpose of this chapter is to integrate production decisions into this analysis. To accomplish this, we must analyze the behavior of firms and, in particular, the relationship between their productive decisions and their market values v^j.

Two sorts of problems can be distinguished:

The essential difficulty stems from the fact that in the absence of complete markets (except for certain particular cases), there exists no objective evaluation of variations in the market value of a firm as a function of variations of its production. Such a change in productive decisions appears to be a public good for which the shareholders have eventually contradictory subjective evaluations. We need to study how a manager aggregates the preferences of the shareholders in order to make his production decisions.

The second difficulty comes from the fact that if the firms are large in relationship to their markets, they will behave monopolistically.

Each agent forms his expectations on the way in which the value of the firm changes with its investment decision y_0^j by combining these two factors. As a first step, we define competitive expectations as those that attempt to express what would be rational expectations for a firm of negligible size in the economy. Rewrite the problem for consumer i by substituting in (3) the value of b^i obtained in (2) to get

$$\text{Max} \sum_{s=1}^{S} \pi_s^i u^i(x_s^i), \tag{4}$$

$$p_s x_s^i \leqslant \left[w_0^i + \sum_{j=1}^{J} (\theta_0^{ij} - \theta^{ij}) v^j \right] (1 + r)$$

$$+ \sum_{j=1}^{J} \theta^{ij}(p_s y_s^j + (1 + r) y_0^j) + p_s w_s^i \qquad s = 1, \dots, S. \tag{5}$$

Denote by R_s^i the right-hand side of (5), that is, income in state s.

As in the preceding chapter, we express the maximum of (4) using indirect utility functions $V^i(p_s, R_s^i)$ for each state s. The above program can then be rewritten:

$$\sum_{s=1}^{S} \pi_s^i V^i(p_s, R_s^i),$$

with

$$R_s^i = \left[w_0^i + \sum_{j=1}^{J} (\theta_0^{ij} - \theta^{ij}) v^j \right] (1 + r) + \sum_{j=1}^{J} \theta^{ij}(p_s y_s^j + (1 + r) y_0^j) + p_s w_s^i.$$

Now we can write the effect that a marginal change $d\lambda^j$ of the production vector of firm j, $(y_0^j, y_1^j, \dots, y_S^j)$, in any direction compatible with the technology, has on agent i as follows:

$$\frac{dU^i}{d\lambda^j} = \sum_{s=1}^{S} \pi_s^i \frac{\partial V^i}{\partial R_s^i}(p_s, R_s^i) \cdot \frac{dR_s^i}{d\lambda^j}$$

$$= \sum_{s=1}^{S} \pi_s^i \frac{\partial V^i}{\partial R_s^i}(p_s, R_s^i) \left\{ (1 + r)(\theta_0^{ij} - \theta^{ij}) \frac{dv^{j(i)}}{d\lambda^j} \right.$$

$$\left. + \theta^{ij} \left(p_s \cdot \frac{dy_s^j}{d\lambda^j} + (1 + r) \frac{dy_0^j}{d\lambda^j} \right) \right\}. \tag{6}$$

Denote by

$$q_s^i = \frac{\pi_s^i(\partial V^i/\partial R_s^i)}{\sum_{s=1}^{S} \pi_s^i(\partial V^i/\partial R_s^i)(1 + r)}$$

the marginal rate of substitution between a unit of good 1 at date 1 in state s and a unit of the good at date 0 for consumer i. Of course, the changes in production $dy_s^j/d\lambda^j, s = 0, \ldots, S$, must be compatible with the technology of firm j. If this technology is characterized by a production function of the form

$$f^j(y_0^j, y_1^j, \ldots, y_S^j) = 0,$$

this constraint is written as

$$\frac{\partial f^j}{\partial y_0^j} \cdot \frac{dy_0^j}{d\lambda^j} + \sum_{s=1}^{S} \frac{\partial f^j}{\partial y_s^j} \cdot \frac{dy_s^j}{d\lambda^j} = 0. \tag{7}$$

Moreover $dv^{j(i)}/d\lambda^j$ expresses agent i's perception (or conjecture) of the change in the value of firm j following a change $d\lambda^j$ of the production program. We say that consumer i's conjecture is *competitive* if he thinks that any change in the discounted expected value of the firm's profits is reflected in a change in the market value of the firm (assuming prices to be fixed and evaluating contingent incomes based on personalized prices q_s^i).

$$\frac{dv^{j(i)}}{d\lambda^j} = \sum_{s=1}^{S} q_s^i \left[p_s \frac{dy_s^j}{d\lambda^j} + (1+r)\frac{dy_0^j}{d\lambda^j} \right]. \tag{8}$$

Substituting (8) into (6) yields

$$\frac{dU^i/d\lambda^j}{\sum_{s=1}^{S} \pi_s^i(dV^i/dR_s^i)(1+r)} = \theta_0^{ij} \left[\sum_{s=1}^{S} q_s^i \left(p_s \frac{dy_s^j}{d\lambda^j} + (1+r)\frac{dy_0^j}{d\lambda^j} \right) \right]$$

$$= \theta_0^{ij} \frac{dv^{j(i)}}{d\lambda^j},$$

that is, the effect on consumer i's utility of a change in production expressed in terms of the marginal utility of the good at date 0. This analysis highlights the fundamental difficulty—namely, that the different shareholders evaluate differently the changes in production under consideration. Notice that this is because they are using different personalized prices q_s^i to evaluate income in different states of nature, and this in turn is due to the absence of contingent markets, which precludes the shareholders from equalizing the marginal rates of substitution between income in different states among themselves.

Several possible solutions are conceivable. For example, consider the behavior proposed by Grossman and Hart (1979) and Drèze (1974).[3] A

---

3. Drèze's criterion refers to new shareholders, and not original shareholders, as we assume here following Grossman and Hart (1979).

production program for firm j is optimal if there exist no transfers t^i of the good at date 0 among the initial shareholders of the firms, A^j, associated to a marginal change in production $d\lambda^j$ such that $\sum_{i \in A^j} t^i > 0$ and all the shareholders favor these transfers where $t^i \geqslant 0$ ($\leqslant 0$) indicates that the shareholder pays (receives) t^i units of the good at date 0. If such were not the case, we could improve the welfare of all the shareholders by combining a program of transfers of the good at date 0 with a change in production.

In other words, the approach taken here is to consider the best possible situation, that is, to assume that the collective decision-making problem posed by firm j's production choice is solved in the best Pareto sense. Therefore for any feasible $d\lambda^j$, we must have

$$\sum_{i \in A^j} \frac{dU^i/d\lambda^j}{\sum_{s=1}^{S} \pi_s^i (dV^i/dR_s^i)(1 + r)} = \sum_{i \in A^j} \theta_0^{ij} \left\{ \sum_{s=1}^{S} q_s^i \left(p_s \frac{dy_s^j}{d\lambda^j} + (1 + r) \frac{dy_0^j}{d\lambda^j} \right) \right\} \leqslant 0.$$

That is, the manager must maximize (locally) over the production set the expression

$$\sum_{i \in A^j} \theta_0^{ij} \left\{ \sum_{s=1}^{S} q_s^i (p_s y_s^j + (1 + r) y_0^j) \right\}, \tag{9}$$

which is an average (weighted by the initial ownership shares of the shareholders) of the firm's profits evaluated by using the personalized prices of each of the shareholders. This leads to the following definition:

A *competitive equilibrium in the stock market* (of the Drèze-Grossman-Hart type) consists of prices at date 0 $(r^*, v^{*1}, \ldots, v^{*J})$, that is, the rate of interest and the market values of the firms, portfolios $(b^{*i}, \theta^{*i1}, \ldots, \theta^{*iJ})$ $i = 1, \ldots, I$ at date 0, investment decisions $(y_0^{*1}, \ldots, y_0^{*J})$ at date 0, expectations of prices at date 1 $(p_1^*, \ldots, p_S^*)$, consumption plans $(x_1^{*i}, \ldots, x_S^{*i})$ $i = 1, \ldots, I$, and production plans $(y_1^{*j}, \ldots, y_S^{*j})$ $j = 1, \ldots, J$ for date 1 such that

(i) $(b^{*i}, \theta^{*i1}, \ldots, \theta^{*iJ}, x_1^{*i}, \ldots, x_S^{*i})$ solves (1) for the prices $(r^*, v^{*1}, \ldots, v^{*J}, p_1^*, \ldots, p_S^*)$;

(ii) each firm j maximizes (9) over its production set;

(iiia) $\sum_{i=1}^{I} b^{*i} = -\sum_{j=1}^{J} y_0^{*j} = \sum_{i=1}^{I} w_0^i, j = 1, \ldots, J,$
(iiib) $\sum_{i=1}^{I} \theta^{*ij} = 1,$
(iiic) $\sum_{i=1}^{I} x_s^{*i} = \sum_{i=1}^{I} w_s^i + \sum_{j=1}^{J} y_s^{*j}, s = 1, \ldots, S.$

Condition (iiia) expresses the equilibrium in the bond market at date 0.

Condition (iiib) is the equilibrium in the stock market at date 0. Condition (iiic) is the equilibrium of consumption and production plans for each state of nature at date 1.

What are the advantages of the Drèze-Grossman-Hart approach? Their definition of equilibrium allows us to generalize the propositions of chapter 6, namely, the equivalence between Nash social optima and equilibria. To the definition of a Nash social optimum, we must add a production planner who can reallocate resources at date 0 and make production plans, taking as given the choices of other planners. Therefore he can improve on the allocation only by changing the flow of dividends and by making transfers at date 0. In particular, there is no simultaneous coordination of the choices of production plans and portfolios in this notion of equilibrium. An asymptotic justification of competitive conjectures has been given by Hart (1979). Moreover this hypothesis appears to be a generalization of several known particular cases.

7.2   Several Special Cases

If, in addition to stocks and bonds, there exists a system of complete Arrow-Debreu contingent markets at date 0, the consumers can equate their marginal rates of substitution between the good at date 0 and good 1 at date 1 in each state s at the contingent price for good 1 in state s, denoted $\tilde{p}_{1s}$:

$$\frac{\pi_s^i(\partial V^i/\partial R_s^i)}{\sum_{s'=1}^{S}(1+r)\pi_{s'}^i(\partial V^i/\partial R_{s'}^i)} = \tilde{p}_{1s},$$

which yields equality between all q_s^i and $\tilde{p}_{1s}$ for all $i = 1, \ldots, I$ and $s = 1, \ldots, S$. The objective function for firm j (equation 9) becomes

$$\sum_{s=1}^{S} \tilde{p}_{1s}p_s y_s^j + y_0^j,$$

that is, the discounted profit calculated by using the contingent prices.

Diamond's pioneering model (1967) also emerges as a particular case. In this model there is only one good at date 1, no initial endowments in period 1, and therefore only technological uncertainty. Moreover Diamond assumes that technological uncertainty is multiplicative so that, in our notation, we would have

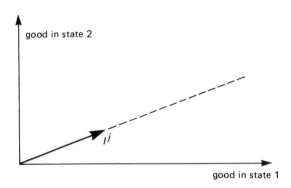

Figure 7.1

$$\begin{bmatrix} y_1^j \\ \vdots \\ y_S^j \end{bmatrix} = \mathbf{l}^j \cdot f^j(y_0^j)$$

where $\mathbf{l}^j$ is a vector in $\mathbf{R}^S$. In $\mathbf{R}^2$ we have figure 7.1. By changing the input, the firm's manager changes outputs but in a proportional manner—that is, the production vector stays in the same linear one-dimensional subspace of $\mathbf{R}^S$.

First, consider the optimizing behavior of consumers:

$$\operatorname*{Max}_{(\theta^{ij})} \sum_{s=1}^S \pi_s^i u^i(x_s^i)$$

subject to

$$x_s^i \leqslant \left[w_0^i + \sum_{j=1}^J (\theta_0^{ij} - \theta^{ij}) v^j \right] (1 + r)$$

$$+ \sum_{j=1}^J \theta^{ij}(y_s^j + (1 + r)y_0^j) \qquad s = 1, \dots, S.$$

By noting that here $\partial V^i/\partial R_s^i(p_s, R_s^i) = u'^i(x_s^i)$ since we have only one good, the first-order conditions for this problem are written as

$$\sum_{s=1}^S \pi_s^i \frac{\partial V^i}{\partial R_s^i}[y_s^j + (1 + r)y_0^j - (1 + r)v^j] = 0 \qquad j = 1, \dots, J,$$

or furthermore by using the definition of (q_s^i) and the assumption of multiplicative uncertainty, we have

$$\sum_{s=1}^{S} q_s^i l_s^j = \frac{(v^j - y_0^j)}{f^j(y_0^j)} \qquad j = 1, \ldots, J. \tag{10}$$

Therefore all the consumers equate their marginal utility from one unit of the composite good l^j to the same quantity $(v^j - y_0^j)/f^j(y_0^j)$ that we will denote by r^j. Consequently there exists an *objective* evaluation of the direction of production l^j, the direction in which firm j must remain because of multiplicative uncertainty. Competitive behavior for producer j involves considering this price r^j (for the basket of contingent goods l^j) to be fixed and maximizing profit given by

$$r^j f^j(y_0^j) + y_0^j.$$

This yields the following first-order condition:

$$r^j = -\frac{1}{df^j/dy_0^j} \qquad j = 1, \ldots, J. \tag{11}$$

The behavior of the firms described here corresponds exactly to competitive behavior in an economy where only baskets of goods whose components are fixed (the l^j) are produced and exchanged. We show that this behavior coincides with that proposed by Drèze-Grossman-Hart in the particular case considered. Here the objective function (9) is written

$$\sum_{i \in A^j} \theta_0^{ij} \left\{ \sum_{s=1}^{S} q_s^i l_s^j f^j(y_0^j) + y_0^j \right\} = \sum_{i \in A^j} \theta_0^{ij} f^j(y_0^j) \sum_{s=1}^{S} q_s^i l_s^j + y_0^j$$

where

$$\sum_{s=1}^{S} q_s^i l_s^j = r^j \qquad \forall i$$

so that the right-hand side becomes

$$r^j f^j(y_0^j) + y_0^j.$$

Because of multiplicative uncertainty, we have unanimity regarding the criterion to be used by firm j. Intuitively, a change in production for firm j is only a change in the number of baskets l^j that it produces. However, since it is already producing, a market price for these baskets exists. The competitive character of the consumers' conjectures regarding the market values of the firms involves only the traditional competitive assumption that this market price is fixed.

Now we examine the normative properties of this equilibrium. From (10) and (11), we have

$$-\frac{1}{df^j/dy_0^j} = \frac{\sum_{s=1}^{S} \pi_s^i(\partial V^i/\partial R_s^i)l_s^j}{(1+r)\sum_{s=1}^{S} \pi_s^i(\partial V^i/\partial R_s^i)} \qquad i = 1, \ldots, I, \tag{12}$$

that is, equality of the marginal rate of transformation in the direction $\mathbf{l}^j$ to the marginal rate of substitution between one unit of good $\mathbf{l}^j$ at date 1 and one unit of the good at date 0. As Diamond shows, this allocation is a constrained optimum in the following sense: it is one of the optima that can be achieved by a planner who limits himself to make only allocations at date 1 that are affine in the production decisions of the firms, that is,

$$x_s^i = \alpha^i + \sum_{j=1}^{J} \alpha^{ij} \mathbf{l}^j f^j(y_0^j) \qquad i = 1, \ldots, I, s = 1, \ldots, S, \tag{13}$$

$$\sum_{i=1}^{I} \alpha^i = 0 \qquad \sum_{i=1}^{I} \alpha^{ij} = 1 \qquad \forall j.$$

The coefficients α^i, (α^{ij}) are noncontingent, but the planner optimizes simultaneously over choices of the levels of production and the fractions α^{ij} (contrary to the NSO).

If we maximize

$$\sum_{i=1}^{I} \lambda^i \left(\sum_{s=1}^{S} \pi_s^i u^i(x_s^i) \right) \qquad \lambda^i \geqslant 0, \sum_{i=1}^{I} \lambda^i = 1,$$

subject to constraints (13), (12) follows immediately.

The concept of optimality defined here is a particular case (when there is only one good at date 1) of Diamond optimality defined in chapter 6. It is well understood that this property of constrained optimality cannot be generalized when there is more than one good at date 1. In this case no participant in the stock market equilibrium effectively takes into account the effects of changes in production on the distribution of prices $(p_1, \ldots, p_S)$ that influence the insurance capabilities of the system of securities that represent the stocks and bonds (see Stiglitz 1982 and the discussion of section 6.3).

In the Diamond model, firms j's production is treated as the production of a particular basket of goods $\mathbf{l}^j$. The firms cannot change the nature of the basket that they produce. By redefining the goods to be the numéraire and these J baskets, the equilibrium market values turn out to be the traditional competitive equilibrium prices for these $(J + 1)$ markets. Therefore the equilibrium is Pareto optimal with respect to these markets, that is, markets in which exchange is constrained to only these baskets. The substantial simplification apparent in this case stems from the fact that when the firm considers a change in its production, by examining how its current production (the baskets that it already produces) is evaluated, it can unambiguously define the effect of its change in production on the change in its market value, given the competitive assumption.

This essential property is preserved in a more general way under the spanning assumption in which all production changes considered by a firm at the equilibrium belong to the subspace of $\mathbf{R}^S$ generated by the already existing production vectors. Therefore we have an objective evaluation by the market that leads to unanimity not only among final shareholders[4] with respect to any change in production but also among initial shareholders[5] under the competitive assumption.

The public good problem referred to above—the fact that each shareholder evaluates differently the effect of a change in the production program —can be treated in several different ways. The Drèze-Grossman-Hart approach amounts to finding transfers such that the sum of the marginal rates of substitution (or Lindahl prices) is equal to marginal cost.[6] Formally,

$$\sum_{i=1}^{I} \left\{ \theta_0^{ij} \cdot \sum_{s=1}^{S} q_s^i p_s \cdot \frac{dy_s^j}{d\lambda^j} \right\} = -\frac{dy_0^j}{d\lambda^j},$$

in other words, the Bowen-Lindahl-Samuelson condition.[7]

An alternative approach is to determine production by a voting mechanism, but then we would encounter Arrow's impossibility theorem.[8] Gevers (1974) explores this path. Helpman and Razin (1978) formalize the choice of inputs as a subscription equilibrium, and Kihlstrom and Laffont (1982) as a Tiebout equilibrium. Having extolled the virtues of the Drèze-Grossman-Hart approach, we must now explore its limitations.

First of all, who is this mystical manager capable of guessing the personal evaluations q_s^i that are unobservable (although this is not required in the multiplicative case or under the spanning assumption) and where are the transfers discussed above that lead to the objective function (9)? On the one hand, the issue of managerial incentives arises, and we shall return to this

4. See Ekern and Wilson (1974), Leland (1974), and Radner (1974).
5. See Grossman and Stiglitz (1976).
6. See Laffont (1988), ch. 2.
7. See Laffont (1988), ch. 2.
8. See Laffont (1988), ch. 4.

shortly. On the other hand, even if we could motivate the manager properly, from where would his mystical power come?

One possible justification for this approach is the possibility of takeover bids. If the manager does not behave properly, another manager is likely to arrive on the scene and obtain the agreement of the shareholders to modify production—an action that is in their self-interest when the appropriate transfers are realized and that also leaves him with a portion of the surplus. Unfortunately, since it is sufficient to have a majority of the shares to implement a takeover, a situation such as that described by Grossman and Hart may not be robust with respect to takeovers. If we allow takeovers, an equilibrium may not exist.[9]

Now we come to another criticism regarding the competitive assumption. Suppose that the fixed costs of establishing a firm are low and the corresponding amounts may be borrowed on capital markets. Then we have free entry of firms, which requires that the evaluation of the firm at date 0 be

$$v^j = y_0^j + c^j$$

where c^j is the fixed cost. Moreover each agent is induced to establish his own firm to produce the basket of goods that he prefers, or at the very least, agents with identical tastes will hold shares in the same type of firms. Therefore we have unanimity concerning production decisions and constrained optimality in the Diamond sense.[10]

Suppose that fixed costs are important and the number of firms is necessarily small. Of course we would have to explain how this came about in a general equilibrium model, but here we will take it as a given. Then firms are likely to behave monopolistically because changes in their production will affect substantially the attainable subspaces of $\mathbf{R}^S$ and therefore the marginal rates of substitution between the different states of nature as well. Then the agents will necessarily take into account this influence when they form their expectations about the market values of the firms.

Stiglitz (1972) examines such a model in the mean-variance framework of finance theory, given multiplicative uncertainty. Since he is able to calculate the explicit dependence of the market value of each firm as a

---

9. See Hart (1977).
10. See Kihlstrom and Laffont (1982) for such a model, as well as Makowski (1983) for a more general model.

function of its investment decisions, he obtains an objective valuation of this market value[11] that managers can use to make their decisions. Surely, the equilibrium obtained no longer has the limited efficiency properties that we highlighted above for competitive expectations.

7.3 The Modigliani-Miller Theorem

We have assumed that firms finance their investments by issuing bonds at the rate of interest r; consequently we have neglected the possibility of firms issuing new equity shares. This approach can be justified by the Modigliani-Miller theorem. Let B^j be the value of the bonds of firm j and v^j be the market value of its equity shares. The total value of the firm at date 0 is

$$T^j = B^j + v^j,$$

which is itself a valuation of future earnings. The distribution of future earnings between shareholders and bond holders is determined by the ratio

$$\frac{\text{bonds}}{\text{stocks}} \quad \text{or} \quad \frac{\text{debt}}{\text{equity}}.$$

Assume that the consumers can borrow and lend at the rate of interest r (that is, at the same interest rate as the firms). If a general equilibrium with a specific debt–equity ratio for each firm exists, there exists another general equilibrium with any other debt–equity ratio in which the total value of the firms is the same and the rate of interest is unchanged. It follows directly that all the real variables are identical in the two equilibria.

At date 1, consumer i's wealth, given by $w^i = w_0^i + \sum_{j=1}^{J} \theta_0^{ij} v^j$, is divided between his bond holdings b^i and his equity holdings $\theta^{ij} v^j$:

$$w^i = \sum_{j=1}^{J} \theta^{ij} v^j + b^i.$$

Therefore his income in state s is given by

$$R_s^i = \sum_{j=1}^{J} [p_s \cdot y_s^j - (r+1)B^j]\theta^{ij} + (r+1)\left(w^i - \sum_{j=1}^{J} \theta^{ij}(T^j - B^j)\right)$$

$$= \sum_{j=1}^{J} (p_s y_s^j) \cdot \theta^{ij} + (r+1)\left(w^i - \sum_{j=1}^{J} \theta^{ij} T^j\right). \tag{14}$$

11. This is the inverse function of objective demand.

If T^j does not vary as B^j changes, the choice set of agent i remains unchanged so that he continues to choose the same shares θ^{ij}. Then we always have

$$\sum_{i=1}^{I} \theta^{ij} = 1.$$

The net demand for bonds is

$$\sum_{i=1}^{I} \left(w^i - \sum_{j=1}^{J} \theta^{ij}(T^j - B^j) \right) - \sum_{j=1}^{J} B^j = \sum_{i=1}^{I} w^i - \sum_{j=1}^{J} T^j.$$

Since the market was in equilibrium in the initial situation, that is,

$$\sum_{i=1}^{I} w^i = \sum_{j=1}^{J} T^j,$$

it remains in equilibrium if the total values of the firms are invariant with respect to changes in the debt–equity ratios.

The possibility that consumers may borrow at the same rate of interest as that applied to bonds means that they can reorganize their initial portfolios when a firm changes its structure of debt financing. If a firm reduces the amount of its bonds and issues new equity shares, the consumers can decrease their purchases of bonds by that much and regain the same portfolios. As equation (14) indicates, income in state s is independent of the debt–equity ratio if consumers purchase the same shares of firms. Moreover the initial shareholders always have the same endowment because if v^j is the initial value of shares and $\tilde{v}^j$ is the new value, they have a share $v^j/\tilde{v}^j$ of the total equity holdings and therefore an unchanged initial wealth since $\tilde{v}^j(v^j/\tilde{v}^j) = v^j$.

7.4   Concluding Remarks

The elegant theoretical construction described in this chapter has led us to realize its deficiency by running head-on into an asymmetry of information between the manager and the shareholders. Furthermore it suggests that we have neglected another asymmetry of information that makes the problem studied perhaps less relevant. Firms are managed by individuals who have private information about the firm and whose relationship with the shareholders is regulated by complex contracts. Therefore the research agenda shifts toward the study of contracts and their resulting performance in a context that reminds us of Radner's (1972) somewhat naive vision. Each manager maximizes his personal utility subject to the constraints imposed on him by the contract drawn up with the shareholders. Nevertheless, we must expect to come across the difficulties encountered in this chapter when we embed these contracts into a general equilibrium analysis.

7.5*   The Capital Asset Pricing Model

The capital asset pricing model (CAPM) can be considered as a special case of the model in this chapter in which particular assumptions imposed on utility functions

(i)   allow us to determine the prices of shares as a function of the rate of interest on bonds r and of the value of a market portfolio by studying only equilibrium in the assets market,

(ii)   reduce the study of general equilibrium to an analysis of an economy with two goods,

(iii)   yield simple formulas for evaluating assets that are amenable to estimation.

We assume that the VNM utility functions of the I consumers are quadratic, that is,

$$u^i(x_s^i) = x_s^i - \tfrac{1}{2}\alpha^i(x_s^i)^2 \quad s = 1, \dots, S, i = 1, \dots, I.$$

Such a property justifies the crucial hypothesis that expected utility depends only on the mean and the variance of consumption. The alternative justification, that is, normality of the distribution of returns (see problem 5), is inconvenient because it requires an infinite number of states of nature and therefore does not lend itself well to a comparison with the model in this chapter.

For simplification, we assume that all the consumers have the same probabilistic perception of the states of nature:

$$\pi_s^i = \pi_s \quad i = 1, \dots, S.$$

Therefore we have

$$\sum_{s=1}^{S} \pi_s u^i(x_s^i) = Ex^i - \tfrac{1}{2}\alpha^i(Ex^i)^2 - \tfrac{1}{2}\alpha^i \operatorname{Var} x^i,$$

and consumer i's optimization problem is written as

$$\text{Max}\{Ex^i - \tfrac{1}{2}\alpha^i(Ex^i)^2 - \tfrac{1}{2}\alpha^i \text{Var}\, x^i\},$$

subject to

$$b^i + \sum_{j=1}^{J} \theta^{ij}v^j = w_0^i + \sum_{j=1}^{J} \theta_0^{ij}v^j, \tag{15}$$

$$x_s^i = b^i(1 + r) + \sum_{j=1}^{J} \theta^{ij}d_s^j \qquad s = 1, \ldots, S, \tag{16}$$

where $d_s^j = y_s^j + (1 + r)y_0^j$ represents the dividends paid out in state s and d^j is a stochastic variable which takes values $d_1^j, \ldots, d_S^j$.

Equation (15) can be rewritten as

$$\frac{b^i}{(w_0^i + \sum_{j=1}^{J} \theta_0^{ij}v^j)} + \sum_{j=1}^{J} \frac{\theta^{ij}v^j}{(w_0^i + \sum_{j=1}^{J} \theta_0^{ij}v^j)} = 1,$$

or

$$a^{i0} + \sum_{j=1}^{J} a^{ij} = 1,$$

where a^{ij} is the proportion of wealth invested in asset j, $j = 0, \ldots, J$, with asset 0 being the certainty asset.

Let $w^i = w_0^i + \sum_{j=1}^{J} \theta_0^{ij}v^j$ be the initial wealth. Let $r_s^i = (d_s^j/v^j) - 1$ be the return from investment in asset j in state s. The stochastic quantity consumed x_s^i can then be written as

$$x_s^i = \left[a^{i0}(1 + r) + \sum_{j=1}^{J} a^{ij}(1 + r_s^j) \right] w^i.$$

Let $v^m = \sum_{j=1}^{J} v^j$ be the market value of risky assets, $d^m = \sum_{j=1}^{J} d^j$ be aggregate market (stochastic) dividends, and $r^m = (d^m/v^m) - 1$ be the market (stochastic) return. From portfolio theory (see problem 5 at the end of the book), there exists a relation that defines the equilibrium value of a firm as a function of the certain rate of interest r, the average market return, and the covariance between the dividends of firm j and also aggregate market dividends given by the following:

$$v^j = \frac{1}{1 + r}\left[Ed^j - (Ed^m - (1 + r)v^m)\frac{\text{Cov}\,(d^j, d^m)}{\text{Var}\,d^m} \right] \qquad j = 1, \ldots, J. \tag{17}$$

Moreover all consumers own a share of the market portfolio:

$$\sum_{j=1}^{J} \theta^{ij} v^{j} = \theta^{i} v^{m} \qquad i = 1, \ldots, I,$$

with $\sum_{i=1}^{I} \theta^{i} = 1$ at the equilibrium. From it follows

$$x^{i} = b^{i}(1 + r) + \theta^{i} d^{m},$$

and consumer i's problem can be simplified to

$$\text{Max} \{ Ex^{i} - \tfrac{1}{2}\alpha^{i}(Ex^{i})^{2} - \tfrac{1}{2}\alpha^{i} \text{Var} \, x^{i} \}$$

subject to

$$x^{i} = (w^{i} - \theta^{i} v^{m})(1 + r) + \theta^{i} d^{m},$$

with the equilibrium condition given by $\sum_{i=1}^{I} \theta^{i} = 1$.

Equilibrium of supply and demand on the bond market allows us to define the value of the market portfolio v^{m} (as a function of r) and then, by using (17), the values of the firms and the expected returns to the risky assets.

Suggested Readings

Diamond, P. (1967).   The pioneering article in general equilibrium.

Drèze, J. (1974).   The fundamental understanding of the public good nature of the input decision in a firm.

Grossman, S., and O. Hart (1979).   A remarkable synthesis, that provides the last word in a certain direction of research.

Modigliani, F., and M. Miller (1969).   A classic article in finance.

Stiglitz, J. (1969).   A modern exposition of the Modigliani-Miller theorem and its limitations.

Stiglitz, J. (1982).   On the inefficiency of equilibrium due to pecuniary externalities.

References

Diamond, P. 1967. "The Role of a Stock Market in a General Equilibrium Model with Technological Uncertainty." *American Economic Review* 57:759–765.

Drèze, J. 1974. "Investment under Private Ownership: Optimality Equilibrium and Stability." In J. Drèze (ed.), *Allocation under Uncertainty*. Macmillan, New York.

Ekern, S., and R. Wilson. 1974. "On the Theory of the Firm in an Economy with Incomplete Markets." *Bell Journal of Economics* 5:1971–1980.

Gevers, L. 1974. "Competitive Equilibrium of the Stock Exchange and Pareto Efficiency." In J. Drèze (ed.), *Allocation under Uncertainty*. Macmillan, New York.

Grossman, S., and O. Hart. 1979. "A Theory of Competitive Equilibrium in Stock Market Economies." *Econometrica* 47:293–330.

Hart, O. 1977. "Take-over Bids and Stock Market Equilibrium." *Journal of Economic Theory*: 53–83.

Hart, O. 1981. "On Shareholder Unanimity in Large Stock Market Economies." *Econometrica* 47:1057–1086.

Helpman, E., and A. Razin. 1978. "Participation Equilibrium and the Efficiency of the Stock Market Allocation." *International Economic Review* 19:129–140.

Kihlstrom, R., and J.-J. Laffont. 1982. "A Competitive Entrepreneurial Model of a Stock Market." In McCall (ed.), *The Economics of Information and Uncertainty*. NBER.

Laffont, J.-J. 1988. *Fundamentals of Public Economics*. MIT Press, Cambridge.

Leland, H. 1974. "Production Theory and the Stock Market." *Bell Journal of Economics and Management Science* 5:125–144.

Makowski, L. 1983. "Competitive Stock Markets." *Review of Economic Studies* 50:305–330.

Modigliani, F., and M. M. Miller. 1958. "The Cost of Capital, Corporation Finance, and the Theory of Investment." *American Economic Reveiw* 48:261–297.

Radner, R. 1972. "Existence of Equilibrium of Plan, Prices and Price Expectations in a Sequence of Markets." *Econometrica* 40:289–303.

Stiglitz, J. 1969. "A Reexamination of the Modigliani-Miller Theorem." *American Economic Review* 59:784–793.

Stiglitz, J. 1972. "On the Optimality of the Stock Market Allocation of Investment." *Quarterly Journal of Economics* 86:25–60.

Stiglitz, J. 1982. "The Inefficiency of the Stock Market Equilibrium." *Review of Economic Studies* 64:241, 262.

8 The Theory of Insurance

Like the stock market, insurance is also a way for society to share risk. Insurance companies are particularly oriented toward handling independent, individual risks that have no effect on society's aggregate resources but can seriously affect the welfare of the unfortunate individuals. In this chapter we pay attention to independent, individual risks that are subject to the law of large numbers, although we point out that the theory can be generalized to some types of dependent risks that do not violate the law of large numbers.[1] After couching insurance in the framework of contingent markets, we analyze several problems of insurance theory generated by the asymmetries of information between insurers and insurees. These asymmetries are the origin of various particular aspects of insurance contracts, such as deductions and bonus-penalty clauses.

8.1 Contingent Markets and Insurance

Consider an exchange economy consisting of I identical consumers and a single good. The endowment of agent i in the good is stochastic; it equals w with probability $(1 - \pi)$ and $w - L$ with probability π. These two possible situations for agent i can be interpreted as the probability π of having an accident that yields a loss L in his income which is originally equal to w. For this agent, state 1 is called the "no-accident" state, and state 2 refers to the accident state. Let $u(.)$ with $u' > 0$ and $u'' < 0$ be the VNM utility function of a typical agent.

The probabilities of an accident for different agents are independent. Initially, we analyze this economy in the framework of contingent markets. A *state of nature* is a complete description of the endowments of all the agents, for example,

Agent 1 has an accident, agent 2 does not have an accident, ..., agent I has an accident.

Therefore there are 2^I states of nature. From the Arrow-Debreu theory, we must organize 2^I markets of contingent goods in order to have a system of complete markets and to achieve an ex ante Pareto optimum.

Let x_s^i be agent i's consumption of the good in state s, $s = 1, \ldots, S$ where $S = 2^I$. Let π_s be the probability of state s:

---

1. For example, see Henry (1981).

$$\pi^{\eta_s}(1 - \pi)^{I - \eta_s}$$

if η_s is the number of agents having an accident in state s.

Let (p_s) be a vector of contingent prices. An Arrow-Debreu competitive equilibrium is a system of prices $p_1^*, \ldots, p_S^*$ and quantities consumed $x^{*i} = \{x_1^{*i}, \ldots, x_S^{*i}\}$ for $i = 1, \ldots, I$ such that

(i) x^{*i} maximizes

$$\sum_{s=1}^{S} \pi_s u(x_s^i)$$

subject to the budget constraint

$$\sum_{s=1}^{S} p_s x_s^i = \sum_{s=1}^{S} p_s w_s^i$$

where $w_s^i = w$ if i does not have an accident in state s, and it equals $w - L$ otherwise,

(ii) $\sum_{i=1}^{I} x_s^{*i} = \sum_{i=1}^{I} w_s^i$, $s = 1, \ldots, S$.

From chapter 5, we know that a competitive equilibrium exists and that it is an ex ante Pareto optimum. Because of the symmetry of the problem, we consider only the symmetric equilibrium that allocates to all agents the same level of expected utility. Can we, nevertheless, claim that this is an appropriate allocation of risk? The huge number of markets required when the number of agents is large contrasts with the simplicity of "quasi-Pareto-optimal allocations."

Indeed, assume that I is large enough so that we can say, as a first approximation, that in most states of nature a proportion π of agents has accidents. Thus for most states of nature—in other words, almost always—the per capita endowment of agents in the economy is

$$(w - L)\pi + w(1 - \pi).$$

Therefore available resources are essentially constant. If we focus on egalitarian allocations, it is preferable to give each agent the same consumption level in each state of nature because of the concavity of the utility functions. Specifically,

$$x_s^i = (w - L)\pi + w(1 - \pi)$$

$$= w - \pi L \qquad \forall i = 1, \ldots, I, \forall s = 1, \ldots, S.$$

When I tends toward infinity, the egalitarian Pareto optima tend toward the constant allocation $w - \pi L$. Then the symmetric competitive equilibrium that is Pareto optimal, and here egalitarian as well, tends toward this same allocation. However, it is possible to achieve this allocation with a much simpler institutional structure.

Consider an insurance company that collects a premium α and reimburses agent i for his loss L when he has an accident. Therefore the insurance company collects premia summing to αI and pays out compensation amounting to $I \pi L$ because the proportion of agents who have accidents is π. The zero profit constraint (in an asymptotic sense) on the insurance company that results from competition between companies or from a regulatory constraint requires that

$$\alpha = \pi L,$$

in other words, the premium is equal to the expected value of the risk.

The income of the agent who is insured in this manner is

$$w - \alpha = w - \pi L \qquad \text{if he does not have an accident,}$$

$$w - L + L - \alpha = w - \pi L \qquad \text{if he has an accident,}$$

that is, the allocation in the asymptotic competitive equilibrium considered above (see figure 8.1).

From chapter 5 we know that the slope of any indifference curve along the 45-degree line, and therefore at point A, is $(1 - \pi)/\pi$. If $\alpha = \pi L$, we have complete insurance. Furthermore the company can allow the consumer to

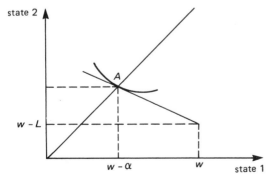

Figure 8.1

choose his own insurance coverage, by setting a price, q, per unit of compensation in the case of an accident so that $q = \pi$. The consumer then solves the following problem:

$$\underset{x_1,x_2,z}{\text{Max}} \; [(1 - \pi)u(x_1) + \pi u(x_2)]$$

subject to

$$x_1 = w - qz$$

$$x_2 = w - L + z - qz$$

or

$$\underset{z}{\text{Max}} \; [(1 - \pi)u(w - qz) + \pi u(w - L + z - qz)].$$

The first-order condition for this solution is

$$(1 - \pi)qu'(w - qz) = \pi(1 - q)u'(w - L + z - qz),$$

which yields, when $q = \pi$,

$$u'(w - qz) = u'(w - L + z - qz)$$

or

$$z = L.$$

In other words, the consumer insures himself completely.

If the agent faces "actuarially fair" insurance, that is, an insurance policy in which the premium per unit of compensation equals the probability of the accident, he will always insure himself completely. It is important to point out that the transaction now takes place between an agent and an insurance company, the behavior of which we have left a bit loose by assuming only that it always makes zero profits. In practice, transaction costs[2] (and the lack of competition) lead to an insurance premium that is greater than the actuarially fair price. Consequently optimal insurance will not be complete (see figure 8.2). Line OA represents the fair price, whereas line OB corresponds to a higher price and leads to an optimal choice below the 45-degree line (unless a two-part tarif with a fair marginal price is used).

2. In fact, these costs may be considerable.

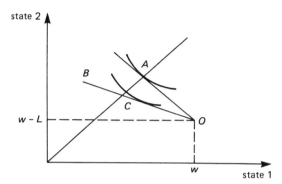

Figure 8.2

8.2   Moral Hazard

In the model of the previous section, assume that the agents can influence their personal probability of an accident by choosing some level of self-protection x expressed in monetary units.[3] Let $\pi(x)$ be the function that describes the way in which the probability of an accident varies with x. First, we analyze the egalitarian Pareto optimum in the limit economy $(I \rightarrow \infty)$, where frequency and probability are identical.

In this economy, income per capita is given by

$$w - \pi(x)L - x.$$

If $u(w - \pi(x)L - x)$ is strictly concave in x, the unique optimum is characterized by

$$(1 + \pi'(x)L)u'(w - \pi(x)L - x) = 0$$

or

$$1 = -\pi'(x)L. \tag{1}$$

In other words, the marginal cost of self-protection must be equated to the marginal social gain, which is determined by multiplying the decrease in the number of accidents (per capita), minus $\pi'(x)$, by the loss per accident L.

Therefore, once we derive an optimal level of self-protection and the accompanying probability of an accident $\pi(x)$, the analysis follows that in the previous section. In particular, insurance is complete at the optimum.

---

3. Some analogous problems arise if the loss incurred depends on the amount of self-insurance chosen (see Ehrlich and Becker 1972).

If the insurance company can observe the level of self-protection x, in order for a Pareto optimum to be achieved, it is sufficient for the company to impose a pricing schedule in the form of a variable premium $\pi(x)$ that depends on the level of self-protection chosen.

The income of the typical consumer is

$w - x - \pi(x)z$ if there is no accident,

$w - x - L - \pi(x)z + z$ if there is an accident.

Then the consumer solves the following optimization problem:

$$\underset{(x,z)}{\text{Max}} \; [\pi(x)u(w - L - x + (1 - \pi(x))z) + (1 - \pi(x))u(w - x - \pi(x)z)].$$

The first-order conditions are

$$[u(2) - u(1)]\pi'(x) - \pi(x)(1 + \pi'(x)z)u'(2)$$

$$- (1 - \pi(x))(1 + \pi'(x)z)u'(1) = 0, \tag{2}$$

$$\pi(x)[1 - \pi(x)]u'(2) - [1 - \pi(x)]\pi(x)u'(1) = 0, \tag{3}$$

where $u(1)$ and $u'(1)$ refer to state 1 (no-accident state), and $u(2)$ and $u'(2)$ refer to state 2 (accident state). Condition (3) implies that $u'(2) = u'(1)$; in other words, insurance is complete and $z = L$. Condition (2) then simplifies to $1 + \pi'(x)L = 0$, which is precisely the optimality condition (1).

The major difficulty with this solution stems from the impossibility of observing x. What happens if the insurance company sets a price q that is independent of x?[4] The optimization problem for any agent becomes

$$\underset{(z,x)}{\text{Max}} \; [\pi(x)u(w - x - L + z(1 - q)) + (1 - \pi(x))u(w - x - zq)],$$

which yields

$$\pi'(x)[u(2) - u(1)] - \pi(x)u'(2) - (1 - \pi(x))u'(1) \leqslant 0$$

$$= 0 \quad \text{if } x > 0, \tag{4}$$

$$\pi(x)(1 - q)u'(2) - (1 - \pi(x))qu'(1) = 0. \tag{5}$$

The zero-profit condition requires that

$$q^* = \pi(x^*)$$

4. See Helpman and Laffont (1976) for the difficulties caused by the nonconcavity of the objective function.

for the level of self-protection x^* chosen at the equilibrium. Condition (5) implies $u'(2) = u'(1)$, that is, complete insurance. Then condition (4) is written as

$$-u'(1) < 0$$
$$= 0 \quad \text{if } x^* > 0.$$

Since $u'(1) > 0$, we must have $x^* = 0$.

In the competitive equilibrium the level of self-protection is zero, and the price of insurance is the actuarially fair price compatible with this level of self-protection, $\pi(0)$.[5] This result occurs because the agent does not take into account the positive pecuniary externality that he has on the insurance "technology" in the competitive equilibrium. An increase in the level of chosen self-protection by all the agents allows the offer of a more favorable price of insurance than $\pi(0)$. The agent who considers $\pi(0)$ to be fixed does not perceive this effect (see problem 7).

One way to improve on the allocation obtained in this problem is to introduce required co-insurance, that is, to make it impossible for an agent to insure himself completely. The optimal level of the deduction is determined from the following program:[6]

$$\text{Max}_{(z,x)} \ [\pi(x)u(w - x - L + z(1 - q)) + (1 - \pi(x))u(w - x - zq)]$$

subject to

$$q = \pi(x), \tag{6}$$

$$\pi'(x)[u(2) - u(1)] - \pi(x)u'(2) - (1 - \pi(x))u'(1) = 0. \tag{7}$$

Condition (6) is the zero profit condition, and condition (7) means that the agent chooses his level of self-protection by himself.

Therefore the deduction (or regulatory charge) appears as a solution to a second-best problem with asymmetric information arising from the non-observability of the levels of self-protection. In a dynamic context we could use past performances to determine the contracts. By choosing the penalties associated with past behavior appropriately, we can restore optimality (in

5. Another competitive equilibrium also exists in which the price of insurance leads to the agents not insuring themselves and choosing a level of self-protection that maximizes

$$\pi(x)u(w - x - L) + (1 - \pi(x))u(w - x).$$

6. See Shavell (1979) for a detailed analysis of this model.

an infinite horizon model). This is the fundamental idea of using bonus-penalty contracts (see chapter 11).

8.3   Adverse Selection

In section 8.1, we made the extreme simplifying assumption that all the agents are identical so that the insurance company could easily know the probability of an accident that is common to all agents. The problem is considerably more complicated when there are many agents having different probabilities of an accident. We take the simplest case of two types with the same VNM utility function but different probabilities of an accident given by π_B and π_H where $\pi_B < \pi_H$. We assume that the agents know their own probability of an accident but that the insurance company cannot distinguish between the two types.[7]

What happens if the company sets a common price q, as in section 8.1, and lets each agent choose his own level of coverage? The type H agent solves the following problem:

$$\text{Max}_z \ [\pi_H u(w - L - qz + z) + (1 - \pi_H)u(w - qz)],$$

which yields

$$\frac{u'(w - L - qz + z)}{u'(w - qz)} = \frac{(1 - \pi_H)q}{\pi_H(1 - q)}.$$

Similarly, for a type B agent we have

$$\frac{u'(w - L - qz + z)}{u'(w - qz)} = \frac{(1 - \pi_B)q}{\pi_B(1 - q)}.$$

Since $(1 - \pi_H)/\pi_H < (1 - \pi_B)/\pi_B$, it follows that $z_H > z_B$ (see figure 8.3).

For a price q corresponding to line OA, insurance yields zero profit with respect to the low-risk agents who choose A but losses with respect to the high-risk agents who choose a point on line OA above the 45-degree line. If we increase the price, the low-risk types buy less insurance (for example, A') and the company makes profit from them, but this may not be sufficient to compensate for the losses still accruing from the high-risk types. Self-selection of this high-risk types who insure themselves more can lead to

---

7. If the insurance company could identify the types, the analysis would be analogous to that in section 8.1. On the other hand, we point out that the opposed asymmetry of information exists often and should merit careful study.

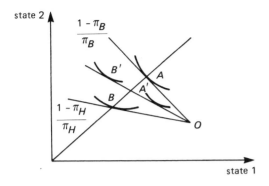

Figure 8.3

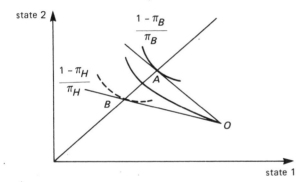

Figure 8.4

either the nonexistence of a zero-profit equilibrium[8] or the existence of an equilibrium with only high-risk types (see figure 8.4).

For the price corresponding to line OB, the high-risk types choose B, and the company makes zero profits on them. The low-risk types prefer not to buy any insurance[9] and they remain at O. This is a clear case of an adverse selection equilibrium, that is, the self-selection of high risks as the only ones to avail themselves of insurance. The same result occurs in Akerlof's model (1970) where only defective used cars (lemons) are traded in equilibrium.[10]

8. See Cresta (1984) for an example.
9. They might actually desire a negative amount of insurance, but this is not allowed here.
10. See problem 7 at the end of the book.

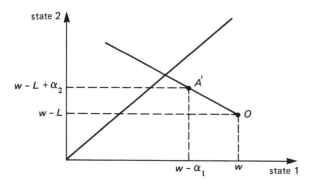

Figure 8.5

In an attempt to overcome this difficulty, the companies will propose price-quantity contracts; in other words, they will no longer allow the insured agents to choose their own level of coverage. Instead of a line segment like OA, they will propose only a point on OA. We will identify such a contract by the premium α_1 and the net coverage α_2 (see figure 8.5). Such a contract, like point A' in figure 8.5, is a particular case of a nonlinear price.

Point A' corresponds to a price $q = \alpha_1/(\alpha_1 + \alpha_2)$ for a quantity of coverage $z = \alpha_1 + \alpha_2$ (then the premium is indeed $qz = \alpha_1$ and the net coverage is $(1 - q)z = \alpha_2$). No other amount of coverage is possible; in other words, it would entail an infinite price. Each insurance company can propose one or several contracts (or points in figure 8.5). We will study how competition among these companies determines the equilibrium contracts.

Since there are only two types of agents, the analysis is limited to two types of contracts: pooling *contracts* (α_1, α_2) designed to pool all the agents and pairs of *separating contracts* $((\alpha_1^H, \alpha_2^H), (\alpha_1^B, \alpha_2^B))$ that lead to self-selection so that the higher-risk types prefer (α_1^H, α_2^H), and the lower-risk types prefer (α_1^B, α_2^B).

First, we look for Nash-equilibrium contracts. It is easy to see that a pooling contract is not robust with respect to competition; in other words, it cannot be a Nash equilibrium here. Such a contract must yield zero profits—that is, it must be on line OD (figure 8.6) which has a slope equal to $(1 - \pi)/\pi$, with $\pi = \lambda\pi_B + (1 - \lambda)\pi_H$ where λ is the proportion of low-risk types. Then π is indeed the average probability of an accident. Take any point C on OD; the indifference curves of the two types of agents passing through C intersect as, for example, in figure 8.6. Any contract in

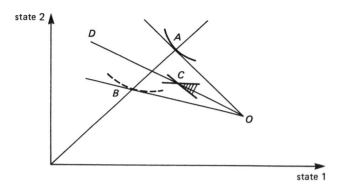

Figure 8.6

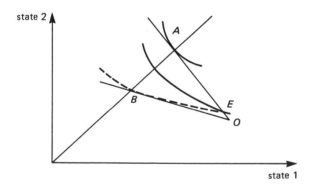

Figure 8.7

the shaded area in the figure will attract low-risk types only (the high-risk types prefer C) and will yield positive profit because these contracts are under OA. A company will therefore propose such a contract. Contract C will incur losses, and therefore it is not viable.

Consider the separating contracts. By an argument analogous to that just stated, it is easy to see that the only serious candidate for equilibrium is the pair of contracts formed by the points B and E (figure 8.7).

The high-risk agents choose B and are completely insured; the low-risk agents[11] choose E and are partially insured (at a lower price per unit). It remains to show that this pair of contracts is not improved upon by a pooling contract.

11. To be sure, high-risk agents are indifferent between B and E. We could define E on OA slightly below the indifference curve passing through B.

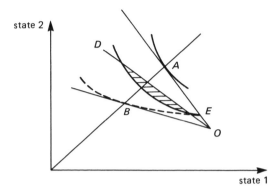

Figure 8.8

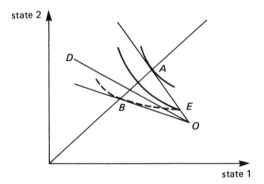

Figure 8.9

There are two cases to consider depending on the value of λ. Let the chord OD of equilibrium pooling contracts intersect the indifference curve of low-risk types passing through E (λ is large). Any contract in the shaded area of figure 8.8 pools the two types and yields positive profit. The contract (B, E) is not viable, but since we know that no pooling contract is viable, this demonstrates that no equilibrium exists.

Alternatively, let the chord OD of pooling contracts pass below the indifference curve of the low-risk agents through E. The pair of separating contracts (B, E) is indeed an equilibrium (see figure 8.9).

When it exists the equilibrium has the following remarkable properties. If we compare (B, E) with the pair of separating contracts under complete information (A, B), we notice that the high-risk agents have the same allocation, and it is the low-risk agents who suffer from the impossibility of being identified as low-risk types. Therefore it will be in the self-interest of the low-risk agents to try to identify themselves as low-risk types by signaling credibly (see chapter 10). Similarly, it is in the insurance companies' self-interest to find criteria that allow them to divide the population into subgroups of different accident probabilities to attract the low-risk types and leave the high-risk types to other companies.

To assume that Nash behavior with respect to price-quantity contracts characterizes competition is rather tenuous. When a company breaks up the pair (B, E) by proposing a pooling contract (see figure 8.9), it is indeed myopic because it should realize that another company will propose a contract that will render this pooling contract nonviable. Similarly, when a company breaks up a pooling contract (see figure 8.6) by attracting only the low-risk types, it should realize that the other company must incur losses from now on so that it will go out of business, and all the agents will choose the first company's contract and it will then incur losses itself.

More sophisticated behavior has been suggested—for example, allowing only the introduction of contracts that will yield profits once any competitors' contracts that make losses are removed. Then certain pooling contracts become equilibrium contracts and the nonexistence of equilibrium disappears.[12] Riley (1979) proposes a notion of reactive equilibrium that makes the pair (B, E) an equilibrium (see chapter 10). Nevertheless, we should point out that these various equilibria are based on very ad hoc, nonequilibrium expectations. Recently, Hellwig (1987) models in a more precise manner the communication of information between the insurance company and the insured and shows the high sensitivity of the results to the particular extensive form of the game used for modeling.

8.4 Concluding Remarks

Economists studying uncertainty are particularly interested in the theory of insurance. Ever since pioneering general equilibrium theorists like Arrow became interested in insurance and actuaries like Borch became interested in economics, the dialogue between actuaries and economists has deepened to the point where the economics of insurance has become a well-known branch of economics.[13] The problems of moral hazard and adverse selec-

12. See Wilson (1977).
13. In particular, see the publications of The International Association for the Study of the Economics of Insurance.

tion that were posed practically for the first time in the context of insurance emerge as fundamental phenomena of economic theory, which has abandoned the simplifying assumption of symmetric information (see chapters 10 and 11).

Suggested Readings

Arrow, K. (1963).   A pioneering article.

Malinvaud, E. (1972).   The theory with complete information.

Helpman, E., and J.-J. Laffont (1976).   Moral hazard in a general equilibrium context.

Shavell, S. (1979).   A principal-agent formulation.

Riley, J., (1979).   Competition with adverse selection.

References

Arrow, K. 1963. "Uncertainty and the Welfare Economics of Medical Care." *American Economic Review* 53:941–973.

Akerlof, G. 1970. "The Market for 'Lemons': Qualitative Uncertainty and the Market Mechanism." *Quarterly Journal of Economics* 89:488–500.

Cresta, J. P. 1984. *Théorie des marchés d'assurance avec information imparfaite*. Economica, Paris.

Ehrlich, I., and G. Becker. 1972. "Market Insurance, Self-insurance, and Self-protection." *Journal of Political Economy* 6:623–648.

Helpman, E., and J.-J. Laffont. 1976. "On Moral Hazard in General Equilibrium Theory." *Journal of Economic Theory* 15:8–23.

Henry, C. 1981. "Critères simples pour la prise en compte du risque." *Econometrica* 49:153–170.

Hellwig, M. 1987. "Some Recent Developments in the Theory of Competition in Markets with Adverse Selection." *European Economic Review* 31:319–325.

Malinvaud, E. 1972. "The Allocation of Individual Risks in Large Markets." *Journal of Economic Theory* 5:312–328.

Riley, J. 1979. "Informational Equilibrium." *Econometrica* 47:331–360.

Rothschild, M., and J. Stiglitz. 1977. "Equilibrium in Competitive Insurance Markets." *Quarterly Journal of Economics* 90:629–649.

Shavell, S. 1979. "On Moral Hazard and Insurance." *Quarterly Journal of Economics* 93:541–562.

Wilson, C. A. 1977. "A Model of Insurance Markets with Incomplete Information." *Journal of Economic Theory* 16:167–207.

9 The Transmission of Information by Prices

When, at the beginning of an exchange process, the information structures of the agents are different and when some agents have information that is pertinent to the others, we should expect the uniformed agents to try to infer information from observing variables influenced by the behavior of informed agents. For example, a stockbroker may think that because the price of a stock increases, agents who are better informed than he is (such as the shareholders of the firm) have received favorable news concerning this firm and are therefore acquiring new shares.

In this chapter we focus more particularly on the problem of the transmission of information by equilibrium prices in existing markets. Other variables, such as the quantities exchanged or the amounts rationed in an equilibrium with rationing, are surely also likely to transmit information. In the first section we show how to modify the concept of Walrasian equilibrium to construct a definition of equilibrium that does represent such an economic system at rest. The second section is devoted to the problems of the nonexistence of equilibrium posed by certain market structures. Finally, the third section studies the normative properties of the equilibria that transmit information by prices.

9.1 The Green-Lucas Equilibrium[1]

Consider an exchange economy with I consumers, a single good, and S states of nature. All the consumers have the same prior distributions $\pi(.)$ on the space of states of nature. We distinguish three dates:

ex ante   interim   ex post

At the ex ante date, denoted date 0, nature selects a state s, but no consumer is informed of it. At the interim date, denoted date 1, each agent observes a private signal $y^i \in Y^i$ that is correlated with the realized state of nature.

By using the Bayesian rule, an agent computes his posterior distribution, which we denote

$$v_s(y^i) = v(\tilde{s} = s | \tilde{y}^i = y^i) \qquad s = 1, \dots, S,$$

with

---

1. Radner (1967) was the first to define this concept.

$$v(y^i) = [v_1(y^i), \ldots, v_S(y^i)].$$

Since all the agents have the same prior distributions, the posterior probabilities depend only on the signals. At the ex post date, denoted date 2, all the consumers observe the realization of the state of nature and then consume the good.

Let $u^i(x_s^i, s)$ be the utility function[2] of consumer i in state s defined over $\mathbf{R}_+$, and let π_s be the prior probability of state s, which is common to all. Notice that the signals y^i, which are correlated with s, influence neither the endowments nor the preferences of the agents. Let w_s^i be the endowment of consumer i in state s for $i = 1, \ldots, I$ and $s = 1, \ldots, S$.

ASSUMPTION A_0

$u'^i(., s) > 0$ and $u''^i(., s) < 0$ $\forall i, \forall s,$

$w_s^i > 0$ $\forall i, \forall s.$

We distinguish three concepts of Pareto optimality depending on the date (ex ante, interim, and ex post) at which the expected utilities of the agents are evaluated.

An allocation (x_s^{*i}) is *ex ante Pareto optimal* if there exists no feasible allocation (x_s^i) such that

$$\sum_{s=1}^{S} \pi_s u^i(x_s^i, s) \geq \sum_{s=1}^{S} \pi_s u^i(x_s^{*i}, s)   \forall i = 1, \ldots, I,$$

with at least one strict inequality.

An allocation (x_s^{*i}) is *interim Pareto optimal* if there exists no feasible allocation (x_s^i) such that

$$\sum_{s=1}^{S} v_s(y^i) u^i(x_s^i, s) \geq \sum_{s=1}^{S} v_s(y^i) u^i(x_s^{*i}, s)   \forall y^i, \forall i = 1, \ldots, I,$$

with at least one strict inequality.

An allocation (x_s^{*i}) is *ex post Pareto optimal* if there exists no feasible allocation (x_s^i) such that

$$u^i(x_s^i, s) \geq u^i(x_s^{*i}, s)   \forall s, \forall i = 1, \ldots, I,$$

with at least one strict inequality.

2. Notice that here we allow the VNM utility function to depend on the state of nature.

First, assume that we have a system of complete contingent markets for values of $\tilde{s}$ at date 0, and consider the competitive equilibrium corresponding to the allocation (e_s^i). Clearly, we cannot improve the ex ante welfare of the agents by exchanges that are conditional on s and y. If we assume the contrary, this would indicate that there exist net trades $z^i(s, y)$ such that

$$e_s^i + z^i(s, y) \geq 0 \qquad \forall s, \forall y,$$

$$\sum_{i=1}^{I} z^i(s, y) \leq 0 \qquad \forall s, \forall y,$$

$$\underset{y}{E} \underset{s}{E} \, u^i(e_s^i + z^i(s, y), s) \geq E \, u^i(e_s^i, s) \qquad \forall i, \tag{1}$$

with at least one strict inequality.

Then consider the net trades that are independent of y:

$$z_s^i = \underset{y}{E} \, z^i(s, y) \qquad i = 1, \ldots, I.$$

Since the utility functions $u^i(., s)$ are strictly concave (risk aversion), we have

$$\sum_{s=1}^{S} \pi_s \underset{y}{E} \, u^i(e_s^i + z^i(s, y), s) < \sum_{s=1}^{S} \pi_s u^i(e_s^i + z_s^i, s) \qquad \forall i,$$

which, given condition (1), contradicts the ex ante Pareto optimality of the Arrow-Debreu equilibria conditional on $\tilde{s}$.

Now suppose that an Arrow-Debreu equilibrium conditional on $\tilde{s}$ has been realized at date 0, and consider date 1 when each agent receives a private signal y^i. Then suppose that the markets conditional on s are reopened at date 1. Let $z^i(s, y)$ be the net trades realized beginning with the allocation in the Arrow-Debreu equilibrium e_s^i. Since the new equilibrium is individually rational, we must have

$$\sum_{s=1}^{S} v_s^i(y^i) u^i(e_s^i + z^i(s, y), s) \geq \sum_{s=1}^{S} v_s^i(y^i) u^i(e_s^i, s) \qquad i = 1, \ldots, I. \tag{2}$$

The net trades are functions of the realized signals. Therefore consider $z_s^i = E_y z^i(s, y)$ computed at date 0. If one of the inequalities in condition (2) is strict, the analysis of the previous paragraph contradicts the ex ante Pareto optimality of e_s^i. Therefore we have equality for all i in condition (2), but the strict concavity of u^i then implies $z^i(s, y) = 0$ for any i, any s, and any y.

To sum up, when an Arrow-Debreu equilibrium has been attained at date 0, opening markets at date 1 does not change the equilibrium allocation.[3] Consequently ex ante Pareto optimality implies interim Pareto optimality, and we can show as well that this implies ex post Pareto optimality.

Now consider the case in which there are no Arrow-Debreu markets organized at date 0, although we have a system of complete contingent markets operating at date 1. Consumer i calculates his demand for the good by solving the following problem:

$$\text{Max} \sum_{s=1}^{S} v_s(y^i)u^i(x_s^i, s) \tag{3}$$

subject to

$$\sum_{s=1}^{S} p_s x_s^i \leqslant \sum_{s=1}^{S} p_s w_s^i$$

where

$$p = (p_1, \ldots, p_S) \in P = \left\{ p : \sum_{s=1}^{S} p_s = 1 \right\}.$$

Notice that the state of nature influences both the preferences and the endowments of the consumer.

An *Arrow-Debreu-Radner equilibrium* is a system of prices $(p_1^*, \ldots, p_S^*) \in P$ and an allocation $(x^{*1}, \ldots, x^{*I})$ such that

(i) $(x_1^{*i}, \ldots, x_S^{*i})$ solves (3) for $i = 1, \ldots, I$,

(ii) $\sum_{i=1}^{I} x_s^{*i} = \sum_{i=1}^{I} w_s^i$, for all s.

The system of prices obtained in this way depends on the vector of signals that have been observed at date 1.[4]

$$p^* = \phi(y^1, \ldots, y^I).$$

Now assume that the consumers have perfect knowledge about the structure of the economy, and that they know the function $\phi(.)$. When an agent sees a price vector p, he can infer that the signals $y \in \phi^{-1}(p)$ have been

---

3. See Milgrom and Stockey (1982).
4. If there are multiple equilibria, we always choose the same equilibrium.

observed. Then he can compute a new posterior distribution, which we denote as

$$v_s(y^i, \phi^{-1}(p)) = v(\tilde{s} = s | \tilde{y}^i = y^i \text{ and } y \in \phi^{-1}(p)) \qquad s = 1, \dots, S.$$

In general, he will then wish to recontract on the basis of his new demand function $x^i(p, y^i, \phi(.))$ which is computed from solving the following optimization problem:

$$\text{Max} \sum_{s=1}^{S} v_s(y^i, \phi^{-1}(p)) u^i(x_s^i, s)$$

subject to

$$\sum_{s=1}^{S} p_s x_s^i \leq \sum_{s=1}^{S} p_s w_s^i.$$

The Arrow-Debreu-Radner prices p^* are no longer equilibrium prices. This leads us to a definition of equilibrium in which no agent desires to recontract.

DEFINITION   A *Green-Lucas equilibrium*[5] is a price function $\phi^*(.)$ from $\prod_{i=1}^{I} Y^i$ to P such that

$$\sum_{i=1}^{I} x_s^i(\phi^*(y), y^i, \phi^*(.)) = \sum_{i=1}^{I} w_s^i \qquad \forall y \in \prod_{i=1}^{I} Y^i.$$

When agents use all the available information—that is, their private information and the information revealed by the price vector—to calculate their demands, the resulting demand functions lead to precisely these prices. Then their expectations are said to be *rational*. Notice that the mathematical concept used to define an equilibrium is no longer a vector, as in the Arrow-Debreu equilibrium, but it is rather a function.

The existence of a Green-Lucas equilibrium will be proved in a constructive way by exhibiting a particular equilibrium—the fully revealing equilibrium—which is nothing other than the Arrow-Debreu equilibrium of the artificial economy in which all the agents know all the signals and S contingent markets have been organized. Notice first that the signals are relevant for the demand functions only because of their effects on the posterior distributions. Therefore we can write the demand functions as

---

5. See Green (1973), Lucas (1972), and problem 10 at the end of the book.

functions of the prices and the posterior probabilities:

$$v_s(y) = v(\tilde{s} = s \mid \tilde{y}^1 = y^1, \ldots, \tilde{y}^I = y^I) \qquad s = 1, \ldots, S,$$

$$y = (y^1, \ldots, y^I),$$

$$v(y) = [v_1(y), \ldots, v_S(y)].$$

In the artificial economy the demand functions $x^i(p, v(y))$ are determined by the following program:

$$\text{Max } \sum_{s=1}^{S} v_s(y) u^i(x_s^i, s) \tag{4}$$

subject to

$$\sum_{s=1}^{S} p_s x_s^i \leqslant \sum_{s=1}^{S} p_s w_s^i \qquad i = 1, \ldots, I.$$

Under assumption A_0, Arrow-Debreu equilibria depending only on $v(y)$ exist for any y. Let $p(v(y))$ be one selection from these equilibria. We will show that the function of prices $\phi^*(y) = p(v(y))$ is a Green-Lucas equilibrium.

First, we show[6] that the signals that give rise to different posterior distributions can lead to different demands only for different prices. Therefore the prices are sufficient statistics for the economic agents to use to determine their behavior.

PROPOSITION 1   Assume that $v_s(y) > 0$, for $s = 1, \ldots, S$ and all y. Consider two vectors of signals y and $\bar{y}$ such that $v(y) \neq v(\bar{y})$. If there exists an agent for whom

$$x^i(p(v(y)), v(y)) \neq x^i(p(v(\bar{y})), v(\bar{y})),$$

then $p(v(y)) \neq p(v(\bar{y}))$.

Proof Suppose, on the contrary, that $p = p(v(y)) = p(v(\bar{y}))$. Since the agents have the same budget constraint in both cases, strict quasi concavity of preferences implies

$$\sum_{s=1}^{S} v_s(y) u^i(x_s^i, s) > \sum_{s=1}^{S} v_s(y) u^i(\bar{x}_s^i, s)$$

6. See Grossman (1981).

for agents who have chosen different consumption bundles in the two cases with

$$x_s^i \equiv x_s^i(p(v(y)), v(y)),$$

$$\bar{x}_s^i \equiv x_s^i(p(v(\bar{y})), v(\bar{y})).$$

For such an agent i we have

$$\sum_{s=1}^{S} v_s(y)[u^i(x_s^i, s) - u^i(\bar{x}_s^i, s)] > 0.$$

Then concavity of preferences yields

$$\sum_{s=1}^{S} v_s(y)(x_s^i - \bar{x}_s^i)\frac{\partial u^i}{\partial x_s^i}(\bar{x}_s^i, s) > 0. \tag{5}$$

The first-order conditions for optimal behavior of consumer i, when $\bar{y}$ is the signal, are written as (see program 4):

$$v_s(\bar{y})\frac{\partial u^i}{\partial x_s^i}(\bar{x}_s^i, s) \leqslant \bar{\lambda}^i p_s \qquad s = 1, \ldots, S \tag{6}$$

(with equality if $\bar{x}_s^i > 0$) where the Lagrangian multiplier $\bar{\lambda}^i$ is positive and represents the marginal utility of income.

Combining conditions (5) and (6) yields

$$\sum_{s=1}^{S} v_s(y)(x_s^i - \bar{x}_s^i)\bar{\lambda}^i\frac{p_s}{v_s(\bar{y})} > 0. \tag{7}$$

Dividing inequality (7) by $\bar{\lambda}^i$ and summing over i, we obtain

$$\sum_{s=1}^{S} p_s\left[\sum_{i=1}^{I}(x_s^i - \bar{x}_s^i)\right]\frac{v_s(y)}{v_s(\bar{y})} > 0,$$

which is a contradiction since $\sum_{i=1}^{I} x_s^i = \sum_{i=1}^{I} \bar{x}_s^i = \sum_{i=1}^{I} w_s^i$ for all s. ∎

The intuition for this result is clear in the case of two states of nature: $v_s(y) > v_s(\bar{y})$ implies $x_s^i > \bar{x}_s^i$ for any i because state s becomes more probable for everybody. If we can find an agent i' for whom $x_s^{i'} > \bar{x}_s^{i'}$, we have

$$\sum_{i=1}^{I} x_s^i > \sum_{i=1}^{I} \bar{x}_s^i,$$

which is a contradiction.

THEOREM 1   Given A_0, if $v_s(y) > 0$, for $s = 1, \ldots, S$ and all y, any selection from the Arrow-Debreu equilibria of the artificial economy where all the agents know y is a Green-Lucas equilibrium of the economy in which each agent i observes y^i and the prices.

Proof   If $p(v)$ from $\mathbf{R}^{S-1}$ to $\mathbf{R}^{S-1}$ is invertible, the agent who maximizes $E[u^i|y^i, p(v(y))]$ has the same demand functions as the agent who maximizes $E[u^i|v(y)]$. Therefore, $p(v(y))$ is indeed an equilibrium of the economy with private signals.

If $p(v)$ is not invertible, assume that there exist a y and a consumer i such that

$$E[u^i|y^i, p(v(y))] \neq E[u^i|v(y)]. \tag{8}$$

Consider the set of signals $\hat{Y} = \{\hat{y}|\hat{y}^i = y^i \text{ and } p(v(y)) \text{ equals a constant}\}$. For agent i these signals generate different posterior probability vectors v^i, $\ldots, v^k$ so that $p(v^1) = \cdots = p(v^k)$.

From proposition 1, $E(u^i|v(\hat{y}))$ is constant for any $\hat{y} \in \hat{Y}$, which contradicts (8) since

$$E[u^i|y^i, p(v)] = E[u^i|\hat{Y}] = E[u^i|v(\hat{y})]   \qquad \forall \hat{y} \in \hat{Y}. \blacksquare$$

The full transmission of information in the fully revealing equilibrium might lead us to think that this equilibrium has attractive normative properties. Notice that there may be other equilibria than fully revealing equilibria that have been ignored in this analysis. More important, the equilibrium may in fact transmit too much information. Since there is no system of complete markets at date 0, at date 1 there are, in general, unexploited insurance possibilities that the fully revealing equilibrium can destroy. This is the Hirshleifer effect that we came across in chapter 5.

We shall return to the normative analysis of this type of model in section 9.3. To conclude this section, we mention the paradox of Grossman-Stiglitz (1980) posed by fully revealing equilibria. Assume that the acquisition of the signal y^i is costly for agent $i, i = 1, \ldots, I$. If each agent becomes informed by observing prices, he will not find it in his self-interest to acquire the signal. However, if all the agents behave in this fashion, the system of prices is not informative. Then it would be beneficial for each agent to acquire a signal. This circular reasoning shows that indeed an equilibrium does not exist.

In order to have a fully revealing equilibrium, we must assume that the private signals are not costly or that they generate more private utility than postulated in the above model—or else that the agents can use the information contained in the prices only with a time lag (see Hellwig 1982). An alternative perspective is to pursue the analysis in situations where the dimensionality of the relevant information is larger than the dimensionality of the space of prices so that prices cannot be fully revealing.

9.2   The Problem of the Existence of Equilibrium in Systems of Incomplete Markets

When the number of states of nature is finite, the nonexistence of a Green-Lucas equilibrium is possible, but rare, as the following example illustrates.

Consider an exchange economy with two goods, two agents, and two states of nature. The VNM utility function of agent i is given by

$$u^i(x_1^i, x_2^i, s) = \alpha_s^i \operatorname{Log} x_{1s}^i + (1 - \alpha_s^i) \operatorname{Log} x_{2s}^i.$$

The initial endowments are

$$w_{1s}^i = w_1^i > 0 \qquad s = 1, 2,$$

$$w_{2s}^i = w_2^i > 0 \qquad s = 1, 2, i = 1, 2.$$

State 1 (2) occurs with probability $\pi_1(\pi_2)$. Let

$$\bar{\alpha}^i = \pi_1 \alpha_1^i + \pi_2 \alpha_2^i \qquad i = 1, 2.$$

At date 1, agent 1 receives a signal y^1 which informs him perfectly of the state of nature. Agent 2 receives an uninformative signal. At date 1, markets (noncontingent) for goods 1 and 2 are organized. Therefore, contrary to section 9.1, we have a system of incomplete markets at date 1.

Let $(p, 1 - p)$ be the price vector. Since consumer 1 is always informed, his demand function is

$$x_{11}^1 = \frac{\alpha_1^1 [pw_1^1 + (1 - p)w_2^1]}{p},$$

$$x_{21}^1 = \frac{(1 - \alpha_1^1)[pw_1^1 + (1 - p)w_2^1]}{1 - p} \qquad \text{in state 1,}$$

and

$$x_{12}^1 = \frac{\alpha_2^1(pw_1^1 + (1 - p)w_2^1)}{p},$$

$$x_{22}^1 = \frac{(1 - \alpha_2^1)(pw_1^1 + (1 - p)w_2^1)}{1 - p} \qquad \text{in state 2.}$$

Consumer 2 has no private information. In the absence of the information revealed by the prices, he maximizes his expected utility from which the demand functions relevant to states 1 and 2 are

$$x_{11}^2 = x_{12}^2 = \frac{\bar{\alpha}^2(pw_1^2 + (1 - p)w_2^2)}{p},$$

$$x_{21}^2 = x_{22}^2 = \frac{(1 - \bar{\alpha}^2)(pw_1^2 + (1 - p)w_2^2)}{1 - p}.$$

The (unique) competitive equilibrium is characterized by the following prices:

$$p_1^* = \frac{\alpha_1^1 w_2^1 + \bar{\alpha}^2 w_2^2}{[\alpha_1^1 w_2^1 + (1 - \alpha_1^1)w_1^1] + [\bar{\alpha}^2 w_2^2 + (1 - \bar{\alpha}^2)w_1^2]} \qquad \text{in state 1,}$$

$$p_2^* = \frac{\alpha_2^1 w_2^1 + \bar{\alpha}^2 w_2^2}{[\alpha_2^1 w_2^1 + (1 - \alpha_2^1)w_1^1] + [\bar{\alpha}^2 w_2^2 + (1 - \bar{\alpha}^2)w_1^2]} \qquad \text{in state 2.}$$

If the values of the parameters (α, w) imply that $p_1^* = p_2^*$, the above equilibrium is a Green-Lucas equilibrium because the prices are not informative and agent 2 cannot acquire any information by observing the prices. On the contrary, if $p_1^* \neq p_2^*$, agent 2 becomes informed and changes his behavior so that the above equilibrium cannot be a Green-Lucas equilibrium. The other candidate for such an equilibrium is the fully revealing equilibrium.

Assume now that the prices are informative. Agent 2 has new demand functions, and these in turn yield the following equilibrium prices:

$$\tilde{p}_1 = \frac{\alpha_1^1 w_2^1 + \alpha_1^2 w_2^2}{[\alpha_1^1 w_2^1 + (1 - \alpha_1^1)w_1^1] + [\alpha_1^2 w_2^2 + (1 - \alpha_1^2)w_1^2]} \qquad \text{in state 1,}$$

$$\tilde{p}_2 = \frac{\alpha_2^1 w_2^1 + \alpha_2^2 w_2^2}{[\alpha_2^1 w_2^1 + (1 - \alpha_2^1)w_1^1] + [\alpha_2^2 w_2^2 + (1 - \alpha_2^2)w_1^2]} \qquad \text{in state 2.}$$

If $\tilde{p}_1 \neq \tilde{p}_2$, this equilibrium is indeed a Green-Lucas equilibrium because

Green-Lucas equilibria

	$p_1^* \neq p_2^*$	$p_1^* = p_2^*$
$\tilde{p}_1 \neq \tilde{p}_2$	$\tilde{p}_1, \tilde{p}_2$	p_1^*, p_2^* $\tilde{p}_1, \tilde{p}_2$
$\tilde{p}_1 = \tilde{p}_2$	inexistence	p_1^*, p_2^*

Figure 9.1

the prices are informative, as we have assumed. However, if $\tilde{p}_1 = \tilde{p}_2$, agent 2 cannot acquire any information concerning the state of nature, as we have assumed, so that there exists no fully revealing equilibrium. If we have simultaneously $p_1^* \neq p_2^*$ and $\tilde{p}_1 = \tilde{p}_2$, no Green-Lucas equilibrium exists. However, this case requires a very particular relationship (equality) among the parameters so that $\tilde{p}_1 = \tilde{p}_2$. If the parameters are drawn in a stochastic way, such an eventuality will be rare. The same comment can be made for the case in which $p_1^* = p_2^*$. Figure 9.1 summarizes our results.

Generically (except for negligible cases), we have $(p_1^* \neq p_2^*, \tilde{p}_1 \neq \tilde{p}_2)$, and we have therefore a fully revealing equilibrium.[7] From the technical perspective, the nonexistence problem arises from the fact that the information structure of agent 2 does not change in a continuous way with the prices. In the preceding example, let $p_1^{(n)}$ and $p_2^{(n)}$ be two sequences of prices such that $p_1^{(n)} \neq p_2^{(n)}$ for any n with $\text{Lim}_{n \to \infty} p_1^{(n)} = p_2^{(n)}$. For any n, the prices are informative, and agent 2 is perfectly informed about the state of nature. But he is uninformed in the limit.

The existence of an equilibrium could be proved in a general manner by using a fixed point argument for the mapping,

$$\phi(.) \xrightarrow{h} z(., \phi(.)) \xrightarrow{g} p = \phi(y),$$

that associates an excess demand function to any price function and the

7. See Radner (1979) for the general analysis.

price function that equates supply and demand for all the signals to this excess demand function. The problem discussed here is that h may be discontinuous. In this case an obvious way to proceed is to introduce noise that makes the outcome $p_1 = p_2$ negligible for agent i. For example, suppose that he can observe prices only with error. This makes $h(.)$ continuous, but the mapping $g \circ h$ has as its domain a vector space that must be convex and compact in order to invoke a fixed-point theorem. These requirements may not be met (see Green 1977).

The introduction of errors in the observation of prices leads to the general case in which the space of the states of nature becomes a continuum and the signals are continuous stochastic variables. If the number of relative prices is greater than or equal to the number of these signals, transmission of all the information remains possible. In the contrary case (when the number of relative prices is less than the number of signals), only nonfully revealing equilibria, which we call "noisy equilibria," may exist. Recent results on the question of existence can be summarized as follows: Let m be the number of stochastic variables and l the number of relative prices. If $m < l$, fully revealing equilibria exist generically. If $m = l$, we have robust counterexamples of nonexistence. If $m > l$, noisy equilibria exist provided we are willing to use quite discontinuous functions of prices.[8]

9.3   Welfare Analysis of Green-Lucas Equilibria

In section 9.1 we introduced three concepts of Pareto optimality depending on the date—ex ante, interim, or ex post—at which we considered welfare analysis. When the relevant information for allocating resources is decentralized, it is important to take into account the incentives that economic agents have to reveal their private information. Indeed, it would not be legitimate to criticize an allocation of resources that could be improved upon by a planner having complete information without constraining him to use mechanisms capable of extracting the information that he does not possess.

So as not to confuse the problems concerning monopolistic behavior, which is inevitable in an economy with a finite number of agents, with the incentive problems based on the decentralization of information, we now

8. See the introduction of Jordan and Radner (1982) in the special volume of the *Journal of Economic Theory*.

assume that there exists a continuum of consumers on the unit interval $I = [0, 1]$. There exist K relevant stochastic variables $\theta_1, \ldots, \theta_K$, and each agent observes unbiased signals of these stochastic variables given by

$$y_k^i = \theta_k + \varepsilon_k^i \qquad k = 1, \ldots, K$$

where the stochastic error terms ε_k^i have zero mean and are independently distributed.

Let $y^i = (y_1, \ldots, y_K)$, and let y be a profile of signals. For simplification, we assume that the stochastic variables $\theta_1, \ldots, \theta_K$ influence only preferences, and not the initial endowments. Therefore the utility function of consumer i depends on the consumption vector $x^i \in \mathbf{R}_+^L$ and on the vector $\theta = (\theta_1, \ldots, \theta_K)$. If we denote the true values of the signals by circumflexes over the variables, we have by the law of large numbers

$$\hat{\theta} = \int_0^1 \hat{y}^i \, di.$$

The utility function of an agent depends on his vector of goods and on the mean of the true observations of the others. In what sense are the Green-Lucas equilibria realizable as equilibria of a game, that is, implementable? To make this point precise, we recall two definitions.[9]

A *social choice function* is a function x^i from $I \times \mathbf{R}^K \times \mathbf{R}^K$ to $\mathbf{R}_+^L$ such that

$$\forall i \in I \qquad x^i(\hat{y}^i, \hat{\theta}) \in X^i \qquad \forall \hat{y}^i \in \mathbf{R}^K, \forall \hat{\theta} \in \mathbf{R}^K$$

and

$$\int_0^1 x^i(\hat{y}^i, \hat{\theta}) \, di = \int_0^1 w^i \, di \qquad \forall \hat{y}, \forall \hat{\theta} \in \mathbf{R}^K.$$

A *direct mechanism* is a mapping ξ^i from $I \times \mathbf{R}^K \times \mathbf{R}^K$ to $\mathbf{R}_+^L$ such that $\forall i \in I$, $\xi^i(y^i, \theta) \in X^i$, $\forall y^i \in \mathbf{R}^K$, $\forall \theta \in \mathbf{R}^K$, and

$$\int_0^1 \xi^i(y^i, \theta) \, di = \int_0^1 w^i \, di \qquad \forall y^i, \forall \theta \in \mathbf{R}^K.$$

The mechanism specifies a feasible allocation of resources for the reports of the characteristics y^i. The social choice function x^i is implementable as a dominant Nash equilibrium if

9. See Laffont (1988), chap. 5.

$\forall i \in I$, $\hat{y}^i$ maximizes $u^i(x^i(y^i, \hat{\theta}), \hat{\theta})$.

Regardless of the characteristics of the other agents, so long as they report their true observations, truthful revelation is a dominant strategy for each agent.

THEOREM 2   The Green-Lucas fully revealing equilibrium, if it exists, is implementable as a dominant Nash equilibrium.

Proof   The equilibrium is implemented by the following mechanism:

Report your characteristics. The mechanism computes the average of these responses, calculates prices using the price function $p^*(\theta)$ corresponding to the equilibrium, and makes the best allocation to each agent i based on his utility function $u^i(x^i, \theta)$, where $\theta = \int_0^1 y^i \, di$, subject to his budget constraint. It is clear that it is in the agent's self-interest to report his true $\hat{y}^i$ so long as he assumes that the mean of the others is the true $\hat{\theta}$.[10] ∎

In section 9.1 we noted that the fully revealing equilibrium might transmit too much information. To demonstrate this, we need to find an incentive compatible mechanism that extracts information and uses it to obtain a socially preferred allocation of resources. We show this possibility in the example that follows, for which the fully revealing equilibrium is not ex ante Pareto optimal.

Consider an exchange economy with two goods in which we have a continuum of agents $I = [0, 1]$ whose utility functions are written as

$$x_1^{i1} + \theta \operatorname{Log} x_2^{i1}   \qquad i \in I$$

and who are perfectly informed about the value of θ that we assume to be equal to 1 with probability $\frac{1}{2}$ and 2 with probability $\frac{1}{2}$. The endowments of a typical agent are $(1, 1)$ in the two states of nature. There exists another continuum of agents on the unit interval $[0, 1]$ whose utility functions are

$$\operatorname{Log} x_1^{i2} + \theta \operatorname{Log} x_2^{i2}   \qquad i \in [0, 1]$$

and whose signals are uninformative. The endowments of a typical agent in this group are $(2, 1)$.

We can verify easily that there exists a fully revealing equilibrium characterized by a price of good 2 in terms of good 1 equal to

10. If the utility function $u^i(.)$ depends directly on y^i, the incentive to tell the truth is strict.

$$p^*(\theta) = \frac{\theta(3 + \theta)}{2 + \theta} \quad \text{with } p^*(1) \neq p^*(2),$$

and allocations given by

$$x_1^{i1} = \frac{2\theta + 2}{\theta + 2} \quad x_2^{i1} = \frac{\theta + 2}{\theta + 3} \qquad \forall i \in [0, 1],$$

$$x_1^{i2} = \frac{\theta + 4}{\theta + 2} \quad x_2^{i2} = \frac{\theta + 4}{\theta + 3} \qquad \forall i \in [0, 1].$$

In this equilibrium all the information is transmitted. However, at date 1 the informed agents are not risk-averse, whereas type 2 agents are risk-averse. Therefore an insurance opportunity can be exploited at date 1. To improve on the above allocation in the ex ante Pareto sense, we construct a new allocation using the following incentive compatible mechanism.

An incentive compatible mechanism for the informed type 1 agent is a pair of functions

$$x_1^{i1}(\theta), x_2^{i1}(\theta)$$

that lead the agent to report his true observation $\hat{\theta}$. Taking a differential approach (see chapter 10 and Laffont 1988, ch. 5), these functions lead to truthful revelation if

$$\frac{dx_1^{i1}}{d\theta}(\theta) + \frac{\theta}{x_2^{i1}(\theta)} \frac{dx_2^{i1}}{d\theta}(\theta) = 0 \tag{9}$$

and

$$\frac{dx_2^{i1}}{d\theta}(\theta) \geq 0.$$

For example, choose the allocation of the Green-Lucas equilibrium for good 2, that is, $x_2^{i1} = (\theta + 2)/(\theta + 3)$. By integrating equation (9), we obtain

$$x_1^{i1}(\theta) = -\int_1^\theta \frac{t}{(2 + t)(3 + t)} \, dt + K.$$

Now K can be chosen so that each type 1 agent has the same level of expected utility with the mechanism as he has in the equilibrium, specifically,

$$K = \frac{17}{12} + \frac{1}{2} \int_1^2 \frac{t}{(2+t)(3+t)} dt.$$

Each type 2 agent can have the same allocation of good 2 that he has in the equilibrium. With respect to good 1, he can obtain $3 - x_1^{i1}(\theta)$, that is,

$$\frac{19}{12} - \frac{1}{2} \int_1^2 \frac{t}{(2+t)(3+t)} dt \quad \text{if } \theta = 1,$$

$$\frac{19}{12} + \frac{1}{2} \int_1^2 \frac{t}{(2+t)(3+t)} dt \quad \text{if } \theta = 2.$$

This allocation has the same mean as the equilibrium one but a smaller variance so that each type 2 agent (who is risk-averse) is strictly better off than he is at the equilibrium.

That the fully revealing equilibrium is not ex ante Pareto optimal may not be terribly surprising in as much as we have foregone the opportunity to organize a system of complete markets at date 0. It is more interesting to show that the equilibrium can be improved upon once private information is acquired—that is, the equilibrium is not even interim Pareto efficient.

This result can be shown by modifying slightly the preceding example. Assume that only a proportion λ of type 1 agents is informed. No matter what value λ takes, the fully revealing equilibrium is unaffected. To show that the equilibrium is not interim efficient, it suffices to show that we can strictly improve the situation of this fraction λ of type 1 agents in *both* states of nature. This is accomplished by adding δ to the allocation of good 1 for these agents so that

$$\frac{17}{12} + \frac{1}{2} \int_1^2 \frac{t}{(2+t)(3+t)} dt + \delta > \frac{4}{3} \quad \text{if } \theta = 1,$$

$$\frac{17}{12} - \frac{1}{2} \int_1^2 \frac{t}{(2+t)(3+t)} dt + \delta > \frac{3}{2} \quad \text{if } \theta = 2.$$

The aggregate amount required for this modification is $\lambda\delta$. Since, in the preceding example, it was possible to improve strictly the expected welfare of type 2 agents, we can take away from each of them a quantity τ of good 1 and still leave their welfare improved. To clinch the result, it is sufficient to take λ small enough so that $\lambda\delta = \tau$. Therefore the fully revealing equilibrium may transmit too much information. If the number of stochastic variables θ_k is greater than the number of relative prices, the opposite problem may arise.[10] Consequently there is no reason to believe that the transmission of information in the Green-Lucas equilibrium is appropriate.

Suggested Readings

Grossman, S., and Stiglitz, J. (1980). The paradox of the transmission of costly information.

Jordan, J., and Radner, R. (1982). A comprehensive survey focused on the problems of existence.

Holmström, B., and Myerson, R. (1983). The general methodology of welfare analysis in economies where information is decentralized.

Laffont, J.-J. (1985). The welfare analysis of Green-Lucas equilibria.

Lucas, R. E. (1972). An example of a non fully revealing equilibrium to analyze the Phillips curve.

References

Green, J. 1973. "Information, Efficiency and Equilibrium." Discussion Paper no. 284. Harvard Institute of Economic Research.

Green, J. 1977. "The Non-existence of Informational Equilibria." *Review of Economic Studies* 44:451–463.

Grossman, S. J., and J. Stiglitz. 1980. "On the Impossibility of Informationally Efficient Markets." *American Economic Review* 70:393–408.

Grossman, S. J. 1981. "An Introduction to the Theory of Rational Expectations under Asymmetric Information." *Review of Economic Studies* 154:541–559.

Hellwig, M. 1980. "On the Agregation of Information in Competitive Markets." *Journal of Economic Theory* 22:477–498.

Hellwig, M. 1982. "Rational Expectations Equilibrium with Conditioning on Past Prices: A Mean-Variance Example." *Journal of Economic Theory* 26:279–312.

Hirschleifer, J. 1971. "The Private and Social Values of Information and the Reward to Inventive Activity." *American Economic Review* 61:561–574.

Holmström, B., and R. Myerson. 1983. "Efficient and Durable Decision Rules with Incomplete Information." *Econometrica* 51:1799–1820.

Jordan, J., and R. Radner. 1982. "Rational Expectations in Microeconomic Models: An Overview." *Journal of Economic Theory* 26:201–223.

Laffont, J.-J. 1985. "On the Welfare Analysis of Rational Expectations Equilibria with Asymmetric Information." Walras Bowley Lecture, *Econometrica* 53:1–30.

Laffont, J.-J. 1988. *Fundamentals of Public Economics*. MIT Press, Cambridge.

Lucas, R. E. 1972. "Expectations and the Neutrality of Money." *Journal of Economic Theory* 4:103–124.

10. See problem 9 at the end of the book.

Milgrom, P., and N. Stockey. 1982. "Information, Trade and Common Knowledge." *Journal of Economic Theory* 26:17–27.

Radner, R. 1967. "Equilibre des marchés à terme et au comptant en cas d'incertitude." *Cahiers du Séminaire d'Econométrie.* CNRS, 35–52.

Radner, R. 1968. "Competitive Equilibrium under Uncertainty." *Econometrica* 36:31–56.

Radner, R. 1979. "Rational Expectations Equilibrium: Generic Existence and the Information Revealed by Prices." *Econometrica* 47:655–678.

10 Adverse Selection and Exchange

In the preceding chapter we saw how agents can involuntarily transmit a portion of their private information to the other market participants by their actions on markets. In that chapter we retained the anonymity of the exchange process so that we were constrained to use prices that are independent of the quantities transacted, that is, "linear prices." On the contrary, when transactions between agents possessing different information structures can be personalized (as in the insurance contracts of chapter 8), we can use contracts that are more complex than linear price contracts.

This chapter is devoted to the study of contracts that govern relationships between an informed agent and an uninformed agent. Initially, we provide a general method of characterizing contracts by borrowing from the theory of incentives[1] a language that focuses on the role of transmission of information in these contracts. This first step allows us to determine the set of feasible allocations subject to incentive constraints due to the decentralization of information. In order to describe the nature of exchange once the feasible contracts have been characterized, a choice must be made between alternative assumptions: either a partner to the exchange optimizes his welfare over the set of contracts if, for example, this agent is a monopolist who chooses the contract, or conflicts arise among the various agents. We also study the case where an uninformed agent can use the competition among informed agents as well as the role played by repeated contracting over time to gain information. Finally, we show how this perspective integrates various key contributions to the economics of information.

10.1 The Characterization of Incentive Compatible Contracts

Consider a supplier with w units[2] of a good of quality θ to sell to a buyer. The seller is the only one who knows the value of θ; however, θ belongs to an open interval of $\mathbf{R}$, denoted Θ, that is itself commonly known. In the exchange relationship between the two agents, two variables are observable—namely, the quantity of the good that the buyer obtains, x, and the monetary payment he makes to the seller, t.

The buyer's utility function is denoted $U(\theta, x, t)$, and the seller's utility is denoted $V(\theta, x, t)$. Both functions are assumed to be twice continuously differentiable. Any type of exchange can be represented by a mechanism.

---

1. See Laffont (1988), ch. 5.
2. w is large so that the buyer is never constrained.

A *mechanism* is a space of strategies for the seller, M, and an outcome function g from M to the space of social states characterized here by a value of x and a value of t. Therefore g maps M into $\mathbf{R}_+ \times \mathbf{R}$.

Assume that faced with such a mechanism the seller[3] has a best strategy m^*:

$$V(\theta, x(m^*), t(m^*)) \geqslant V(\theta, x(m), t(m)) \qquad \forall m \in M.$$

The revelation principle indicates that there exists a direct mechanism in which the space of strategies is equivalent to the space of characteristics Θ, which leads the seller to report the true value of his characteristic and which is equivalent to the preceding mechanism.

For each value of θ, consider the best message $m^*(\theta)$ in the original mechanism; $m^*(.)$ defines a mapping from Θ to M. Consider the direct mechanism defined by the resulting function $g \circ m^*$ from Θ to $\mathbf{R}_+ \times \mathbf{R}$. Then, revealing θ is the best strategy for the seller. Indeed, suppose that there exists $\tilde{\theta} \neq \theta$ that is a better response. Then

$$V(\theta, x(m^*(\tilde{\theta})), t(m^*(\tilde{\theta}))) > V(\theta, x(m^*(\theta)), t(m^*(\theta))). \tag{1}$$

Let $m^*(\tilde{\theta}) = m$ and $m^*(\theta) = m^*$ so that condition (1) can be written as

$$V(\theta, x(m), t(m)) > V(\theta, x(m^*), t(m^*)),$$

which contradicts the assumption that m^* is the best strategy given the mechanism (M, g).

This result allows us to restrict the analysis to direct mechanism $(x(\tilde{\theta}), t(\tilde{\theta}))$ that induce truthful revelation of θ by the seller. Such contracts are called *incentive compatible contracts*.

For simplification, we limit our analysis to continuously differentiable mechanisms. The seller maximizes $V(\theta, x(\tilde{\theta}), t(\tilde{\theta}))$ with respect to his response $\tilde{\theta}$. Then the mechanism specifies a quantity exchanged $x(\tilde{\theta})$ and a monetary payment $t(\tilde{\theta})$. The first-order necessary condition of this optimization problem is written as

$$\frac{\partial V}{\partial x}(\theta, x(\tilde{\theta}), t(\tilde{\theta})) \frac{dx}{d\theta}(\tilde{\theta}) + \frac{\partial V}{\partial t}(\theta, x(\tilde{\theta}), t(\tilde{\theta})) \frac{dt}{d\theta}(\tilde{\theta}) = 0. \tag{2}$$

A necessary condition for truthful revelation to be an optimal response is then

---

3. Remember that the seller is completely informed.

$$\frac{\partial V}{\partial x}(\theta, x(\theta), t(\theta))\frac{dx}{d\theta}(\theta) + \frac{\partial V}{\partial t}(\theta, x(\theta), t(\theta))\frac{dt}{d\theta}(\theta) = 0. \tag{3}$$

Since truthful revelation must obtain for any value of θ, equation (3) can be considered to be an identity in θ, that is, as the following differential equation:

$$\frac{\partial V}{\partial x}(\theta, x(\theta), t(\theta))\frac{dx}{d\theta}(\theta) + \frac{\partial V}{\partial t}(\theta, x(\theta), t(\theta))\frac{dt}{d\theta}(\theta) = 0 \quad \forall \theta \in \Theta. \tag{4}$$

The local second-order necessary condition for the optimization problem of the seller evaluated at $\tilde{\theta} = \theta$ is written as

$$\frac{\partial^2 V}{\partial x^2}\left(\frac{dx}{d\theta}\right)^2 + 2\frac{\partial^2 V}{\partial x \partial t}\cdot\frac{\partial x}{\partial\theta}\cdot\frac{\partial t}{\partial\theta} + \frac{\partial^2 V}{\partial t^2}\left(\frac{dt}{d\theta}\right)^2 + \frac{\partial V}{\partial x}\frac{d^2 x}{d\theta^2} + \frac{\partial V}{\partial t}\frac{d^2 t}{d\theta^2} \leqslant 0, \tag{5}$$

which, from using equation (4) (the derivative of which can be equated to 0 because it is an identity), reduces to

$$\frac{\partial V}{\partial t}\cdot\frac{dx}{d\theta}\cdot\frac{\partial}{\partial\theta}\left(\frac{\partial V/\partial x}{\partial V/\partial t}\right) \geqslant 0. \tag{6}$$

Here it is natural to assume that $\partial V/\partial t > 0$. Then under the assumption that[4]

$$\frac{\partial}{\partial\theta}\left(\frac{\partial V/\partial x}{\partial V/\partial t}\right) > 0 \quad \forall\theta, \forall x, \forall t, \tag{7}$$

the second-order condition reduces to the condition of monotonicity, that is,

$$\frac{dx}{d\theta}(\theta) \geqslant 0 \quad \forall\theta \in \Theta. \tag{8}$$

We now show that conditions (4) and (8) are indeed sufficient conditions for the agent to report his true θ. In other words, the local necessary conditions are sufficient globally. Let $\phi(\tilde{\theta}, \theta) = V(\theta, x(\tilde{\theta}), t(\tilde{\theta}))$; we wish to show that

$$\phi(\theta, \theta) \geqslant \phi(\tilde{\theta}, \theta) \quad \forall\tilde{\theta} \in \Theta \tag{9}$$

---

4. For $dx/d\theta \geqslant 0$ to summarize the second-order necessary condition (6), it is sufficient that (7) hold for only $x(\theta)$ and $t(\theta)$. We show later that by invoking (7) for all θ, x, and t, $dx/d\theta \geqslant 0$ and conditions (4) become sufficient as well.

knowing that

$\phi_1(\theta, \theta) = 0$ (first-order condition),

$\phi_{11}(\theta, \theta) \leqslant 0$ (local second-order condition).

Suppose that $\tilde{\theta} < \theta$. Then we have

$\phi(\theta, \theta) - \phi(\tilde{\theta}, \theta)$

$$= \int_{\tilde{\theta}}^{\theta} \phi_1(\tau, \theta) \, d\tau$$

$$= \int_{\tilde{\theta}}^{\theta} \frac{\partial V}{\partial t}(\theta, x(\tau), t(\tau)) \left\{ \frac{(\partial V/\partial x)(\theta, x(\tau), t(\tau))}{(\partial V/\partial t)(\theta, x(\tau), t(\tau))} \cdot \frac{dx}{d\tau}(\tau) + \frac{dt}{d\tau}(\tau) \right\} d\tau. \tag{10}$$

For any $\tau < \theta$,

$$\frac{(\partial V/\partial x)(\tau, x(\tau), t(\tau))}{(\partial V/\partial t)(\tau, x(\tau), t(\tau))} < \frac{(\partial V/\partial x)(\theta, x(\tau), t(\tau))}{(\partial V/\partial t)(\theta, x(\tau), t(\tau))}.$$

Then (4) and (8) imply

$$0 = \frac{(\partial V/\partial x)(\tau, x(\tau), t(\tau))}{(\partial V/\partial t)(\tau, x(\tau), t(\tau))} \frac{dx}{d\theta}(\tau) + \frac{dt}{d\theta}(\tau)$$

$$\leqslant \frac{(\partial V/\partial x)(\theta, x(\tau), t(\tau))}{(\partial V/\partial t)(\theta, x(\tau), t(\tau))} \frac{dx}{d\theta}(\tau) + \frac{dt}{d\theta}(\tau).$$

Moreover, since $\partial V/\partial t > 0$, we can conclude that (10) is positive. A symmetric argument in the case when $\tilde{\theta} > \theta$ completes the demonstration of (9). Note that in view of the first-order condition $\phi_1(\theta, \theta) = 0$, the second-order condition can be rewritten $\phi_{12}(\theta, \theta) \geqslant 0$. This formulation is in general more convenient. It gives us a shorter proof of the above global sufficiency result. For $\tilde{\theta} < \theta$, $\phi(\theta, \theta) - \phi(\tilde{\theta}, \theta) = \int_{\tilde{\theta}}^{\theta} \phi_1(\tau, \theta) \, d\tau \geqslant \int_{\tilde{\theta}}^{\theta} \phi_1(\tau, \tau) \, d\tau = 0$.

Assumption (7)—namely, that the marginal rate of substitution between the good and money is monotonic in θ—simplifies greatly the analysis of contracts because it affords a simple characterization of feasible allocations in the class of differentiable or piecewise differentiable contracts so that the techniques of optimal control may be used.[5]

---

5. When this assumption is not satisfied, we must abandon the differentiable approach and revert to a discrete formulation of the space of characteristics in order to write explicitly the set of incentive compatible constraints.

An incentive compatible mechanism can be represented as follows: Choose any increasing function $x(.)$. The monetary payment is defined by integrating equation (4). Notice that integrating (4) yields a degree of freedom due to the constant of integration, that is,

$$t(\theta) = \phi(\theta) + K \tag{11}$$

where $\phi(\theta)$ is a particular solution of equation (4). The constant K can be chosen in such a way as to satisfy a minimum utility constraint (called the "individual rationality constraint") for one of the two agents, for example, the seller (if the contract is designed by the buyer). Then we would have

$$V(\theta, x(\theta), \phi(\theta) + K) \geqslant \bar{v} \qquad \forall \theta \in \Theta$$

where $\bar{v}$ indicates the utility level that the seller can obtain outside of the exchange relationship with the buyer. In a general equilibrium model this parameter is surely an endogenous variable.[6]

Notice as well that, since $x(\theta)$ is monotonic, it is invertible, and equation (11) can be rewritten as $t(x) = \phi(x) + K$ to define a particular class of nonlinear price schedules given by

$$p(x) = \frac{t(x)}{x} = \frac{\phi(x) + K}{x}.$$

Indeed, it is clear that, in the final analysis, exchange between the two agents involves a quantity exchanged and a price. Therefore we can approach the problem more directly by saying that the buyer, for example, selects a nonlinear price schedule $p(x)$ and lets the seller determine the quantity exchanged—and from $p(x)$ the price of the transaction—according to the value of θ.

A nonlinear price schedule $p(x)$ defines the frontier of exchanges proposed by the buyer, such as AB in figure 10.1, where $t(x) = p(x) \cdot x$. Depending on the value of θ, the seller chooses a quantity to be exchanged on AB, $x(\theta)$, at the corresponding price $p(\theta) = t(\theta)/x(\theta)$. Any nonlinear price schedule (and, more generally, any compact subset of the space (x, t)) defines a contract.

---

6. This individual rationality constraint may also be satisfied, on average, as we express it in the following section. Enforcing this constraint for each value of θ corresponds to either the case in which the seller is informed when he decides whether or not to accept the contract or the case in which the seller can break the contract once he discovers θ.

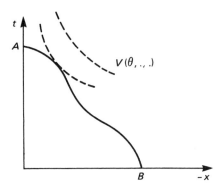

Figure 10.1

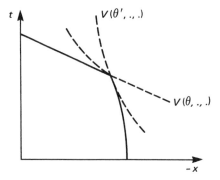

Figure 10.2

The preceding approach allows us to determine necessary and sufficient conditions that characterize the differentiable contracts and are also easy to analyze. If we consider the set of nonlinear contracts, it is difficult to go beyond existence proofs without reintroducing the restrictive assumptions that the preceding approach already led us to impose. Nevertheless, the object of the analysis is the nonlinear contract that is equivalent to an incentive compatible mechanism (of transmission of information). When the frontier $t(x)$ is nondifferentiable at some points, we treat different agents identically (see figure 10.2). This property of bunching occurs in the mechanism approach if $x(.)$ is constant on an interval.

10.2 The Selection of a Contract

Let us first note that by assuming that the contract is offered ex ante before θ is known or that the contract is offered by the uninformed party, we eliminate the difficulties due to informed principals. In this latter case the analysis must take into account the information transmitted by the contract proposal (see, for example, Laffont and Maskin 1987). Reconsider now the problem of exchange in the preceding section, and assume that the contract is selected ex ante at date 0. At date 1 the seller discovers the true value of θ, the quantity $x(\theta)$ is exchanged, and the monetary amount $t(\theta)$ is paid. Finally, at date 2 the buyer discovers the value of θ for himself and consumes:

ex ante	interim	ex post
date 0	date 1	date 2

Therefore at date 0 we have a bilateral monopoly situation. We shall examine only the case where we have a "natural" principal, that is, an agent who is a Stackelberg leader. This agent will select the best contract from his perspective, given that he must secure the participation of his partner in the exchange.

Assume that the buyer selects the contract. Let $F(\theta)$ be his subjective cumulative distribution[7] over the values of θ for which the density function $f(\theta)$ is strictly positive on $\Theta = [\underline{\theta}, \bar{\theta}]$. He will maximize his expected utility subject to the incentive constraints obtained in section 10.1 and to the individual rationality constraint of the seller (which is also a type of incentive constraint):[8]

$$\text{Max} \int_{\Theta} U(\theta, x(\theta), t(\theta)) \, dF(\theta) \tag{12}$$

subject to

$$\frac{dx}{d\theta}(\theta) \geqslant 0, \tag{13}$$

7. $F(\theta)$ can also be interpreted as the objective distribution over a large population of sellers as long as we assume that the buyer has an additive utility function. A similar problem of optimization in the theory of optimal income taxation appears in this form as well (see Laffont 1988, problem 4 and also section 3.1) or in the theory of the discriminating monopolist.
8. Notice that the individual rationality constraint is expressed here on average. The seller accepts the contract before knowing θ, over which he has the same expectations as the buyer.

$$\frac{dV}{dx}\frac{dx}{d\theta} + \frac{dV}{dt}\cdot\frac{dt}{d\theta} = 0, \tag{14}$$

$$\int_{\Theta} [V(\theta, x(\theta), t(\theta))]\, dF(\theta) \geq \bar{v}. \tag{15}$$

For simplification, consider the particular case where U and V are quasi linear:[9]

$$U(\theta, x, t) = u(\theta, x) - t,$$

$$V(\theta, x, t) = v(\theta, x) + t.$$

Equation (14) then becomes a differential equation that is easy to integrate in t. We solve for

$$t(\theta) = -\int_{\underline{\theta}}^{\theta} \frac{\partial v}{\partial x}\cdot\frac{dx}{ds}\, ds - K.$$

Then the objective function of the buyer is

$$\int_{\Theta} \left\{ u(\theta, x(\theta)) + \int_{\underline{\theta}}^{\theta} \frac{\partial v}{\partial x}\frac{dx}{ds}\, ds + K \right\} dF(\theta).$$

At date 1 the utility of the seller is

$$v(\theta, x(\theta)) - \int_{\underline{\theta}}^{\theta} \frac{\partial v}{\partial x}\frac{dx}{ds}\, ds - K.$$

The constant K is determined by the buyer so as to satisfy the individual rationality constraint of the seller; hence,

$$K = \int_{\Theta} \left[v(\theta, x(\theta)) - \int_{\underline{\theta}}^{\theta} \frac{\partial v}{\partial x}\frac{dx}{ds}\, ds - \bar{v} \right] dF(\theta),$$

so that the optimization problem becomes

$$\text{Max} \int_{\Theta} \{ u(\theta, x(\theta)) + v(\theta, x(\theta)) \}\, dF(\theta) \tag{16}$$

$$\frac{dx}{d\theta}(\theta) \geq 0.$$

9. See Guesnerie and Laffont (1984) for a more general analysis.

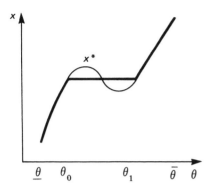

Figure 10.3

Let $x^*(\theta)$ be an unconstrained solution to problem (16); this is the first-best optimum for the problem. If $x^*(\theta)$ is increasing, we indeed have the solution to the above problem. Here asymmetric information does not hinder the achievement of a first-best optimum. If $x^*(.)$ is not increasing (for example, see figure 10.3), the optimum is the bold curve $\bar{x}(.)$ which coincides with $x^*(.)$ on all of its increasing portions. The interval where $x(\theta)$ is constant $[\theta_0, \theta_1]$ is defined by

$$\int_{\theta_0}^{\theta_1} \left(\frac{\partial u}{\partial x} + \frac{\partial v}{\partial x} \right) dF(\theta) = 0$$

$$x^*(\theta_1) = x^*(\theta_0),$$

and we have $\bar{x}(\theta) = x^*(\theta_1) = x^*(\theta_0)$ for any θ in $[\theta_0, \theta_1]$.

These results are obtained by applying control theory[10] to the following problem:

$$\text{Max} \int_{\underline{\theta}}^{\bar{\theta}} \{u(x(\theta), \theta) + v(x(\theta), \theta)\} \, dF(\theta)$$

$$\frac{dx}{d\theta} = \mu(\theta), \quad \mu(\theta) \geqslant 0.$$

We have a control theory problem with free end points and an inequality constraint on the control variable μ; x is the state variable. The Hamiltonian

---

10. For an introduction to optimal control theory, see M. Kamien and N. Schwartz, *Dynamic Optimization*, North-Holland, 1981.

is written

$$H(\theta, x, \mu, \lambda) = \{u(x(\theta), \theta) + v(x(\theta), \theta)\}f(\theta) + \lambda(\theta)\mu(\theta).$$

If $u(.)$ and $v(.)$ are strictly concave in x, according to Pontryagin's principle, the necessary and sufficient conditions for an optimum are written

$$\frac{d\lambda}{d\theta}(\theta) = -\left\{\frac{\partial u}{\partial x}(\bar{x}(\theta), \theta) + \frac{\partial v}{\partial x}(\bar{x}(\theta), \theta)\right\}f(\theta), \tag{17}$$

$$\frac{d\bar{x}}{d\theta}(\theta) = \mu(\theta), \tag{18}$$

$$\lambda(\underline{\theta}) = \lambda(\bar{\theta}) = 0 \qquad \text{(transversality conditions)} \tag{19}$$

and

$$\mu(\theta) \quad \text{maximizes} \quad H(\theta, x, \mu, \lambda) \quad \text{subject to the constraint} \quad \mu(\theta) \geqslant 0. \tag{20}$$

By using (19) and integrating (17), we have

$$0 = \lambda(\bar{\theta}) - \lambda(\underline{\theta}) = -\int_{\underline{\theta}}^{\bar{\theta}} \left(\frac{\partial u}{\partial x}(\bar{x}(\theta), \theta) + \frac{\partial v}{\partial x}(\bar{x}(\theta), \theta)\right)dF(\theta).$$

Integrating (17) between $\underline{\theta}$ and θ yields

$$\lambda(\theta) = -\int_{\underline{\theta}}^{\theta} \left\{\frac{\partial u}{\partial x}(\bar{x}(\theta), \theta) + \frac{\partial v}{\partial x}(\bar{x}(\theta), \theta)\right\}dF(\theta).$$

From the linearity of H in μ and from (20), $\lambda(\theta) \leqslant 0$ and $\lambda(\theta) < 0$ implies $\mu(\theta) = 0$. Therefore

$$\int_{\underline{\theta}}^{\theta} \left(\frac{\partial u}{\partial x} + \frac{\partial v}{\partial x}\right)dF(\theta) \geqslant 0 \qquad \forall \theta \in [\underline{\theta}, \bar{\theta}]. \tag{21}$$

If we have a strict inequality in (21), $\mu(\theta) = (d\bar{x}/d\theta)(\theta) = 0$. Then we can summarize these conditions by

$$\frac{d\bar{x}}{d\theta}(\theta) \int_{\underline{\theta}}^{\theta} \left\{\frac{\partial u}{\partial x}(\bar{x}(\theta), \theta) + \frac{\partial v}{\partial x}(\bar{x}(\theta), \theta)\right\}dF(\theta) = 0 \qquad \forall \theta \in [\underline{\theta}, \bar{\theta}].$$

In particular, we can conclude from these conditions that if $\bar{x}(\theta)$ is strictly increasing, it coincides with $x^*(\theta)$. Indeed, if $\mu(\theta) > 0$ over an interval, $\lambda(\theta) = 0$ in this interval; therefore $(d\lambda/d\theta)(\theta) = 0$, which yields, from (17),

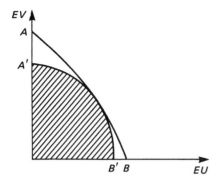

Figure 10.4

$$\frac{\partial u}{\partial x} + \frac{\partial v}{\partial x} = 0,$$

defining $x^*(\theta)$ over this interval.

To determine the intervals over which $\bar{x}$ is constant (for example, as in figure 10.3), it is sufficient to notice that by the continuity of the multiplier $\lambda(\theta)$, $\lambda(\theta_0) = \lambda(\theta_1) = 0$, which yields

$$\int_{\theta_0}^{\theta_1} \left(\frac{\partial u}{\partial x} + \frac{\partial v}{\partial x} \right) d\theta \geq 0. \tag{22}$$

Moreover, continuity of $\bar{x}$ requires that

$$x^*(\theta_1) = x^*(\theta_0), \tag{23}$$

which yields two equations in two unknowns θ_0 and θ_1.[11]

A zone in which $\bar{x}(\theta)$ is constant identifies a zone of bunching that reveals here an inefficiency in comparison with the world of complete information.

More generally, in the space of expected utilities at date 0, we can draw the feasible set both with ($A'B'$) and without (AB) asymmetric information (see figure 10.4). The shaded area represents the attainable set given the incentive constraints. Its frontier $A'B'$ represents the set of "incentive-efficient" utility allocations. It may partially coincide with AB as the preceding analysis shows. Point $A'(B')$ is obtained if the seller (buyer) selects the contract. In other cases the determination of exchange is very difficult given the nature of the bilateral monopoly situation.

11. See Guesnerie and Laffont (1984) for a rigorous treatment of the general case.

From the perspective of social welfare (see chapter 9), it is important to understand that the relevant feasible set is defined by $A'B'$ and that it is with regard to this set (unless other methods of obtaining information are available) that the performance of institutions should be evaluated (continuing to ignore other transaction costs). There are particular cases in which the complete information optimum is attainable. In the preceding example we see that when the utility functions are quasi-linear and the individual rationality constraint is satisfied on average, the second-order incentive conditions are the sole obstacle to the achievement of a complete information optimum. If the individual rationality constraint were imposed for each value of θ, the seller would be in a position to extract a rent above and beyond his individually rational level for favorable values of θ. To attenuate this loss, the buyer would deviate from the complete information optimum even in the absence of a second-order problem (see the example in section 10.4). Similarly, when the principal is a utilitarian government maximizing social welfare (see problem 12 at the end of the book), and if transfers between the agents are not costly and therefore the above rent has no social cost, the complete information optimum is attained provided there is no second-order condition problem.

10.3   Competition among Agents

Consider the case where the principal is a firm with a constant marginal production cost, c, and it faces a continuum of buyers. Each buyer has a utility function of the form

$$\theta x - \frac{x^2}{2} - t$$

where x is the quantity consumed of the good produced by the firm, t is the payment made, and θ is a characteristic of taste.[12] The distribution of tastes is known by the firm, and it is characterized by the cumulative distribution function $F(.)$ over the interval $[\underline{\theta}, \overline{\theta}]$. The tastes of different agents can be considered to be independent random draws from this distribution.

Now, a priori, a revelation mechanism makes the allocation that an agent receives, (x, t), depend on the set of responses from the other agents. Because

---

12. Notice that here it is the seller who suffers from asymmetric information and who is the principal, contrary to the situation in section 10.2.

of the law of large numbers, the distribution of characteristics is fixed. Therefore, for the allocation that an agent receives to be dependent on these responses, it would have to depend on the profile of these responses in an nonanonymous manner. If we neglect this possibility, in this context we are restricted to contracts $x(\theta)$ and $t(\theta)$ that depend only on the agent's own responses, that is, again to nonlinear prices (see Roberts 1984). Then the dominant-strategy incentive compatible contracts are characterized by

$$\theta \frac{dx}{d\theta} - x \frac{dx}{d\theta} - \frac{dt}{d\theta} = 0, \tag{24}$$

$$\frac{dx}{d\theta} \geq 0, \tag{25}$$

and the firm's objective is to maximize its average profit

$$\int_{\underline{\theta}}^{\bar{\theta}} (t(\theta) - cx(\theta)) \, dF(\theta)$$

subject to these incentive constraints (24) and (25) and to an individual rationality constraint.

Since the objective function of the principal is additive, the analysis is equivalent to the case of a single agent with average profit replacing expected profit. In numerous contexts the objective function of the principal cannot be considered additive. Take the case where the seller has only one unit of the good to sell, and assume that this good is indivisible. The seller's problem is to determine the best feasible auction for selling this good. Assume that he faces n potential buyers where the willingness to pay of buyer i, θ^i, results from an independent draw from the distribution $F(.)$. Since the problem is no longer additive, the allocation that an agent receives necessarily depends on the responses of the other agents.

From the revelation principle, an auction is a revelation mechanism,

$$x^i(\theta^1 \ldots \theta^n): [\underline{\theta}, \bar{\theta}]^n \rightarrow \{0, 1\},$$

$$t^i(\theta^1 \ldots \theta^n): [\underline{\theta}, \bar{\theta}]^n \rightarrow \mathbf{R} \qquad i = 1, \ldots, n,$$

that associates a winner (if $x^i = 1$, agent i receives the good) and a payment t^i for each participant i in the auction to a profile of bids. We may be interested in dominant-strategy auctions. The Vickrey auction (Laffont 1988, ch. 5) that allocates the good to the highest bidder and requires him to pay the second highest price bid is a dominant-strategy auction. We can

complete the description of this auction by assuming that the seller announces a reservation price, r, below which he will not sell the object.

We may also weaken the incentive concept and consider Bayesian equilibria for auctions (Laffont 1988, ch. 5). Consider, for example, the highest
bidder auction,[13] and let $b^i(\theta^i)$ be the bid of agent i when his willingness
to pay is equal to θ^i. Restrict the analysis to symmetric strategies (the
function $b^i(.) = b(.)$ for any i) with $b(.)$ increasing. Since $b(.)$ is increasing,
the agent with characteristic θ^i has a probability of winning given by
$[F(\theta^i)]^{n-1}$ at the equilibrium.

Let $P^i(b^1,\ldots,b^i,\ldots,b^n)$ be the payment that agent i must make if the bids
are $b^1, \ldots, b^i, \ldots, b^n$ (in the highest-bidder auction, $P^i(b^1,\ldots,b^n) = b^i$ if
$b^i = \text{Max}_j\, b^j$; or otherwise $P^i = 0$). The expected utility of an agent θ^i who
bids $b^i = b(x)$ is

$$\theta^i \cdot [F(x)]^{n-1} - \underset{\theta^{-i}}{\text{E}}\; P^i(b(\theta^1),\ldots,b(x),\ldots,b(\theta^n))$$

if he assumes that the other agents use the bidding strategy given by $b(.)$.

A symmetric Bayesian equilibrium is a function $b^*(.)$ such that:[14]

$$\forall i,\; \forall \theta^i \quad \theta^i \in \underset{x}{\text{Argmax}} \left\{ \theta^i [F(x)]^{n-1} - \underset{\theta^{-i}}{\text{E}}\; P^i(b^*(\theta^1),\ldots,b^*(x),\ldots,b^*(\theta^n)) \right\};$$

in other words, if he anticipates that the other agents use the bidding
strategy $b^*(.)$, it is in his self-interest to use it as well. Let

$$\bar{P}^i(x) = \underset{\theta^{-i}}{\text{E}}\; P^i(b^*(\theta^1),\ldots,b^*(x),\ldots,b^*(\theta^n)).$$

The first-order condition for this revelation mechanism is

$$\theta^i \frac{d}{dx}[F(x)]^{n-1} = \frac{d\bar{P}^i}{dx}, \tag{26}$$

which yields

$$\theta^i \frac{d}{d\theta^i}[F(\theta^i)]^{n-1} = \frac{d\bar{P}^i}{d\theta^i} \qquad \forall \theta^i.$$

The second-order (sufficient) condition is satisfied here because

---

13. Here we consider sealed-bid auctions. The Vickrey auction is equivalent to the ascending-
bid oral auction; the highest-bidder auction is equivalent to the descending-bid oral auction.
14. In the following expression, argmax indicates "the set of elements that maximize ...."

$$\frac{d}{dx}[F(x)]^{n-1} \geqslant 0.$$

Let θ^* be the largest value below which the agent has no interest in participating in the auction. By continuity, we must have

$$\theta^*[F(\theta^*)]^{n-1} - \bar{P}^i(\theta^*) = 0. \tag{27}$$

By using (27) to integrate (26), we obtain

$$\bar{P}^i(\theta^i) = \theta^i[F(\theta^i)]^{n-1} - \int_{\theta^*}^{\theta^i} [F(\theta)]^{n-1}\, d\theta. \tag{28}$$

Therefore the expected payment from buyer i is

$$\bar{P}^i = \int_{\theta^*}^{\bar{\theta}} \bar{P}^i(\theta)\, dF(\theta),$$

and the expected aggregate payment is n times this term. It is remarkable that this amount is independent of the strategies except through θ^*. All auctions that lead to the same θ^* yield the same expected payments.

Now return to the Vickrey auction and to the highest-bidder auction with reservation price r. It is easy to show that in both cases $\theta^* = r$. Therefore we obtain the result that the Vickrey auction (in which the agents report their true willingness to pay but pay only the second highest bid if they win) and the highest-bidder auction (in which the agents pay the amount that they bid and therefore bid an amount less than their true willingness to pay) are equivalent from the seller's perspective.

We compute the extent of the underbidding in the highest-bidder auction. Here

$$\bar{P}^i(\theta^i) = b(\theta^i)[F(\theta^i)]^{n-1}$$

since the agent pays his bid $b(\theta^i)$ if he wins—an outcome that occurs with probability $[F(\theta^i)]^{n-1}$. By using (28), we derive

$$b(\theta^i) = \theta^i - \int_r^{\theta^i} \frac{[F(\theta)]^{n-1}}{[F(\theta^i)]^{n-1}}\, d\theta.$$

If the buyers are risk-averse, the highest-bidder auction is preferable to the Vickrey auction. In essence, in the highest-bidder auction, the buyer can reduce the chance of losing by restricting the extent of his underbidding with respect to his willingness to pay. This course of action is surely beneficial to the seller. For the Vickrey auction, revelation of θ^i remains a dominant strategy. In the case of risk-averse buyers the derivation of the best auction from the seller's perspective is a complex optimal control problem (Maskin and Riley 1984).

Here we have assumed that the willingnesses to pay of the individual buyers are independent and perfectly known to them. Crémer and McLean (1985) show that if the buyers' willingnesses to pay are correlated with each other, the seller is able to take advantage of this correlation and often extract all of the surplus (this result uses the assumption of risk neutrality in an extreme manner).

Auctions are often used in a situation where agents have the same objective evaluation of the good (drilling rights) but different subjective evaluations because they have different information. The bids of other agents carry information about one's own valuation so that oral auctions and sealed-bid auctions are no longer equivalent (see Milgrom and Weber 1982).

To sum up, in the case of a continuum of independent agents, or in the case of the sale of an indivisible object, the characterization of competition among agents is relatively simple if we ignore collusion as we have done. We can surely generalize the approach to consider the case of the sale of a divisible good to a finite number of agents.

The next step consists of analyzing competition that can result from the agents' choosing among many principals. Since each principal selects a contract, an analysis of Nash equilibria in which the space of strategies of each player is the space of incentive contracts that can be implemented follows naturally. By adopting the naive Nash equilibrium, if it exists, we are led to a Bertrand equilibrium of zero profit contracts for all the principals. In chapter 8 we stressed the problem of nonexistence of pure strategy Nash equilibria in the particular case of the Rothschild-Stiglitz model when the proportion of low-risk agents is high. Riley (1979) shows that there exists no Nash equilibrium when the support of the unknown parameter θ is an interval, as it is in this chapter, because one can always destroy the equilibrium by attacking the high-risk market. On the contrary, Riley shows that when a Pareto-optimal contract exists (like the one described in section 10.2), this contract may be considered to be a *reactive equilibrium* in the following sense:

A contract $(x(\theta), t(\theta))$ where $\theta \in \Theta$ is a reactive equilibrium if, for any offer $(x(\theta), t(\theta))$ where $\theta \in \Theta$ that generates an expected gain for the principal who makes the offer, there exists another offer that can be made by a second principal, yielding a gain for him and generating a loss for the first principal. Moreover any other profitable addition to the set of offers is not allowed to cause losses for the second principal. To be sure, these conjectures are too particular for the notion of reactive equilibrium to be satisfactory. See the emerging literature on multiple principals.

10.4 Repeated Contracts

To illustrate the role played by repeated contracts in adverse selection models, consider the particular case in which the principal is a government that contracts with a firm to produce a public good, although it does not know the firm's marginal cost. The firm plays here the role of the seller in section 10.1 and the government the role of the buyer. The public good generates, for the consumers, utility equal to $S(x)$ for the quantity x with $S' > 0$ and $S'' < 0$. The cost function of the firm is $C = \theta x$, with $\theta \in [\underline{\theta}, \bar{\theta}]$ and $\bar{\theta} - \underline{\theta} = 1$ where the parameter θ is known only to the firm. The government has a uniform prior distribution over θ.

For an output level x of the public good, social welfare according to the utilitarian criterion is

$$S(x) - (1 + \lambda)t + t - \theta x$$

where t is the monetary transfer paid to the firm, $t - \theta x$ is the utility of the firm's manager, and $S(x) - (1 + \lambda)t$ is the net utility of the consumers taking into account the opportunity cost $1 + \lambda > 1$ of public funds ($\lambda > 0$ due to fiscal distortions).

If the government is completely informed, the optimum is characterized by the following problem:

$$\text{Max } \{S(x) - (1 + \lambda)t + t - \theta x\}$$

subject to

$$t - \theta x \geqslant 0 \tag{29}$$

where condition (29) represents the individual rationality constraint of the firm. The solution to this problem is given by

$$S'(x) = (1 + \lambda)\theta, \tag{30}$$

$$t - \theta x = 0. \tag{31}$$

Equation (30) expresses the necessary equality between the marginal utility of the good and its marginal social cost. Equation (31) indicates that it is necessary to saturate the individual rationality constraint of the agent with equality because transfers are costly.

Under incomplete information the government maximizes the expected social welfare subject to the first- and second-order incentive constraints, and to the individual rationality constraint of the firm. Formally, we have

$$\text{Max} \int_{\underline{\theta}}^{\bar{\theta}} [S(x(\theta)) - \theta x(\theta) - \lambda t(\theta)] \, d\theta$$

subject to

$$\frac{dt}{d\theta}(\theta) = \theta \frac{dx}{d\theta}(\theta), \tag{32}$$

$$\frac{dx}{d\theta}(\theta) \leqslant 0, \tag{33}$$

$$t(\theta) - \theta x(\theta) \geqslant 0 \qquad \forall \theta. \tag{34}$$

Let $\Pi(\theta)$ be the profit of the firm, given θ. From (32), $\dot{\Pi}(\theta) = -x(\theta) \leqslant 0$. Therefore the individual rationality constraint (34) can be replaced by

$$t(\bar{\theta}) - \bar{\theta}x(\bar{\theta}) \geqslant 0. \tag{35}$$

By choosing Π as a state variable and x as a control variable, the optimization problem is transformed to the following:

$$\text{Max} \int_{\underline{\theta}}^{\bar{\theta}} [S(x(\theta)) - (1 + \lambda)\theta x(\theta) - \lambda\Pi(\theta)] \, d\theta$$

subject to

$$\dot{\Pi}(\theta) = -x(\theta), \tag{36}$$

$$\dot{x} \leqslant 0, \tag{37}$$

$$t(\bar{\theta}) - \bar{\theta}x(\bar{\theta}) \geqslant 0. \tag{38}$$

For the moment we neglect (37) and write the Hamiltonian as

$$H = S(x(\theta)) - (1 + \lambda)\theta x(\theta) - \lambda\Pi(\theta) - \mu(\theta)x(\theta).$$

By applying Pontryagin's principle, we derive

$$\dot{\mu} = -\frac{\partial H}{\partial \Pi} = \lambda. \tag{39}$$

Since we have $\mu(\underline{\theta}) = 0$ by the transversality condition, integrating (39) yields

$$\mu(\theta) = \lambda(\theta - \underline{\theta}),$$

$$\frac{\partial H}{\partial x} = S'(x(\theta)) - (1 + \lambda)\theta - \mu(\theta) = 0, \tag{40}$$

or

$$S'(x(\theta)) = (1 + \lambda)\theta + \lambda(\theta - \underline{\theta}). \tag{41}$$

Since the solution to (41) satisfies (37), we have now obtained the desired result. The government reduces output compared to the complete information optimum to attenuate the social loss due to the rent $\Pi(\theta)$ from asymmetric information.

Now suppose that the contract is repeated over two periods with the same value of θ, and let δ be the discount factor common to both the government and the firm. The complete information optimum is obviously obtained from equations similar to (30) and (31). Consequently we have

$$S'(x_1) = (1 + \lambda)\theta, \quad S'(x_2) = (1 + \lambda)\theta, \tag{42}$$

$$t_1 = \theta x_1, \quad t_2 = \theta x_2. \tag{43}$$

To determine the optimum under incomplete information, we must know whether or not the government can commit itself for two periods. Can it implement in the beginning of period 1 a revelation mechanism $t(\theta)$, $x_1(\theta)$, and $x_2(\theta)$ that specifies an aggregate discounted transfer and outputs to be produced at dates 1 and 2? In other words, does the government have enough credibility to convince the agent that after the revelation of θ at date 1, it will still request $x_2(\theta)$ from him in the second period and not demand an output that instead forces him to his individually rational level of utility?

Initially, we assume that the government can make a credible commitment, and we characterize the incentive compatible mechanisms. The agent solves the following problem:

$$\underset{\tilde{\theta}}{\text{Max}} \; \{t(\tilde{\theta}) - \theta x_1(\tilde{\theta}) - \delta\theta x_2(\tilde{\theta})\}$$

which yields

$$\frac{dt}{d\theta} = \theta \frac{dx_1}{d\theta} + \delta\theta \frac{dx_2}{d\theta}$$

and

$$\frac{dx_1}{d\theta} + \delta \frac{dx_2}{d\theta} \leqslant 0.$$

By a similar reasoning we obtain the government's problem:

$$\text{Max} \int_{\underline{\theta}}^{\bar{\theta}} \{S(x_1(\theta)) + \delta S(x_2(\theta)) - (1 + \lambda)\theta x_1(\theta) - (1 + \lambda)\delta\theta x_2(\theta)$$

$$- \lambda\Pi(\theta)\} \, d\theta$$

subject to

$$\dot{\Pi}(\theta) = -x_1(\theta) - \delta x_2(\theta)$$

$$t(\bar{\theta}) - \bar{\theta} x_1(\bar{\theta}) - \delta\bar{\theta} x_2(\bar{\theta}) \geqslant 0,$$

which yields

$$S'(x_1(\theta)) = (1 + \lambda)\theta + \lambda(\theta - \underline{\theta}), \tag{44}$$

$$S'(x_2(\theta)) = (1 + \lambda)\theta + \lambda(\theta - \underline{\theta}). \tag{45}$$

Therefore, if the government commits itself credibly, the optimum is stationary with the same distortion, in both the first and second periods, compared to the complete information case.

If the government does not have the credibility required to commit itself for more than one period, the problem is much more complex. When he transmits information in the first period, the agent must take into account the use to which the government will put this information in the second period. This dynamic game can be formalized by using the concept of a perfect Bayesian equilibrium (see Laffont and Tirole 1988a). In the first period the agent reveals only a part of the information so that, in general, he retains some rent from asymmetric information in the second period. The optimal contract will no longer be the same over the two periods. Therefore it is impossible to separate completely firms of different types in the first period. This nonseparation result can be explained intuitively as follows: If a firm reveals its characteristic θ in the first period, it earns no profit in the second period. Therefore it must maximize its first-period utility. By pretending to have a smaller characteristic, $\theta - d\theta$, a firm loses nothing in the first period to a first-order approximation (by the envelope theorem) and ensures for itself a profit in the second period.

Thus far we have assumed a perfect correlation between marginal cost in the first period and in the second period. Suppose, on the other hand, that these costs can be considered to be independent draws θ_1 and θ_2 from a uniform distribution over $[\underline{\theta}, \bar{\theta}]$. The agent discovers θ_2 only at the beginning of the second period. Therefore the incentive mechanism for period 2 is characterized by

$$\frac{dt_2}{d\theta_2}(\theta_2) = \theta_2 \frac{dx_2}{d\theta_2}(\theta_2), \quad \frac{dx_2}{d\theta_2}(\theta_2) \leqslant 0,$$

and the one for period 1 by

$$\frac{dt_1}{d\theta_1}(\theta_1) = \theta_1 \frac{dx_1}{d\theta_1}(\theta_1), \quad \frac{dx_1}{d\theta_1}(\theta_1) \leqslant 0.$$

If we assume that the government can commit itself credibly for the two periods, we can write its problem as

$$\text{Max} \int_{\underline{\theta}}^{\bar{\theta}} [S(x_1(\theta_1)) - (1 + \lambda)\theta_1 x_1(\theta_1) - \lambda \Pi_1(\theta_1)] \, d\theta_1$$

$$+ \delta \int_{\underline{\theta}}^{\bar{\theta}} [S(x_2(\theta_2)) - (1 + \lambda)\theta_2 x_2(\theta_2) - \lambda \Pi_2(\theta_2)] \, d\theta_2$$

subject to

$$\dot{\Pi}_1(\theta_1) = -x_1(\theta_1), \quad \dot{x}_1 \leqslant 0,$$

$$\dot{\Pi}_2(\theta_2) = -x_2(\theta_2), \quad \dot{x}_2 \leqslant 0,$$

$$\Pi_1(\theta_1) + \delta \int_{\underline{\theta}}^{\bar{\theta}} \Pi_2(\theta_2) \, d\theta_2 \geqslant 0 \qquad \forall \theta_1.$$

The most noteworthy of the conditions is the firm's individual rationality constraint, now written as an expectation over θ_2 which is unknown to the firm in period 1. For this reason the solution of this problem, which is left as an exercise, involves no distortion in the contract in the second period, unlike the case of perfect correlation. Finally, notice that, by symmetry, the optimal contract is the same in the two periods if the government cannot commit itself for more than one period. Then this contract is identical to the optimal static contract, that is, the solution that we found in the case of perfect correlation with government commitment. This example illustrates the crucial role played by the possibility of the principal to make a credible commitment.

The case of two-period commitment with perfect correlation leads to the curious result that the firm and the government may use in period 2 a contract that they both know is inefficient. Indeed, if the firm has revealed it is bad in period 1, equation (45) shows that an inefficient allocation is selected in period 2 even though the value of θ is common knowledge. An intermediary assumption between commitment and noncommitment is to assume that the parties can commit, but not commit not to renegotiate. Their commitments must be renegotiation proof (see Laffont and Tirole 1988b).

10.5   Examples

Insurance Contracts

Consider an insurance company dealing with an individual who has the probability θ of having an accident that costs him L (see chapter 8), where θ takes its values in the interval $[\underline{\theta}, \overline{\theta}]$. The company proposes a revelation mechanism $(x_1(\theta), x_2(\theta))$ that specifies a net return in state 1 (accident state) and a net return in state 2 (no-accident state) for each report of θ by the agent.

Such a mechanism is an incentive compatible one if

$$\theta u(w - L + x_1(\theta)) + (1 - \theta)u(w + x_2(\theta))$$

$$\geq \theta u(w - L + x_1(\tilde{\theta})) + (1 - \theta)u(w + x_2(\tilde{\theta})) \qquad \forall \tilde{\theta} \in [\underline{\theta}, \overline{\theta}].$$

Using the method described here, we can show immediately that the continuously differentiable incentive contracts are characterized by the following two conditions:[15]

$$\theta u'(1) \cdot \frac{dx_1}{d\theta}(\theta) + (1 - \theta)u'(2)\frac{dx_2}{d\theta}(\theta) = 0, \tag{46}$$

15. Notice that condition (7) is always satisfied here.

$$\dot{x}_2(\theta) \geq 0. \tag{47}$$

If we impose the actuarially fair constraint on the contract, we have, moreover,

$$\theta x_1(\theta) + (1 - \theta)x_2(\theta) = 0.$$

By setting

$$x_1(\theta) = a(\theta)L,$$

$$x_2(\theta) = -\frac{\theta}{(1 - \theta)}a(\theta)L,$$

(46) and (47) become

$$\theta a'(\theta)\left\{u'(w - L + a(\theta)L) - u'\left(w - \frac{\theta}{1 - \theta} \cdot a(\theta)L\right)\right\}$$

$$= \frac{a(\theta)}{(1 - \theta)}u'\left(w - \frac{\theta}{1 - \theta} \cdot a(\theta)L\right), \tag{48}$$

$$a'(\theta) \geq 0 \qquad \forall \theta \in [\underline{\theta}, \bar{\theta}]. \tag{49}$$

Equation (48) defines a differential equation that we can integrate for each terminal value $a(\bar{\theta})$ and that satisfies (49).

The solution associated with $a(\bar{\theta}) = 1 - \bar{\theta}$ for which the agent who has a probability of an accident given by $\bar{\theta}$ is completely insured dominates in the Pareto sense the other solutions. It is represented in figure 10.5 by AB which has the property that the indifference curve of agent θ is tangent to

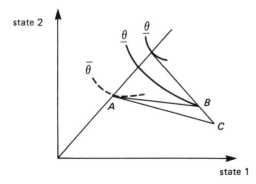

Figure 10.5

AB at the intersection of AB and the locus of equilibrium contracts passing through C and associated with probability θ.[16]

Spence's Signaling Equilibrium

Assume that here the agent is a worker who wants to sell his unit of labor of quality θ known only to him. His utility function depends on the amount x of work that he provides and the monetary compensation t that he receives, but not on θ. From the characterization of incentive compatible contracts, the agent is indifferent between all the responses because

$$\frac{dV}{d\theta} = \frac{\partial V}{\partial x}\frac{dx}{d\theta} + \frac{\partial V}{\partial t}\frac{dt}{d\theta} = 0. \tag{50}$$

Moreover, if we wish to implement the function $x(\theta) = 1$ ($dx/d\theta = 0$) corresponding to full employment of the worker, it is clear from (50) that the wage must be independent of θ. In the absence of other observable variables, the wage common to all workers will be the expected value of their productivity (due to competition among workers and employers).

As we stressed in chapter 8, the high-productivity workers find it beneficial to identify themselves. Spence's contribution is to introduce another variable, the level of education s, and a cost of education that *depends on* θ, to enlarge the class of incentive compatible contracts.

The worker's utility function becomes

$$V(x, t) - C(s, \theta).$$

Here an incentive compatible mechanism is a three-tuple of functions $x(\tilde{\theta})$, $t(\tilde{\theta})$, and $s(\tilde{\theta})$ that satisfy the following first-order condition

$$\frac{\partial V}{\partial x}\cdot\frac{dx}{d\theta} + \frac{\partial V}{\partial t}\cdot\frac{dt}{d\theta} - \frac{\partial C}{\partial s}(s, \theta)\frac{ds}{d\theta} = 0.$$

The second-order condition is

$$\frac{ds}{d\theta}(\tilde{\theta})\cdot\frac{\partial^2 C}{\partial\theta\partial s}(s, \theta) \leqslant 0 \qquad \forall\theta,\ \forall\tilde{\theta}.$$

16. In Cresta and Laffont (1987) this class of contracts is compared to the equilibrium contracts of the Rothschild-Stiglitz model studied in chapter 8 where the company knows that the agent has only two possible probabilities of an accident.

The famous Spence condition, according to which the marginal cost of transmitting the signal must decrease with quality $(\partial^2 C/\partial\theta\partial s)(s, \theta) \leqslant 0$, corresponds to our assumption (7). Then the second-order condition becomes $(ds/d\theta)(\theta) \leqslant 0$. In our notation Spence imposes $x(\theta) = 1$ so that the characterization of the optimum reduces to

$$\frac{\partial V}{\partial t}\frac{dt}{d\theta} - \frac{\partial C}{\partial s}(s, \theta)\frac{ds}{d\theta} = 0 \tag{51}$$

There still exists the possibility of choosing the function t and deriving s from (51). In the spirit of a Bertrand equilibrium, competition among the workers leads Spence to equate the wage $t(\theta)$ to the true productivity:

$$t(\theta) = \Psi(\theta).$$

Then $s(.)$ is obtained by integrating the following equation:

$$\frac{\partial V}{\partial t}(1, \Psi(\theta))\frac{d\Psi}{d\theta}(\theta) - \frac{\partial C}{\partial s}(s, \theta)\frac{ds}{d\theta}(\theta) = 0,$$

whose solution contains a constant of integration. If we accept the concept of reactive equilibrium, competition among employers (see section 10.2) leads to the selection of the Pareto-efficient equilibrium, that is, the choice of a particular constant of integration. Since education has no social utility here, the best equilibrium in which the education signal is perfectly informative corresponds to a specification for the constant of integration so that the lowest-quality agent is the only one to choose no education. Since $s(.)$ is invertible, it is also clear that this equilibrium can be interpreted as a wage $t(s)$ that is a nonlinear function of the level of education.

Employment Contracts

Consider the contract between a worker who provides a quantity of labor x and an employer who uses this labor in a production function of the following type:

$$y = \theta f(x), \quad f'(x) > 0$$

where θ is a variable observed only by the employer. Let ω be the wage. An incentive compatible contract $\omega(\theta)$ and $x(\theta)$ for an employer who maximizes his profit will have the following characteristics:

$$\theta f'(x)\frac{dx}{d\theta}(\theta) - x(\theta)\frac{d\omega}{d\theta}(\theta) - \omega(\theta)\frac{dx}{d\theta} = 0,$$

$$\frac{dx}{d\theta}(\theta) \geqslant 0.$$

Assume that the opportunity cost of work in the remainder of the economy is λ, and consider the particular case $f(x) = \text{Log}\, x$. The first-best allocation under complete information would be $x = \theta/\lambda$ which is increasing in θ and can therefore be realized as an incentive compatible contract. The wage is defined by the following equation:

$$\frac{\theta}{\lambda}\frac{d\omega}{d\theta} = (\lambda - \omega)\frac{1}{\lambda},$$

which can be solved to obtain

$$\omega = \lambda - \frac{K}{\theta} = \lambda - \frac{K}{\lambda x}.$$

where K would be determined by an individual rationality constraint. As the above equation shows, the wage increases with the quantity of work. Therefore the employer is led to report truthfully the marginal productivity because, in order to increase employment in favorable periods, he must increase the wage.

When the two agents are risk-averse, it is desirable that the contract shares risk between them. For this to occur, the wage must vary with θ. For the contract to be an incentive compatible contract, it must vary with x. In particular, if the agents have no disutility from work, there is an ex post divergence between the marginal disutility of work and the marginal productivity of work. In other words, an ex post inefficiency arises in the allocation of work and may take the form of unemployment (see the special issue of the *Quarterly Journal of Economics* in 1983).

Suggested Readings

Spence, M. (1974). A classic reference.

Guesnerie, R., and J.-J. Laffont (1983). A more rigorous synthesis than this chapter.

Riley, J. (1979). A survey about competition with contracts.

Green, J., and C. Kahn (1983). An application to labor markets.

Riley, J., and W. Samuelson (1981). Auction theory.

References

Crémer, J., and R. McLean. 1985. "Optimal Selling Strategies under Uncertainty for a Discriminating Monopolist When Demands Are Interdependent." *Econometrica* 53:345–361.

Cresta, J. P., and J.-J. Laffont. 1987. "Incentive Compatibility of Insurance Contracts and the Value of Information." *Journal of Risk and Insurance* 54:520–540.

Green, J., and S. Honkapohja. 1983. "Bilateral Contracts." *Journal of Mathematical Economics* 11:171–188.

Green, J., and C. Kahn. 1983. "Wage Employment Contracts." *Quarterly Journal of Economics* 98:173–189.

Guesnerie, R., and J.-J. Laffont. 1984. "Control of Firms under Incomplete Information." *Journal of Public Economics* 25:329–369.

Laffont, J.-J. 1988. *Fundamentals of Public Economics.* MIT Press, Cambridge.

Laffont, J.-J., and E. Maskin. 1987. "Monopoly with Asymmetric Information about Quality." *European Economic Review* 31:483–489.

Laffont, J.-J. and J. Tirole 1988a "The Dynamics of Incentive Contracts," *Econometrica*

Laffont, J.-J., and J. Tirole. 1988b. "Adverse Selection and Renegotiation in Procurement." Discussion Paper 665. Caltech.

Maskin, E., and J. Riley. 1984. "Optimal Auctions with Risk Averse Buyers." *Econometrica* 52:1473–1518.

Milgrom. P., and R. Weber. 1982. "A Theory of Auctions and Competitive Bidding." *Econometrica* 50:1089–1122.

Riley, J. 1979. "Informational Equilibrium." *Econometrica* 47:331–359.

Riley, J., and W. Samuelson. 1981. "Optimal Auctions." *American Economic Review* 71:381–392.

Roberts, K. 1977. "The Theoretical Limits to Redistribution." *Review of Economic Studies* 51:177–196.

Spence, M. 1974. *Market Signalling: Informational Transfer in Hiring and Related Processes.* Harvard University Press, Cambridge.

11 Moral Hazard and Exchange

The simplest organization imaginable is undoubtedly a two-party contractual relationship as, for example, between an employer and a worker, a landlord and a tenant farmer, a lawyer and a client, an insurance company and an insured person, a firm manager and the group of shareholders. Often one of the parties, the *principal*, delegates to the other, the *agent*, an action that influences his welfare, such as output for the employer, the harvest for the landlord, and the court's judgment for the client. If the agent's action is observable, the principal can control the agent so long as he has the power to enforce the penalties necessary to punish any deviant behavior on the agent's part.

In general, however, the action of the agent (for example, the level of his effort) is only imperfectly observable. In essence, the result observed by the principal is the joint product of an action which only the agent knows and of uncertainty (known or unknown to the agent at the time that he chooses his action). The product achieved by the agent on behalf of the principal is therefore stochastic. It depends directly on an action variable taken by the agent that is unobservable by the principal and costly to the agent. The basic problem for this mini-organization is to define the rules of sharing the product.

From chapter 5 we know that sharing stochastic income between economic agents achieves an ex ante Pareto optimum if the marginal rates of substitution between the income in the different states of nature are equalized between the economic agents. In particular, if the principal is risk-neutral while the agent is risk-averse, the agent must receive a *constant* return to be completely insured by the principal. This Pareto-optimal risk sharing involves one major inconvenience: the agent no longer has any incentive to exert effort since his income does not depend on his effort. On the other hand, linking the income of the agent to the final outcome deviates from Pareto-optimal risk sharing.

The purpose of this chapter is to show in a detailed enough way how optimal contracts for this organization[1] must be constructed in the presence of *moral hazard*[2]—the combination of the unobservability of the

1. The literature has meandered about considerably before arriving at a satisfactory formulation of the solution to this problem (see Simon 1951; Arrow 1963; Pauly 1968; Stiglitz 1971; Ross 1973; and Harris and Raviv 1979).
2. The qualifier "moral" is awkward but can be explained in the following way. The agent could commit himself morally to pursue an action that is determined jointly with the principal. Then it is the principal's doubt concerning the morality of the agent that creates the problem.

action and of the uncertainty about the outcome that renders the interpretation of the outcome in terms of the action difficult.

In the first section we summarize the most important economic results
obtained by an approach called the *first-order condition approach* that
neglects the second-order conditions of the agent's maximization problem.
The second section provides the sufficient conditions under which this
approach is valid and reviews the attempts to extend these results. Section
11.3 analyzes the way in which competition among many agents can be
exploited by the principal. Finally, the repeated principal–agent relation
opens up new contract possibilities that are explained in section 11.4. The
conclusion mentions the research trends currently under exploration.

11.1   The First-Order Condition Approach

Let $\tilde{y}$ be a stochastic variable that represents the gross income of the
principal, such as the output of a production process owned by the principal. The probability distribution of $\tilde{y}$ is influenced by a variable a that is
controlled by an agent and not observable by the principal—for example,
a might be the agent's effort level. Let $F(y, a)$ be the distribution function
of $\tilde{y}$ and $f(y, a)$ be its probability density function. We assume that the
support of this distribution is independent of a.

The problem posed is to determine the payment t (expressed in units of
y) offered to the agent to compensate him for the disutility of his action a.
We assume that the agent's utility function is separable, that is,

$$V(t, a) = v(t) - w(a) \qquad \text{with } v' > 0, v'' \leqslant 0; w' > 0, w'' > 0. \tag{1}$$

To ensure the agent's participation, we must give him in expected terms a
level of utility greater than that which he could obtain outside the relationship with the principal. This level of utility is called the agent's "individual
rationality level"; it is exogenous here and normalized to be zero. Thus our
analysis is of a partial equilibrium nature. We assume that

$$EV(t, a) \geqslant 0. \tag{2}$$

The utility of the principal is given by

$$u(y - t) \qquad u' > 0, u'' \leqslant 0. \tag{3}$$

Initially, assume that the principal observes and thus controls a. He can choose the level of a and determine the function $t(y)$ that best shares risk. His optimization problem is written as

$$\text{Max}_{(a,t(.))} Eu(\tilde{y} - t(\tilde{y})) \tag{4}$$

subject to

$$Ev(t(\tilde{y})) - w(a) \geqslant 0. \tag{5}$$

The Lagrangian is written as

$$L = \int u(y - t(y))f(y, a)\, dy + \lambda \left[\int v(t(y))f(y, a)\, dy - w(a) \right]. \tag{6}$$

The first-order conditions are

$$\frac{u'(y - t(y))}{v'(t(y))} = \lambda \qquad \forall y, \tag{7}$$

$$\int [u(y - t(y)) + \lambda v(t(y))]f_a(y, a)\, dy = \lambda w'(a). \tag{8}$$

Equation (7) can be rewritten as

$$\frac{u'(y - t(y))}{u'(y' - t(y'))} = \frac{v'(t(y))}{v'(t(y'))} \qquad \forall y, \forall y'. \tag{9}$$

In other words, the marginal rates of substitution of income are equated between the different states of nature characterized here by the value of y. Therefore risk is shared optimally. Equation (8) expresses the equality between the marginal social utility of a and the agent's marginal disutility weighted by λ. Here this weight is endogenous so that constraint (5) will be satisfied with equality. If both the agent and the principal are risk-averse ($v'' < 0$ and $u'' < 0$), by differentiating (7), we observe that the agent's income and the principal's income increase strictly with y.

Now assume that a is not observable by the principal. Nevertheless, the principal realizes that when faced with a transfer function $t(.)$, the agent chooses the a that is in his best interest. Consequently the agent solves

$$a \in \underset{a'}{\text{Argmax}} \int [v(t(y)) - w(a')]f(y, a')\, dy. \tag{10}$$

Now (10) is added to the individual rationality constraint (5).

The *first-order condition approach* consists in replacing (10) by the first-order condition of this maximization problem and assuming that this condition defines a unique solution. Then the optimization problem of the principal is written as

$$\underset{(a,\,t(.))}{\text{Max}} \int u(y - t(y))f(y, a)\,dy \tag{11}$$

subject to

$$\int [v(t(y)) - w(a)]f(y, a)\,dy \geqslant 0 \qquad (\lambda), \tag{12}$$

$$\int v(t(y))f_a(y, a)\,dy - w'(a) = 0 \qquad (\mu). \tag{13}$$

We have assumed that the support of the distribution of $\tilde{y}$ is independent of a. Otherwise, the complete information allocation can be achieved in a trivial way by taking high enough penalties. Intuitively, if the agent does not choose the action a^0 specified by the principal, there exists a nonzero probability that he will be detected because the support of $\tilde{y}$ is not what it should be. Then, in these cases of detection, it suffices to take a penalty large enough to inhibit the agent from taking an action different from a^0. Therefore we obtain the optimum.

The first-order conditions for problem (11) can be written as

$$\frac{u'(y - t(y))}{v'(t(y))} = \lambda + \mu\frac{f_a(y, a)}{f(y, a)} \qquad \forall y, \tag{14}$$

$$\int u(y - t(y))f_a(y, a)\,dy + \mu\left[\int v(t(y))f_{aa}(y, a)\,dy - w''(a)\right] = 0. \tag{15}$$

Action a has a well-defined negative effect on the agent's utility. So that it has a well-defined positive effect on output, we assume that an increase in a generates an improvement in y in the first-order stochastic dominance sense (see chapter 2), or

$$F_a(y, a) \leqslant 0 \tag{16}$$

(with one strict inequality for a set having positive probability).

Then we can show that the risk sharing implied by this solution is not Pareto optimal (that is, $\mu \neq 0$) when the agent is risk-averse. Moreover, by deviating from the Pareto-optimal risk-sharing solution, the principal can induce the agent to choose a better (higher) level of effort.

THEOREM (Holmström 1979; Shavell 1979)   Under the preceding assumptions and if, moreover, $v'' < 0$, then $\mu > 0$.

Proof   Suppose, on the contrary, that $\mu \leqslant 0$. From the first-order condition (14), and by letting $r(y) = y - t(y)$, we have

$$\frac{u'(r(y))}{v'(y - r(y))} = \lambda + \mu \frac{f_a(y, a)}{f(y, a)} \tag{17}$$

where $r(y)$ is the principal's income at the optimum for the incomplete information problem. Let $r_\lambda(y)$ be his income under complete information when the multiplier associated with the individual rationality constraint is λ (see equation 7).
   Then for $y \in \{y | f_a(y, a) \geqslant 0\}$

$$\frac{u'(r(y))}{v'(y - r(y))} \leqslant \lambda = \frac{u'(r_\lambda(y))}{v'(y - r_\lambda(y))}. \tag{18}$$

Therefore, since $u'' \leqslant 0$ and $v'' < 0$, $r_\lambda(y) \leqslant r(y)$.
   Similarly, we show that for $y \in \{y | f_a(y, a) \leqslant 0\}$, $r_\lambda(y) \geqslant r(y)$. Consequently

$$\int u(r(y)) f_a(y, a)\, dy \geqslant \int u(r_\lambda(y)) f_a(y, a)\, dy. \tag{19}$$

We show that the right-hand side of (19) is strictly positive by letting $[\alpha, \beta]$ be the support of $\tilde{y}$:

$$\int_\alpha^\beta u(r_\lambda(y)) f_a(y, a)\, dy = u(r_\lambda(y)) F_a(y, a)\Big|_\alpha^\beta - \int_\alpha^\beta F_a(y, a) u'(r_\lambda(y)) r_\lambda'(y)\, dy. \tag{20}$$

Since $F(\beta, a) = 1$ for all a, $F_a(\beta, a) = 0$ for all a, and since $F(\alpha, a) = 0$ for all a, $F_a(\alpha, a) = 0$ for all a. On the other hand, $u' > 0$ and $r_\lambda' > 0$ from the remark following (9). Since $F_a(y, a)$ is strictly negative on a set of positive probability, we have

$$\int u(r(y)) f_a(y, a)\, dy > 0. \tag{21}$$

   Now consider the second first-order condition (15). Since the action chosen is a (interior) maximum for the agent's optimization problem, the coefficient of μ (which is the second derivative of this problem) is negative or zero. Then, from (15) and (21), we must have $\mu > 0$, which is a contradiction. ∎

To understand this result intuitively, take the case where the principal is not risk-averse ($u'' = 0$). Optimal risk sharing requires complete insurance for the agent. Moreover the agent's income will then be independent of his action, and he will choose the action that is most favorable to him—that is, a zero level of effort if we interpret this variable as effort. To lead the agent to choose a level of effort more favorable to the principal, we must make his income depend on the only observable variable, the output y. Since this is stochastic, such an arrangement cannot share risk optimally.

Notice that if the agent is risk neutral, the complete information optimum is obtained by giving the agent an amount equal to $\bar{y}$ minus a constant (that is, the principal's income is fixed) where the constant is determined to satisfy the individual rationality constraint. Since the agent receives all the benefit of his action, his chosen action will be optimal.

Intuitively, we expect the transfer received by the agent to increase with y. This can be shown by differentiating (14) subject to the additional assumption that $(\partial f(y,a)/\partial a)/f(y,a)$ is an increasing function of y.[3] This condition, called the *monotone likelihood ratio condition* (ML), has the following intuitive interpretation. $\text{Log} f(y,a)$ is the likelihood function for the model in which y is the endogenous variable and a is the parameter to be estimated. The greater this value is for a given (y,a^0), the more this value of y suggests that the true value of a is indeed a^0. Therefore $(\partial f(y,a^0)/\partial a)/f(y,a^0) = \partial \text{Log} f(y,a^0)/\partial a$ measures how inclined we are to think that the observed value y did not come from a model whose value is a^0. The first-order condition (14) indicates that we must accept deviations

3. This condition can also be expressed in the following form:

$$\frac{f(y,a_2)}{f(y,a_1)} \quad \text{is increasing in } y \text{ for } a_1 < a_2;$$

in other words, observing higher values of y means that it is more plausible that the action taken had been a_2 rather than a_1. Notice that $f(y,a_2)/f(y,a_1)$ increasing in y is equivalent to

$$\frac{(f(y,a_2)/f(y,a_1)) - 1}{a_2 - a_1} = \frac{(f(y,a_2) - f(y,a_1))/(a_2 - a_1)}{f(y,a_1)}$$

increasing in y, which is the discrete version of the assumption in the text.

from first-best solutions that are larger when this measure is large. Indeed, y is used as an informative signal concerning the value of a chosen by the agent. If the signal is less informative (the likelihood function $\text{Log} f(y, a)$ is very flat in a), we certainly cannot expect to induce much effort, and we would be better off giving him his individual rationality utility level by insuring him.

Is it useful to take into account other variables denoted z, whose distribution depends on a, to control better the agent by using a transfer function with arguments y and z? Holmström (1979) shows the intuitive result that if y is not a sufficient statistics for the pair (y, z) with respect to a, observing z is valuable to the principal and the optimal transfer depends on y and z. We show how such a theory justifies co-insurance.

Consider an agent who has an accident with probability $1 - F(0, a)$. Let the loss x that he sustains if he has an accident be variable, and let $f(x, a)$ be the probability density of this loss with $\int f(x, a) dx = 1 - F(0, a)$. Here the principal is the insurance company, and x plays the role of $-y$. The agent reduces the probability of having an accident by his action so that $\partial F(0, a)/\partial a > 0$, and he reduces the probability of a loss of size x, $x + dx$ for any x, $\partial f(x, a)/\partial a < 0$. This corresponds to the assumption of first-order stochastic dominance in the more general context where the distribution of y has positive measure (that is, a positive probability mass) at 0. Consider the first-order condition (14). Since the left-hand side of (14) is continuous in t and the right-hand side has a discontinuity at $x = 0$, $t(x)$ must have a discontinuity at $x = 0$. Moreover, by comparing with the first-order condition under complete information, we see that $t(0) > t(x)$ for any x. Therefore

$$t(x) = \begin{cases} t_0 & \text{if } x = 0, \\ t_0 - h(x) & \text{if } x < 0. \end{cases}$$

The agent's income is t_0 if he does not have an accident—that is, after he pays only the premium. If he has an accident, he must share the loss due to the accident with the company; therefore we have co-insurance. This risk sharing, which is nonoptimal if the agent is risk-averse, leads him to behave more prudently. Finally, notice that if the action does not influence the probability of an accident (and also not the amount of the loss if there is an accident), $h(x)$ is constant. Then we have a justification for the deductibles that is different from the one given by Arrow (1963), who bases it on the existence of an administrative cost.

11.2   Validity and Limitations of the First-Order Condition Approach

The first-order condition approach consists of replacing the constraint

$$a \in \operatorname*{Argmax}_{a'} EV(t(y), a') \tag{22}$$

by the first-order condition of this maximization program, that is, by the constraint

$$E \frac{\partial V}{\partial a}(t(y), a) = 0. \tag{23}$$

Diagrammatically, let $-t$ be (symbolically) the abscissa and a be the ordinate (see figure 11.1). Represent the set of all a satisfying the first-order condition by the curve AA'. Since the agent tries to minimize a for given t, only the bold portion of the curve characterizes true maxima.

Trace the indifference curves of the principal as well. If the principal maximizes his utility subject to the first-order condition (that is, subject to AA'), he then obtains B, whereas the true optimum is C. Not only is B not the optimum, but C does not satisfy the first-order conditions of the principal's problem (only B and D do). Since the agent's optimization problem is not always concave in a, the first-order condition does not always characterize the optimum (see Laffont 1988, chap. 3). Then we can either look for sufficient conditions to validate the first-order condition approach or adopt a more general approach.

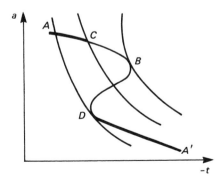

Figure 11.1

Mirrlees (1975) and Rogerson (1985b) provide sufficient conditions, at least for an interior solution. A proof of the sufficient character of these conditions may be sketched when we know that the optimal solution is *one* of the solutions of the first-order conditions for the principal's problem. Then, from the preceding section, we know that $t(y)$ is increasing given the ML assumption. The problem will be concave if

$$\int \left[v(t(y)) - w(a) \right] f_{aa}(y, a) \, dy - w''(a) \leqslant 0. \tag{24}$$

Integrating by parts, we obtain

$$- \int F_{aa}(y, a) v'(t(y)) t'(y) \, dy - w''(a) \leqslant 0. \tag{25}$$

Since $w'' > 0$, the assumption that the distribution function is convex in a along with ML is sufficient to ensure the concavity in a of the problem (see Rogerson 1985b for a more general proof).

What should be done if F is not convex in a? Grossman and Hart (1983) try to progress along these lines by decomposing the principal's problem into two stages. They consider a discrete framework with a finite number of values of y, $y_1, \ldots, y_n$ and a risk-neutral principal. For each action a in the set of feasible actions A, the principal can compute the expected cost $C(a)$ that he must bear to induce the agent to choose a. In the second stage the principal chooses the action that he prefers by comparing the benefits $B(a)$, $a \in A$ and the costs $C(a)$, $a \in A$. The advantage of this method is that the first problem is simple enough because it can be rewritten as a problem of minimizing a convex function over a convex set.

Let $t_1, \ldots, t_n$ be the vector of transfers associated with the observation of $y_1, \ldots, y_n$. Let $\pi_i(a)$ (> 0 for all $a \in A$) be the probability of y_i if the agent chooses a for $i = 1, \ldots, n$. To induce the agent to choose a, the principal bears a cost $C(a)$ that is the value of the objective function at the optimum in the following problem:

$$\text{Min} \sum_{i=1}^{n} \pi_i(a) t_i \tag{26}$$

subject to

$$\sum_{i=1}^{n} \pi_i(a) \left[v(t_i) - w(a) \right] \geqslant 0, \tag{27}$$

$$\sum_{i=1}^{n} \pi_i(a)[v(t_i) - w(a)] \geqslant \sum_{i=1}^{n} \pi_i(a')[v(t_i) - w(a')] \qquad \forall a' \in A. \qquad (28)$$

The individual rationality constraint is given by (27) and (28) is the set of incentive constraints.

Let $v(t_i) = v_i$ and $t_i = v^{-1}(v_i)$. Since $v(.)$ is concave and increasing, $v^{-1}(.)$ is convex, and the problem can be written as

$$\text{Min } \sum_{i=1}^{n} \pi_i(a)v^{-1}(v_i) \qquad (29)$$

subject to

$$\sum_{i=1}^{n} \pi_i(a)[v_i - w(a)] \geqslant 0, \qquad (30)$$

$$\sum_{i=1}^{n} \pi_i(a)[v_i - w(a)] \geqslant \sum_{i=1}^{n} \pi_i(a')[v_i - w(a')] \qquad \forall a' \in A. \qquad (31)$$

The objective function is convex in $(v_1, \ldots, v_n)$, and the constraints are linear. Let λ be the multiplier for (30) and $\mu(a')$, $a' \in A$ be the multipliers for (31). By dividing by $\pi_i(a)$, the first-order conditions (necessary and sufficient) are written as

$$\frac{1}{v'(t_i)} = \lambda + \sum_{a' \in K(a)} \mu(a') \left(\frac{\pi_i(a) - \pi_i(a')}{\pi_i(a)} \right) \qquad i = 1, \ldots, n \qquad (32)$$

where $K(a)$ is the subset of A at which the incentive constraints are binding.

A comparison with (14) indicates that the difference from the first-best approach is that some incentive constraints, other than the local ones (that is, some a' not in the neighborhood of a), can be binding so that we obtain the sum $\sum_{a' \in K(a)}$. By working only with problem (29), Grossman and Hart (1983) obtain several results. They show the equivalent of theorem 1—that is, the nonoptimality of risk-sharing when the agent is risk-averse. They also show that the principal's income and the agent's income cannot always be negatively correlated and that the transfer cannot be nonincreasing throughout. However, to show that the transfer is increasing in y, they must make some assumptions, which in turn validate the first-order condition approach. Consequently in the absence of some very restrictive sufficient conditions that in any case validate the first-order condition approach, we have very little information about the optimal solution other than that it implies a trade-off between encouraging effort and sharing risk optimally.

11.3   Competition among Agents

In numerous contexts the principal may be dealing with many agents, and
the relevant question is whether or not he can use the competition that
takes place among the agents. The basic intuition is simple enough. If the
observable output of agent j is not "informative" about agent i's effort, to
make the payment to i depend on the output of j can only increase the
uncertainty that i faces without inducing him to greater effort. On the
contrary, if it is informative, then we must determine the optimal trade-off
between inducing effort and sharing risk in the spirit of section 11.1. It goes
without saying that the problems related to the first-order condition approach remain here as well.

Let $\tilde{y}^i$ be the stochastic variable that represents the output due to agent
i, $i = 1, \ldots, I$. The joint distribution of $\tilde{y} = (\tilde{y}^1, \ldots, \tilde{y}^I)$ depends on the
actions of the agents $a = (a^1, \ldots, a^I)$ and is denoted $F(y, a)$ with density
$f(y, a)$. The transfer t^i that agent i receives is now a function of the vector
of observables, that is, the individual outputs $y^1, \ldots, y^I$, $i = 1, \ldots, I$. Given
a system of transfers $(t^i(.))$, the agents' choice of actions is characterized by
a Nash equilibrium. Formally,

$$a^{*i} \in \underset{a^i}{\text{Argmax}} \int [v^i(t^i(y)) - w^i(a^i)] \, dF(y, a^i, a^{*-i}) \qquad i = 1, \ldots, I,$$

where $(a^i, a^{*-i}) = (a^{*1}, \ldots, a^{*i-1}, a^i, a^{*i+1}, \ldots, a^{*I})$.

The first complication stems from the possibility of multiple equilibria;
however, we will neglect this problem by assuming that the agents coordinate
on a particular equilibrium. The principal's problem can then be written:

$$\underset{(t^i(.))}{\text{Max}} \int u\left(\sum_{i=1}^I (y^i - t^i(y)) \right) dF(y, a^*)$$

subject to

$$\int [v^i(t^i(y)) - w^i(a^{*i})] \, dF(y, a^*) \geq 0,$$

$$a^{*i} \in \underset{a^i}{\text{Argmax}} \int [v^i(t^i(y)) - w^i(a^i)] \, dF(y, a^i, a^{*-i}) \qquad i = 1, \ldots, I.$$

An initial justification for the principal to have transfers t^i that depend on
the set of y^i is his concern for insurance. We eliminate this consideration

by assuming from now on that the principal is risk-neutral. In general, the transfers depend nonlinearly on the set of observations $y^1, \ldots, y^l$, and the very limited results in section 11.1 and 11.2 can be generalized.

Mookherjee (1984) generalizes the Grossman-Hart approach. Assume that there are two agents, and let

$$\pi_{ij}(a^1, a^2) = \Pr(\tilde{y}^1 = y_i^1, \tilde{y}^2 = y_j^2 | a^1, a^2) \qquad i = 1, \ldots, n, \, j = 1, \ldots, n.$$

With the obvious adaptation of the notation, the cost minimization problem (analogous to equation 26) can be written as

$$\underset{(v_{ij}^1, v_{ij}^2)}{\text{Min}} \sum_i \sum_j \pi_{ij}(a^1, a^2)\{(v^1)^{-1}(v_{ij}^1) + (v^2)^{-1}(v_{ij}^2)\}$$

$$\sum_i \sum_j \pi_{ij}(a^1, a^2)[v_{ij}^1 - w^1(a^1)] \geq 0,$$

$$\sum_i \sum_j \pi_{ij}(a^1, a^2)[v_{ij}^2 - w^2(a^2)] \geq 0,$$

$$\sum_i \sum_j \pi_{ij}(a^1, a^2)(v_{ij}^1 - w^1(a^1))$$

$$\geq \sum_i \sum_j \pi_{ij}(a'^1, a^2)(v_{ij}^1 - w^1(a'^1)) \qquad \forall a'^1 \in A^1,$$

$$\sum_i \sum_j \pi_{ij}(a^1, a^2)(v_{ij}^2 - w^2(a^2))$$

$$\geq \sum_i \sum_j \pi_{ij}(a^1, a'^2)(v_{ij}^2 - w^2(a'^2)) \qquad \forall a'^2 \in A^2.$$

By observing that the individual rationality constraints are satisfied with equality at the optimum, the problem can be rewritten as

$$\underset{(v_{ij}^1, v_{ij}^2)}{\text{Min}} \sum_i \sum_j \pi_{ij}(a^1, a^2)\{(v^1)^{-1}(v_{ij}^1) + (v^2)^{-1}(v_{ij}^2)\}$$

subject to

$$\sum_i \sum_j \pi_{ij}(a^1, a^2)[v_{ij}^1 - w^1(a^1)] = 0 \qquad (\lambda^1),$$

$$\sum_i \sum_j \pi_{ij}(a^1, a^2)[v_{ij}^2 - w^2(a^2)] = 0 \qquad (\lambda^2),$$

$$\sum_i \sum_j \pi_{ij}(a'^1, a^2)[v_{ij}^1 - w^1(a'^1)] \leq 0 \qquad (\mu^1(a'^1)), \forall a'^1 \in A^1,$$

$$\sum_i \sum_j \pi_{ij}(a^1, a'^2)[v_{ij}^2 - w^2(a'^2)] \leq 0 \qquad (\mu^2(a'^2)), \forall a'^2 \in A^2.$$

The first-order conditions for this convex problem are written as

$$\frac{1}{v'^1(t_{ij}^1)} = \lambda^1 - \sum_{a'^1 \in A^1} \mu^1(a'^1) \frac{\pi_{ij}(a'^1, a^2)}{\pi_{ij}(a^1, a^2)},$$

$$\frac{1}{v'^2(t_{ij}^2)} = \lambda^2 - \sum_{a'^2 \in A^2} \mu^2(a'^2) \frac{\pi_{ij}(a^1, a'^2)}{\pi_{ij}(a^1, a^2)}.$$

Given $a^2 \in A^2$, we say that y^2 is an uninformative signal on a^1 if

$$\pi_{ij}(a'^1, a^2) = h(y_i^1, y_j^2, a^2) \cdot f(y_i^1, a'^1, a^2) \qquad \forall a'^1 \in A^1.$$

In other words, y^1 is a sufficient statistics for the pair y^1, y^2 with respect to a^1. Then

$$\frac{\pi_{ij}(a'^1, a^2)}{\pi_{ij}(a^1, a^2)} = \frac{f(y_i^1, a'^1, a^2)}{f(y_i^1, a^1, a^2)},$$

and therefore, from the first-order conditions, t_{ij}^1 does not depend on j.

Therefore, if, for a given a^2, the knowledge of y^2 does not provide any information about the relative likelihoods of the values of a^1, it is inappropriate to use the observation of y^2 in the payment to agent 1. For example, if

$$\tilde{y}^1 = r(a^1) + \tilde{\varepsilon}^1,$$

$$\tilde{y}^2 = r(a^2) + \tilde{\varepsilon}^2,$$

where $\tilde{\varepsilon}^1$ and $\tilde{\varepsilon}^2$ are independent stochastic variables, there is nothing to be gained from using the performances of one agent to control the other.

On the other hand, if we add a common noise $\tilde{\varepsilon}$ to the idiosyncratic noises $\tilde{\varepsilon}^1$ and $\tilde{\varepsilon}^2$, y^2 becomes informative about a^1 in general. Intuitively, if y^2 is large, there is a certain probability that this is due to the fact that $\tilde{\varepsilon}$ is large. Therefore there is a certain probability that y^1 is also large. Then the agent will be penalized if y^1 and y^2 differ significantly. If $\tilde{\varepsilon}^1$ and $\tilde{\varepsilon}^2$ are perfectly correlated, then it is possible to obtain the complete-information optimum, at least when the agents behave in a Nash way (therefore noncooperatively) with respect to each other. Deviating from the action recommended by the principal creates a nonzero probability that this behavior will be detected in light of the output of the other agent. Therefore a sufficiently large penalty prevents this behavior.

In addition to these general considerations about optimal mechanisms, the literature examines closely a particular class of contracts, namely, tournaments (Lazear and Rosen 1981; Green and Stockey 1983; Stiglitz and Nalebuff 1983). In a tournament the payments to the agents depend uniquely on the order of their performances $y^1, \dots, y^I$. It is clear that these mechanisms are not optimal in general. Regarding the preceding example, the object of a tournament is to eliminate from the payment scheme variability due to the *common noise* $\tilde{\varepsilon}$. This variability exists in a nonlinear contract that depends only on the agent's own performance. An inconvenient aspect of tournaments compared with nonlinear "independent" contracts is the increase in variability due to the *idiosyncratic noises of the other agents*. However, as Green and Stockey (1983) have shown, when the number of agents is large, the order of their performances becomes a very precise estimator of the agents' outputs net of common noises. Tournaments are then approximately optimal.

11.4   Repeated Principal–Agent Relations

In a number of circumstances the principal–agent relation is of long duration (insurer–insuree, shareholders–manager, etc.). In these situations our intuition indicates that, in a stationary model, the repeated observation of output y_t allows us to eliminate noise by the law of large numbers and to detect, with a probability as close to 1 as we wish, a deviation from the action recommended by the principal. Then by choosing a large enough penalty in the case of a deviation, we can convince the agent to choose any action that ensures him a level of utility larger than his individual rationality level. In particular, we can achieve the complete-information optimum.

This intuition has been formalized by using the law of the iterated logarithm, which yields a measure of the speed of convergence of the calculated mean of a sequence of independent, identically distributed variables toward the true mean. Here the stochastic variable $\tilde{y}_t$ represents the damage sustained by the agent in period t. Without insurance, his utility is[4]

$$\operatorname*{Lim}_{T \to \infty} \frac{1}{T} \sum_{t=1}^{T} \int [v(-y_t) - w(a_t)] f(y_t, a_t) \, dy_t$$

where a_t is the level of effort chosen in period t and affecting the distribution of damages.

---

4. We use the limit criterion of the mean and therefore do not discount the future.

The principal, the insurance company, is not risk-averse. Therefore the complete-information optimum involves complete insurance and an action level a^* characterized by

$$\underset{a}{\text{Max}} \left\{ v\left(-\int y_t f(y_t, a)\, dy_t \right) - w(a) \right\}.$$

The actuarially fair insurance premium is the expected value of the damage:

$$\Pi^* = \int y_t f(y_t, a)\, dy_t.$$

Therefore the agent's utility level is (if insurance companies are competitive)

$$\underset{T \to \infty}{\text{Lim}} \frac{1}{T} \sum_{t=1}^{T} [v(-\Pi^*) - w(a^*)]$$

and the expected utility level of the insurance company is zero. The agent's utility level tends toward zero with probability 1 when T tends toward infinity.

In the presence of moral hazard, Rubinstein and Yaari (1983) show that the following insurance policy achieves this complete-information optimum. In each period t the premium paid by the agent is either:

• the actuarially fair premium Π^* corresponding to the level of care a^* if the agent's record is satisfactory—that is, if the average damage up to period t does not deviate very much from Π^*, or more formally,

$$\frac{1}{t} \sum_{s=1}^{t} y_s < \Pi^* + \alpha^t,$$

with

$$\alpha^t = \sqrt{\frac{2\lambda\sigma^2 \, \text{Log log } t}{t}}$$

and

$$\lambda > 1, \sigma^2 = \text{Var } \tilde{y}_t \qquad \text{for } a = a^*,$$

or

• a premium Π_* yielding a level of instantaneous utility lower than the individually rational level if the record is not satisfactory.

With such a policy, the agent is penalized only a finite number of times with probability 1 if he chooses $a = a^*$, whereas he would be penalized an infinite number of times if he were to choose $a < a^*$. The choice of the series α^t is delicate (even though any series converging toward zero but larger than the one chosen would suffice). On the one hand, α^t must converge to zero to ensure that the agent does not choose an action level less than a^*. On the other hand, α^t must not converge to zero too quickly because, otherwise, the agent would be penalized too often when he chooses a^* and he would therefore prefer $a > a^*$.

The mathematical tool that allows us to choose the correct speed of convergence is the law of the iterated logarithm which may be stated in the following way: Let $\{y^t\}$ be a sequence of independent stochastic variables drawn from the same distribution with finite mean μ and finite variance σ^2. Then, for any $\lambda > 1$, we have

$$\underset{T}{\text{Lim sup}} \left[\frac{\left| \mu - \dfrac{1}{T} \sum_{t=1}^{T} y^t \right|}{\left(\dfrac{2\lambda\sigma^2 \, \text{Log} \log T}{T} \right)^{1/2}} \right] < 1$$

with probability 1.

When the agents discount the future (Radner 1985) or when the horizon is finite (Lambert 1983; Rogerson 1985a; Henriet and Rochet 1986), the complete-information optimum can no longer be achieved and the optimal contract shares risk intertemporally by making the allocation in period t depend on the sequence of past events (which we can interpret as a justification for bonus–penalty contracts).

11.5   Concluding Remarks

In this chapter we have intentionally treated the topic of repeated contracts briefly for two reasons. First, the essential results may still not be well stated. Second, to delve into the pertinent literature profitably, we must refer in detail to the theory of repeated games which is beyond the scope of this book. We shall mention only a few additional topics of current interest.

In our argument we have assumed implicitly that the principal can *commit himself* not only for one period, as we have always assumed, but also for all future periods. In a credible way he can propose intertemporal contracts without the agent fearing that, in some future period, the principal will change the contract based on the information he has accumulated by this time. Recent work shows that the time dependence of optimal contracts in finite horizon models comes from mixing moral hazard with income-smoothing considerations. When perfect capital markets exist, short-run contracts (without any long-run commitment) quite generally perform as well as long-run contracts.[5] On the other hand, the results are very different when there are several sources of moral hazard.[6] For example, if both the principal and the agent take nonobservable actions or if we study Nash equilibria in a team where each agent chooses a nonobservable action, the complete information optimum cannot be sustained in general.

We have a long way to go to develop a satisfactory economic theory of organizations. Nevertheless, thanks to progress in the theory of incentives, the transaction costs due to informational asymmetries of a moral hazard or adverse selection type can be the object of a qualitative evaluation that allows us to study analytically some problems that we only recently learned how to formalize. However, we must not forget that this approach leaves aside for the time being other transaction costs, in particular, those associated with the costs of optimization and with the complexity of the constraints. Even though several pioneering works exist (Reichelstein 1985; Green and Laffont 1986), we have here an intellectual challenge for future research.

Suggested Readings

Arrow, K. (1963).   A pioneering article.
Holmström, B. (1979).   The best analysis of the first-order approach.

5. Note also that in the particular context of the shareholder–manager relation, Fama (1980) suggests that the manager's concern for his career combined with the forces of the market for managers must also restore the complete-information optimum. Nevertheless, as Holmström (1983) has shown, this result is far from obvious because, in general, risk-aversion and discounting the future limit the ability of the market to police perfectly the manager's incentives.

6. Holmström (1981) points out that, in an organization where all the agents control a moral-hazard variable, the impossibility to commit oneself credibly not to distribute the entire common product, which excludes collective penalties, makes the complete-information optimum impossible in general. Holmström even sees in this result a justification for the role of an outside monitor who can make credible the assessment of collective penalties.

Green, J., and N. Stockey (1983). The analysis of tournaments.

Henriet, D., and J. C. Rochet (1986). A theoretical analysis of bonus–penalty contracts.

References

Arrow, K. 1963. "Uncertainty and the Welfare Economics of Medical Care." *American Economic Review* 53:941–973.

Fama, E. 1980. "Agency Problems and the Theory of the Firm." *Journal of Political Economy* 88.

Green, J., and J.-J. Laffont. 1986. "Incentive Theory with Data Compression." In Heller, W., R. Starr, and D. Starrett (eds.), *Uncertainty, Information and Communication.* Cambridge University Press, chapter 10.

Green, J., and N. Stockey. 1983. "A Comparison of Tournaments and Contracts." *Journal of Political Economy* 91:349–364.

Grossman, S. J., and O. D. Hart. 1983. "An Analysis of the Principal–Agent Problem." *Econometrica* 51:7–45.

Harris, M., and A. Raviv. 1979. "Optimal Incentive Contracts with Imperfect Information." *Journal of Economic Theory* 20:231–259.

Heller, W., R. Starr, and D. Starrett (eds.). 1986. *Uncertainty, Information and Communication.* Essays in Honor of K. J. Arrow. Vol. 3. Cambridge University Press.

Henriet, D. and J. C. Rochet. 1986. "La Logique des systèmes bonus–malus en assurance automobile: une approche théorique." *Annales d'Economie et de Statistique* 1:133–152.

Holmström, B. 1979. "Moral Hazard and Observability." *Bell Journal of Economics* 10:74–91.

Holmström, B. 1982. "Moral Hazard in Teams." *Bell Journal of Economics* 13:324–340.

Holmström, B. 1983. "Managerial Incentives Problems: A Dynamic Perspective." Mimeo.

Laffont, J.-J. 1988. *Fundamentals of Public Economics.* MIT Press, Cambridge.

Lambert, R. 1983. "Long Term Contracts and Moral Hazard." *Bell Journal of Economics* 14:441–452.

Lazear, E., and S. Rosen. 1981. "Rank-Order Tournaments as Optimum Labor Contracts." *Journal of Political Economy* 89:841–864.

Mirrlees, J. 1975. "The Theory of Moral Hazard and Unobservable Behavior, Part I." Mimeo.

Mookherjee, D. 1984. "Optimal Incentive Schemes in Multi-agent Situations." *Review of Economic Studies* 51:433–446.

Nalebuff, B., and J. Stiglitz. 1983. "Prizes and Incentives: Towards a General Theory of Compensation and Competition." *Bell Journal of Economics* 14:21–43.

Pauly, M. V. 1968. "The Economics of Moral Hazard: Comment." *American Economic Review* 58:531–537.

Radner, R. 1985. "Repeated Principal-Agent Games with Discounting." *Econometrica* 53:1173–1198.

Reichelstein, S. 1984. "Incentive Compatibility and Informational Requirements." *Journal of Economic Theory* 34:32–51.

Rogerson, W. 1985a. "Repeated Moral Hazard." *Econometrica* 53:69–76.

Rogerson, W. 1985b. "The First Order Approach to Principal Agent Problems." *Econometrica* 53:1357–1367.

Ross, S. 1973. "The Economic Theory of Agency: The Principal's Problem." *American Economic Review* 63:134–139.

Rubinstein, A., and M. Yaari. 1983. "Insurance and Moral Hazard." *Journal of Economic Theory* 14:441–452.

WORKED PROBLEMS

Problem 1
Taxation and Its Effect on Economic Behavior

Statement of the Problem

Consider an economic agent (representing private investors) who has at his disposal, at the beginning of the period, an amount of wealth equal to W. He can invest his wealth in a riskless asset at an interest rate equal to r and in a risky asset, yielding a return that is a stochastic variable $\tilde{e}$ with finite mean and finite variance. The portion of his wealth invested in the risky asset will be denoted a.

1. Show that the wealth of the agent at the end of the period is

$$W(e) = W_0[1 + ae + (1 - a)r]$$

where e is the realization of the stochastic variable $\tilde{e}$.

Faced with uncertainty, the agent's behavior satisfies the Von Neumann-Morgenstern axioms. Let $u(.)$ be his VNM utility function with $u' > 0$ and $u'' < 0$. Assuming (as we do in the whole problem) that the maxima are interior ones, show that the first-order condition of the agent's problem is written as

$$E\{(\tilde{e} - r)u'(W(\tilde{e}))\} = 0 \tag{1}$$

where E is the expectation's operator with respect to the probability distribution of $\tilde{e}$. Verify that this condition does indeed characterize a maximum.

2. Recall the definition of the coefficient of absolute risk aversion $r_a(.)$. Assume that $r_a(.)$ is a decreasing function and show that for any value of $(e - r)$ we have

$$(e - r)u''[W_0(1 + r + a(e - r))]$$
$$> -(e - r)r_a[W_0(1 + r)]u'[W_0(1 + r + a(e - r))].$$

Using condition (1), derive

$$E\{(\tilde{e} - r)u''[W(\tilde{e})]\} > 0.$$

After differentiating (1) in a and r, find a sufficient condition for $da/dr < 0$ in question 1. Interpret this result.

3. Now introduce a proportionate tax on the final wealth position. Net final wealth will be denoted $W^d(e)$. As a measure of private risk, use the standard deviation of net final wealth, denoted Δ. Then determine the

dependence of both this measure of private risk and the investment in the risky asset (that is, a) on t. By using the new first-order condition, show that the sign of $d\Delta/dt$ depends on $E\{(\tilde{e} - r)u''(W^d(\tilde{e}))\}$. What assumption is required on $r_a(.)$ to yield a determinate result?

4.   Now consider a proportionate tax t_r on income given by $R = W - W_0$ under the assumption that the government will subsidize losses. Show that the sign of $d\Delta/dt_r$ still depends on the sign of $E\{(\tilde{e} - r)u''(W^d(\tilde{e}))\}$. Recall the definition of the coefficient of relative risk aversion $r_r(.)$. Show that

$$\frac{da}{dt_r} = \frac{1}{W_0(1 - t_r)^2} \frac{E\{[W_0 r_a(W^d(\tilde{e})) - r_r(W^d(\tilde{e}))]u'(W^d(\tilde{e}))(\tilde{e} - r)\}}{E\{u''(W^d(\tilde{e}))(\tilde{e} - r)^2\}}.$$

We assume that $r_r(.)$ is a nondecreasing function and that $r_a(.)$ is a nonincreasing function. Show that

$$\frac{da}{dt_r} \geqslant 0, \quad \frac{d\Delta}{dt_r} \leqslant 0.$$

5.   What happens if we decide to tax only income from nonrisky assets at the rate t_{nr}? Compare the various results.

Solution

1.   The agent invests aW_0 in the risky asset; he obtains $aW_0(1 + e)$ at the end of the period. He invests $(1 - a)W_0$ in the riskless asset for a combined wealth at the end of the period of

$$W(e) = W_0 a(1 + e) + (1 - a)W_0(1 + r)$$

$$= W_0(1 + ae + (1 - a)r).$$

He determines his optimal portfolio by maximizing the following with respect to a:

$$Eu(W(\tilde{e})) = Eu(W_0(1 + a\tilde{e} + (1 - a)r)).$$

If the optimum is an interior one and if u is concave, the optimum is characterized completely by the first-order condition:

$$E\{W_0(\tilde{e} - r)u'(W(\tilde{e}))\} = 0. \tag{1}$$

2.   The coefficient of absolute risk aversion at a given level of wealth W is

$$r_a(W) = -\frac{u''(W)}{u'(W)}.$$

If $r_a(.)$ is decreasing, we have for any value of e such that $(e - r) \geqslant 0$:

$$r_a(W_0(1 + r)) \geqslant r_a(W_0(1 + r + a(e - r))).$$

If $(e - r) < 0$, we have

$$r_a(W_0(1 + r)) < r_a(W_0(1 + r + a(e - r))).$$

Therefore in all cases

$$(e - r)r_a(W_0(1 + r)) \geqslant (e - r)r_a(W_0(1 + r + a(e - r))),$$

and by multiplying both sides by $u'(W_0(1 + r + a(e - r)))$, we have

$$(e - r)u''(W_0(1 + r + a(e - r)))$$

$$\geqslant -(e - r)r_a(W_0(1 + r))u'(W_0(1 + r + a(e - r))). \tag{2}$$

Since (2) holds for all e, we can take expectations and derive

$$E(\tilde{e} - r)u''(W_0(1 + r + a(\tilde{e} - r))) \geqslant 0 \tag{3}$$

by using the first-order condition (1).

To determine the way in which risky investment is affected when r increases, we differentiate the first-order condition (1) to derive

$$\frac{da}{dr} = \frac{Eu'(W(\tilde{e})) - W_0(1 - a)E\{(\tilde{e} - r)u''(W(\tilde{e}))\}}{W_0 E\{(\tilde{e} - r)^2 u''(W(\tilde{e}))\}}.$$

The denominator is negative, but the sign of the numerator is ambiguous. A sufficient condition to yield the unambiguous sign $da/dr < 0$ would be that $r_a(.)$ be increasing, which by applying the same reasoning as above, would then imply $E\{(\tilde{e} - r)u''(W(\tilde{e}))\} \leqslant 0$. However, the text leads us to believe that the opposite assumption is more reasonable even though this yields an ambiguous sign for da/dr. Intuitively, an increase in r makes the riskless asset relatively more profitable than the risky asset, which tends to reduce the portion of wealth allocated to risky investment (the *substitution effect*). However, an increase in r leads to an increase in final wealth which, if $r_a(.)$ is decreasing, leads in turn to a reduction in the agent's risk aversion (the *wealth effect*). These two effects are countervailing so that the total effect is ambiguous. If $r(.)$ were increasing, the wealth effect would have the same directional influence as the substitution effect.

3. Now final wealth is given by

$W^d(e) = (1 - t)W(e).$

The new first-order condition is

$E\{(\tilde{e} - r)u'(W^d(\tilde{e}))\} = 0.$

Differentiating this yields

$E\{u''(W^d(\tilde{e}))(\tilde{e} - r)^2\}[(1 - t)\,da - adt] = E\{u''(W^d(\tilde{e}))(\tilde{e} - r)\}(1 + r)\,dt$

or

$$\frac{da}{dt} = \frac{a}{1 - t} + \frac{1 + r}{1 - t} \cdot \frac{E\{u''(W^d(\tilde{e}))(\tilde{e} - r)\}}{E\{u''(W^d(\tilde{e}))(\tilde{e} - r)^2\}}. \tag{4}$$

The sign of (4) depends on $E\{u''(W(\tilde{e}))(\tilde{e} - r)\}$.
  By definition,

$\Delta^2 = E[W^d(\tilde{e}) - E(W^d(\tilde{e}))]^2$

$= \text{Var}\,(1 - t)W(\tilde{e}) = (1 - t)^2 a^2 W_0^2 \sigma_e^2$

where σ_e is the standard deviation of the stochastic variable $\tilde{e}$. Now $\Delta = (1 - t)aW_0\sigma_e$, which yields

$$\frac{d\Delta}{dt} = -W_0 a\sigma_e + (1 - t)W_0\sigma_e\frac{da}{dt}$$

$$= W_0\sigma_e(1 + r)\frac{E\{u''(W^d(\tilde{e}))(\tilde{e} - r)\}}{E\{u''(W^d(\tilde{e}))(\tilde{e} - r)^2\}}. \tag{5}$$

The sign of $d\Delta/dt$ is therefore determined unambiguously by an assumption of increasing or decreasing absolute risk-aversion, whereas the sign of da/dt remains ambiguous when $r_a(.)$ is decreasing.
  As the first term in the middle expression of (5) indicates, an increase in t tends to reduce the standard deviation of final wealth (since the tax is *multiplicative*) which makes the risky asset more *attractive* than the riskless asset on the margin. This tends to increase a as the first term on the right-hand side of (4) indicates. However, an increase in t also reduces final

wealth. If $r_a(.)$ is decreasing, risk aversion increases and a decreases. Once again the *income and substitution effects* are countervailing, leading to the sign ambiguity of da/dt. On the other hand, private risk decreases because the direct effect dominates.

4. If we assume that the government subsidizes losses, the tax is $t_r(W(\tilde{e}) - W_0)$, which leads to a final wealth of

$$W^d(\tilde{e}) = W_0 a(\tilde{e} - r)(1 - t_r) - rW_0 t_r + W_0(1 + r).$$

By differentiating the first-order condition as above, we obtain

$$\frac{da}{dt_r} = \frac{a}{1 - t_r} + \frac{r}{1 - t_r} \cdot \frac{E\{u''(W^d(\tilde{e}))(\tilde{e} - r)\}}{E\{u''(W^d(\tilde{e}))(\tilde{e} - r)^2\}} \tag{6}$$

$$\frac{d\Delta}{dt_r} = W_0 r \sigma_e \frac{E\{u''(W^d(\tilde{e}))(\tilde{e} - r)\}}{E\{u''(W^d(\tilde{e}))(\tilde{e} - r)^2\}}.$$

The coefficient of relative risk aversion is $r_r(W) = -W \cdot (u''(W)/u'(W))$. From (6), simple calculations yield

$$\frac{da}{dt_r} = \frac{1}{W_0(1 - t_r)^2} \frac{E\{[W_0 r_a(W^d(\tilde{e})) - r_r(W^d(\tilde{e}))]u'(W^d(\tilde{e}))(\tilde{e} - r)\}}{E\{u''(W^d(\tilde{e}))(\tilde{e} - r)^2\}}. \tag{7}$$

If $r_r(.)$ is decreasing, by an argument equivalent to that in question 2, we have for any value of e:

$$-r_r(W^d(e))(e - r) \leqslant -r_r(W^d(r))(e - r).$$

From question 2 we have

$$W_0 r_a(W^d(e))(e - r) \leqslant W_0 r_a(W^d(r))(e - r).$$

Therefore

$$[W_0 r_a(W^d(e)) - r_r(W^d(e))](e - r) \leqslant (W_0 r_a(W^d(r)) - r_r(W^d(r)))(e - r).$$

Since $W_0 r_a(W^d(r)) - r_r(W^d(r))$ is nonstochastic, we have

$$E[W_0 r_a(W^d(\tilde{e})) - r_r(W^d(\tilde{e}))](\tilde{e} - r)u'(W^d(\tilde{e}))$$

$$\leqslant (W_0 r_a(W^d(r)) - r_r(W^d(r)))E\{(\tilde{e} - r)u'(W^d(\tilde{e}))\}.$$

Since the denominator of (7) is negative, we may conclude that

$$\frac{da}{dt_r} \geqslant \frac{1}{W_0(1 - t_r)^2} \frac{[W_0 r_a(W^d(r)) - r_r(W^d(r))]E\{(\tilde{e} - r)u'(W^d(\tilde{e}))\}}{E\{u''(W^d(\tilde{e}))(\tilde{e} - r)^2\}},$$

or by using the first-order condition, we have

$$\frac{da}{dt_r} \geqslant 0.$$

Furthermore, if $r_a(.)$ decreases with wealth, we have

$$\frac{d\Delta}{dt_r} \leqslant 0.$$

5. If we decide to tax income from riskless assets only at a rate t_{nr}, the fiscal policy involves replacing the rate of interest r by the rate $r(1 - t_{nr})$, and the results are equivalent to those in question 2.

From this problem we learned that even in a very simple partial-equilibrium framework, unambiguous results are attainable only at the cost of very restrictive assumptions on the third derivatives of the utility functions.

Supplementary Readings

Stiglitz, J. 1970. "The Effects of Income, Wealth and Capital Gains Taxation and Risk Taking." *Quarterly Journal of Economics* 83:263–283.

Kihlstrom, R., and J.-J. Laffont. 1983. "Taxation and Risk Taking in General Equilibrium Models with Free Entry." *Journal of Public Economics* 21:159–181.

Problem 2
Savings under Uncertainty

Statement of the Problem

We analyze the savings behavior of a consumer whose homothetic preferences are represented by a twice-differentiable, increasing, concave utility function $u(c_1, c_2)$ defined over the consumption levels c_1 and c_2 in periods 1 and 2, respectively. In an uncertain world, his optimization problem is characterized by

$$\text{Max } u(c_1, c_2)$$

subject to

$$c_1 + pc_2 = R$$

where R is his discounted income in period 1 and $p = 1/(1 + r)$ is the discounted price of consumption in period 2, in units of period 1 consumption when r is the interest rate.

Savings, denoted e, is defined as $e = R - c_1$. The above optimization problem may be rewritten as

$$\text{Max } u(R - e, e(1 + r)) \qquad 0 \leqslant e \leqslant R.$$

We let $h(e, r) \equiv u(R - e, e(1 + r))$. Verify that h is concave in e and increasing in r. Let $e(r, R)$ be the savings function that solves the above problem and assume an interior maximum.

1. Initially assume that r is certain. For a homothetic utility function, show that the elasticity of substitution between c_1 and c_2 with respect to the price $q = 1/p$ is written as

$$\sigma = \frac{u_1 u_2}{c_2(u_2 u_{12} - u_1 u_{22})}.$$

Show that $\partial e/\partial r < 0 \, (> 0)$ as $\sigma < 1 \, (> 1)$.

2. Now consider the case where r is stochastic with density $g(r)$ and $r \geqslant 0$ with probability 1. Let u^1 and u^2 be two cardinal representations of the homothetic preferences of question 1. We will show that if u^1 is more risk-averse than u^2 (in the sense that u^1 is a concave increasing transformation of u^2), then the savings associated with u^1, denoted e^1, is higher than the savings associated with u^2, denoted e^2, if and only if $\sigma > 1$. We denote as $e(r)$ savings when r is certain and e^i the savings associated with u^i when r is stochastic for $i = 1$ and 2.

(a)   We consider the sure value $\bar{r}$ which yields the same savings in a certain world as in the stochastic world with the function u^2, that is,

$$Eh_1^2(e^2, \tilde{r}) = 0,$$

$$h_1^2(e(\bar{r}), \bar{r}) = 0,$$

$$e(\bar{r}) = e^2,$$

where $h^i(e, r) = u^i(R - e, e(1 + r))$, $i = 1, 2$. Show that

$$h_1^2(e^2, r) < 0 \qquad \text{if } r < \bar{r}$$

$$> 0 \qquad r > \bar{r}.$$

(b)   Since u^1 is more risk-averse than u^2, there exists a concave increasing transformation f so that $u^1 = f(u^2)$. Conclude from this that $f'(h^2(e, r)) > (<)f'(h^2(e, \bar{r}))$ if $r < (>)\bar{r}$.
(c)   By using the results in (i) and (ii), show that

$$Eh_1^1(e, \tilde{r}) < f'(h^2(e, \bar{r}))Eh_1^2(e, \tilde{r}).$$

Conclude that $e^2 > e^1$.

3.   Now assume that $u = f(u^*)$ where u^* is the least concave representation. We will show that if f exhibits increasing (decreasing) relative risk aversion and if $\sigma > 1$, then the savings rate $s(R) = e/R$ decreases (increases) with R.

(a)   Let $R^1 < R^2$. By definition, $s(R^i)$ maximizes $Ef(u^*((1 - s)R^i, (1 + \tilde{r})sR^i))$. (See section 2.7.) Show that $s(R^i)$ maximizes $E\tilde{u}^i((1 - s), (1 + \tilde{r})s)$ for $i = 1$ and 2 with $\tilde{u}^i(c_1, c_2) = f(R^iu^*(c_1, c_2))$ for $i = 1$ and 2.
(b)   Show that $\tilde{u}^1$ is a concave transformation of $\tilde{u}^2$.
(c)   Conclude by applying the result in question 2.

Solution

To verify that h is concave in e and increasing in r, compute

$$h_2 = eu_2 > 0; \quad h_{11} = u_{11} - 2(1 + r)u_{21} + (1 + r)^2u_{22} < 0.$$

1.   For a homothetic function, the marginal rate of substitution is constant along a ray from the origin given by $c_2 = kc_1$, which yields

$$\frac{u_1(c_1, kc_1)}{u_2(c_1, kc_1)} = q \qquad \forall c_1. \tag{1}$$

By definition,

$$\sigma = \frac{q}{c_2/c_1} \cdot \frac{d(c_2/c_1)}{dq} = \frac{q}{k} \frac{dk}{dq},$$

which from differentiating (1) yields

$$\sigma = \frac{u_1 u_2}{c_2(u_2 u_{12} - u_1 u_{22})}.$$

The first-order conditions of the consumer's maximization problem are

$$u_1(c_1, c_2) = \lambda,$$

$$u_2(c_1, c_2) = \lambda p, \tag{2}$$

$$c_1 + pc_2 = R.$$

By differentiating (2), we obtain

$$\frac{\partial c_1}{\partial p} = \frac{1}{\lambda \Delta} [u_1 u_2 - c_2(u_2 u_{12} - u_1 u_{22})],$$

with

$$\Delta = -u_{11} p^2 + 2u_{21} p - u_{22} > 0,$$

from the concavity of u. The desired result follows from observing that

$$\frac{\partial e}{\partial p} = -\frac{\partial c_1}{\partial p}$$

and

$$\frac{\partial e}{\partial r} = -\frac{1}{(1 + r)^2} \cdot \frac{\partial e}{\partial p}.$$

2.

(a)   Since the two utility functions u^1 and u^2 represent the same ordinal preferences, they are associated with the same savings function $e(r)$ when r is certain. By definition,

$h_1^i(e(r), r) = 0$ $i = 1, 2,$

$Eh_1^1(e^1, \tilde{r}) = 0,$

$Eh_1^2(e^2, \tilde{r}) = 0.$

Recall that h^i is concave in e and increasing in r; from question 1, $e(r)$ is increasing if $\sigma > 1$. By continuity, there exists a value $\bar{r}$ such that $e(\bar{r}) = e^2$, with

$e(r) < (>) e(\bar{r})$ if $r < (>) \bar{r}$.

Since e is increasing and $h_{11}^2 < 0$,

$$r < \bar{r} \Rightarrow e(r) < e(\bar{r}) \Rightarrow h_1^2(e^2, r) = h_1^2(e(\bar{r}), r) < h_1^2(e(r), r) = 0$$
$$r > \bar{r} \Rightarrow e(r) > e(\bar{r}) \Rightarrow h_1^2(e^2, r) = h_1^2(e(\bar{r}), r) > h_1^2(e(r), r) = 0. \tag{3}$$

(b)   On the other hand, $h^1(e, r) = f(h^2(e, r))$ with f concave and increasing. Therefore

$$f'(h^2(e, r)) > (<) f'(h^2(e, \bar{r}))   \text{if } r < (>) \bar{r} \tag{4}$$

since h^2 is increasing in r.

(c)

$$Eh_1^1(e, \tilde{r}) = \int_0^{\bar{r}} f'(h^2(e, r)) h_1^2(e, r) g(r) \, dr + \int_{\bar{r}}^\infty f'(h^2(e, r)) h_1^2(e, r) g(r) \, dr$$

$$< f'(h^2(e, \bar{r})) Eh_1^2(e, \tilde{r})   \text{from (3) and (4)}.$$

Since Eh^1 is concave in e, Eh_1^1 is decreasing in e and

$Eh_1^1(e^2, \tilde{r}) < f'(h^2(e^2, \bar{r})) Eh_1^2(e^2, \tilde{r}) = 0.$

Therefore $e^2 > e^1$ (see figure P2.1).

3.
(a) $s(R^i)$ maximizes $Ef(u^*((1 - s)R^i, (1 + \tilde{r})sR^i))$. From section 2.7 of chapter 2, u^* is homogeneous of degree 1. Therefore

$u^*((1 - s)R^i, (1 + \tilde{r})sR^i) = R^i u^*(c_1, c_2),$

with $c_1 = (1 - s)$ and $c_2 = (1 + \tilde{r})s$. Therefore $s(R^i)$ maximizes $E\tilde{u}^i((1 - s), (1 + \tilde{r})s)$, with $\tilde{u}^i(., .) = f(R^i u^*(., .))$.
(b)   Consider the function $g^i(u) = f(R^i u)$ for $i = 1$ and 2 with $R^1 < R^2$.

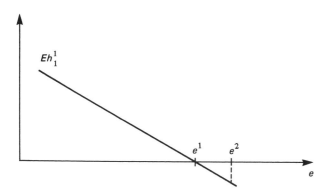

Figure P2.1

Now g^1 is a concave increasing transformation of g^2. Indeed, for any u,

$$-\frac{ug''^1}{g'^1} = -\frac{R^1uf''(R^1u)}{f'(R^1u)} > -\frac{R^2uf''(R^2u)}{f'(R^2u)} = -\frac{ug''^2}{g'^2}$$

since f exhibits increasing relative risk aversion. Therefore, for any u,

$$-\frac{g''^1}{g'^1} > -\frac{g''^2}{g'^2}.$$

From Pratt's theorem, g^1 is an increasing concave transformation of g^2, and there exists $\tilde{f}$ such that $g^1 = \tilde{f} \circ g^2$, which yields

$$\tilde{u}^1(.,.) = \tilde{f}(\tilde{u}^2(.,.)).$$

(c)   We apply the result from question 2.

Supplementary Reading

Kihlstrom, R., and L. Mirman. 1981. "Constant, Increasing and Decreasing Risk Aversion with Many Commodities." *Review of Economic Studies* 48:271–280.

Problem 3
Risk Aversion and the Theory of the Firm

Statement of the Problem

We consider an economy consisting of a continuum of identical agents represented by the interval $[0,1]$. The measure of the set of agents is therefore 1. Each agent is endowed with one unit of work that he can use either by acquiring the production technology, and thus becoming an *entrepreneur*, or by offering his work on the labor market, and thus becoming a *wage earner*. Each agent has a VNM utility function $e^{-\rho x}$ that depends on his consumption, x, where ρ is the coefficient of risk aversion.

The technology acquired by an entrepreneur is stochastic and written as

$$f(L, \theta) = \theta L^{1/2}$$

where L is the quantity of labor and θ is a normally distributed stochastic variable with mean $\bar{\theta}$ and variance σ^2 (ignore the problems of negative values for θ). We assume that the risks affecting the different entrepreneurs are perfectly correlated and that the choice of the level of input must be made before the value of θ is realized. Furthermore we assume that $\bar{\theta}/\rho\sigma^2 < \frac{1}{2}$.

1. Determine the proportions of entrepreneurs α_1 and α_2 in the two egalitarian Pareto optima.

2. We now organize a competitive labor market and define a fixed-wage, free-entry equilibrium as a proportion α^e of entrepreneurs, a proportion $1 - \alpha^e$ of wage earners and a wage w^e such that

(a) the supply of labor equals the demand for labor,
(b) no agent wishes to change his vocation (free-entry condition).

Determine the characteristics of the equilibrium. Explain why this equilibrium is not an egalitarian Pareto optimum.

3. Now assume that the agents coalesce in self-managed firms. They determine the size of the firm in order to maximize the expected utility of the firm's per capita value added. Determine the level of activity of the typical self-managed firm. Discuss this result. (*Hint*: If X is normally distributed with mean θ and variance σ^2, then $Ee^{\rho X} = e^{\rho\mu + \rho^2\sigma^2/2}$.)

Solution

1. Let α be the proportion of entrepreneurs. Due to decreasing returns, all the firms must have the same input of work, L. The aggregate resource constraint from the labor market imposes the following:

$$\alpha L = 1 - \alpha \quad \text{or} \quad L = \frac{1 - \alpha}{\alpha}.$$

Output per capita is then

$$\theta \alpha \left(\frac{1 - \alpha}{\alpha}\right)^{1/2},$$

and the egalitarian Pareto optimum is obtained by maximizing

$$E - e^{(-\rho \theta \alpha^{1/2}(1-\alpha)^{1/2})},$$

or by using the normality of the distribution

$$= - e^{(-\rho \bar{\theta}(1-\alpha)^{1/2}\alpha^{1/2} + 1/2\rho^2\sigma^2(1-\alpha)\alpha)}$$

which yields

$$\alpha^{1/2}(1 - \alpha)^{1/2} = \frac{\bar{\theta}}{\rho \sigma^2}.$$

This equation has two possible solutions for α, namely

$$\alpha_1 = \frac{1}{2} + \frac{1}{2}\sqrt{1 - \frac{4\bar{\theta}^2}{\rho^2\sigma^4}}, \quad L_1 = \frac{1 - \sqrt{1 - (4\bar{\theta}^2/\rho^2\sigma^4)}}{1 + \sqrt{1 - (4\bar{\theta}^2/\rho^2\sigma^4)}},$$

$$\alpha_2 = \frac{1}{2} - \frac{1}{2}\sqrt{1 - \frac{4\bar{\theta}^2}{\rho^2\sigma^4}}, \quad L_2 = \frac{1 + \sqrt{1 - (4\bar{\theta}^2/\rho^2\sigma^4)}}{1 - \sqrt{1 - (4\bar{\theta}^2/\rho^2\sigma^4)}}.$$

In the first solution there are many firms, each operating at relatively low level and therefore with high productivity. In the second solution there are fewer firms (and therefore less fixed costs) with lower productivity in each firm.

2. Given a wage w, the expected utility of a wage earner is simply $-e^{-\rho w}$. An entrepreneur decides his demand for labor by solving the following problem:

$$\underset{L}{\text{Max}} \; - E e^{-\rho(\theta L^{1/2} - wL)},$$

which, by using the first-order condition, yields

$$L = \left(\frac{\bar{\theta}}{2w + \rho\sigma^2}\right)^2. \tag{1}$$

Equality of supply and demand in the labor market implies $\alpha L = 1 - \alpha$. The free-entry condition requires that wage earners and entrepreneurs have the same utility, that is,

$$-e^{-\rho w} = -e^{\rho w L - \rho\bar{\theta}L^{1/2} + \rho^2 L \sigma^2/2},$$

which, by using (1), yields

$$w^e = \frac{\sqrt{\rho^2\sigma^4 + 4\bar{\theta}^2} - \rho\sigma^2}{4}$$

and

$$L^e = \frac{4\bar{\theta}^2}{(\rho\sigma^2 + \sqrt{\rho^2\sigma^4 + 4\bar{\theta}^2})^2}.$$

Therefore, the fixed-wage, free-entry equilibrium is inefficient. Risk sharing is not optimal. Indeed, the entrepreneurs bear all the risk, and the wage earners bear none.

3.   If $L + 1$ agents coalesce in a self-managed firm, they can devote one unit of labor to acquire the technology and L units of labor can be used as an input. The per capita value added is therefore $\theta L^{1/2}/(1 + L)$. Maximizing the expected value of the per capita value added then yields

$$\underset{L}{\mathrm{Max}} \; -Ee^{-\rho(\theta L^{1/2}/(1+L))} = e^{-\rho(\bar{\theta}L^{1/2}/(1+L)) + (\rho^2\sigma^2/2)(L/(1+L)^2)}$$

yielding

$$L = \frac{1 - \sqrt{1 - (4\bar{\theta}^2/\rho^2\sigma^4)}}{1 + \sqrt{1 - (4\bar{\theta}^2/\rho^2\sigma^4)}} \quad \text{or} \quad \frac{1 + \sqrt{1 - (4\bar{\theta}^2/\rho^2\sigma^4)}}{1 - \sqrt{1 - (4\bar{\theta}^2/\rho^2\sigma^4)}},$$

which are the optimal levels.

Here we generalize to a case of uncertainty a classic result: the competitive equilibrium in a labor-managed economy with free entry is Pareto optimal. We can show that these allocations also coincide with the equilibria obtained if we organize a stock market that allows wage earners to share risks with entrepreneurs.

Supplementary Readings

Kihlstrom, R. E., and J.-J. Laffont. 1979.   "A General Equilibrium Entrepreneurial Theory of Firm Formation Based on Risk Aversion." *Journal of Political Economy* 87:719–748.

Kihlstrom, R. E., and J.-J. Laffont. 1982.   "A Competitive Entrepreneurial Model of a Stock Market." In J. McCall (ed.), *Economics of Information and Uncertainty*. University of Chicago.

Problem 4
Increasing Risk and the Value of Information

Statement of the Problem

Consider a family of distribution functions $F(x, r)$ on $[0, 1]$ that are twice differentiable and indexed by r where an increase in r indicates an increase in risk in the Rothschild-Stiglitz sense.

1. Show that if $v(x)$ is a convex function, the function $G(.)$ defined by

$$G(r) = \int_0^1 v(x) \, dF(x, r)$$

is an increasing function.

2. Consider the decision-making problem

$$\underset{a}{\text{Max}} \int_0^1 u(x, a) \, dF(x, r).$$

Let $a^*(r)$ be the solution.

If the agent is informed about the value of x, he solves the problem $\text{Max}_a \, u(x, a)$, whose solution we denote $\bar{a}(x)$. We define the value of information as

$$V(r) = \int_0^1 u(x, \bar{a}(x)) \, dF(x, r) - \int_0^1 u(x, a^*(r)) \, dF(x, r).$$

By using the result in question 1, show that $V(r)$ increases with r if $u(x, a) = x\psi(a) + \xi(a)$, with u strictly concave in a.

Solution

1.

$$G'(r) = \int_0^1 v(x) \, dF_r(x, r) = v(x) F_r(x, r)|_0^1 - \int_0^1 F_r(x, r) v'(x) \, dx$$

$$= - \int_0^1 F_r(x, r) v'(x) \, dx = - \int_0^1 v'(x) \, d \int_0^x F_r(y, r) \, dy$$

$$= -v'(x) \int_0^x F_r(y, r) \, dy|_0^1 + \int_0^1 v''(x) \int_0^x F_r(y, r) \, dy \, dx.$$

By definition of increasing risk in the Rothschild-Stiglitz sense,

$$\int_0^x F_r(y,r)\,dy \geqslant 0 \qquad \forall x \in [0,1]$$

$$= 0 \qquad \text{if } x = 1,$$

Therefore $G'(r) > 0$ if $v'' > 0$.

2.

$$V(r) = \int_0^1 [u(x,\bar{a}(x)) - u(x,a^*(r))]\,dF(x,r).$$

Let

$$v(x) = u(x,\bar{a}(x)) - u(x,a^*(r)),$$

$$v''(x) = u_{11}(x,\bar{a}(x)) - u_{11}(x,a^*(r)) + u_{12}\bar{a}'(x) + u_2\bar{a}''(x).$$

By definition,

$$u_2(x,\bar{a}) = 0,$$

$$\bar{a}'(x) = -\frac{u_{21}}{u_{22}}.$$

Therefore

$$v''(x) = -u_{11}(x,a^*(r)) - \left(\frac{u_{21}^2 - u_{11}u_{22}}{u_{22}}\right)$$

$$= -\frac{u_{21}^2}{u_{22}} > 0$$

in the particular case considered. Therefore, in this case, the value of information increases when risk increases in the Rothschild-Stiglitz sense.

Supplementary Reading

Laffont, J.-J. 1976. "Risk, Stochastic Preference and the Value of Information." *Journal of Economic Theory* 8:64–84.

Problem 5
Portfolio Analysis

Statement of the Problem

1. A stock portfolio consists of wealth that, at the beginning of the period, is represented by a stochastic variable $\tilde{x}$. Show that if $\tilde{x}$ is distributed normally, the Savage-von Neumann-Morgenstern theory leads to expected utilities that depend only on the mean and variance of $\tilde{x}$. Determine the shape of the indifference curves by assuming that all portfolios are distributed normally.

2. In what follows, we assume that the indifference curves have the shape exhibited in question 1. Initially, assume that there exist only risky assets with stochastic returns given by $\tilde{r}^1$ and $\tilde{r}^2$. Show that by varying the composition of his portfolio, the agent who has one dollar to invest can generate a subset in the space (μ, σ). Characterize the efficiency frontier of this set (use the following particular cases: the correlation coefficient between $\tilde{r}^1$ and $\tilde{r}^2$ denoted $\rho = 1$, 0, and -1). How would the optimum portfolio be determined?

3. Assume that in addition to the two preceding risky assets, we introduce a riskless asset yielding r per dollar invested (assume also that it is possible to hold a negative quantity of this new asset, that is, to borrow). What happens to the efficiency frontier? Show graphically that the composition of the risky portfolio chosen is independent of the preferences at the optimum.

4. We generalize the problem to the case of a finite number of risky assets J and a riskless asset yielding r. The return to asset j is denoted $\tilde{r}^j$. Let $\tilde{R} = (\tilde{r}^1, \ldots, \tilde{r}^J)$, and let V be the covariance matrix (symmetric and nonsingular) of $\tilde{R}$. For a given mean, write the problem that minimizes one-half of the variance to generate the efficiency frontier. Determine the composition of the portfolios on this frontier. Show that this composition is independent of preferences and that the efficiency frontier is a half-line. From this, derive the result that the composition of the risky portfolio for each agent reflects the market portfolio.

Let a^e be the optimal risky portfolio yielding $\tilde{r}^e$. From the first-order conditions of the preceding problem, show that

$$E\tilde{r}^j - r = \frac{\text{Cov}(\tilde{r}^e, \tilde{r}^j)}{\text{Var}\,\tilde{r}^e}(E\tilde{r}^e - r).$$

Interpret this result.

5.   Now we will determine the equilibrium prices in a stock market on which J firms are quoted when there are I investors. Investor i holds an initial share θ_0^{ij} of firm j's stock and b_0^i of the riskless asset, $i = 1, \ldots, I$ and $j = 1, \ldots, J$. Let v^j be the market value of the firm, that is, the market value of the set of stock entitlements to firm j at the beginning of the period. Let $\tilde{d}^j$ be the market value of these entitlements for firm j at the end of the period (this value includes dividends and appreciation).[1] Assume that all the investors have the same expectations about future market values.

The return to stock j is therefore defined as

$$\tilde{r}^j = \frac{\tilde{d}^j - v^j}{v^j}.$$

The set of available risky assets in the economy is called the risky market portfolio. Its yield is written as

$$\tilde{r}^m = \frac{\sum_{j=1}^{J} \tilde{d}^j - \sum_{j=1}^{J} v^j}{\sum_{j=1}^{J} v^j} = \frac{\tilde{d}^m - v^m}{v^m}.$$

Assume that investor i has a utility function $U^i(\mu, \sigma) = \mu - \alpha^i \sigma^2$. Write his optimization problem by using the results of the preceding question. Then determine v^m as a function of r from the equilibrium condition on the market for the riskless asset. Use the formula obtained in question 4 to determine the "prices," that is, the initial market values, v^j, as a function of r.

Solution

1.   If $\tilde{x}$ is distributed normally with mean μ and variance σ^2, we have

$$Eu(x) = \int_{-\infty}^{+\infty} u(x) \frac{1}{\sqrt{2\pi}\sigma} e^{-((x-\mu)/\sigma)^2/2} \, dx = U(\mu, \sigma).$$

Let

$$v = \frac{x - \mu}{\sigma}$$

$$U(\mu, \sigma) = \int_{-\infty}^{+\infty} u(v\sigma + \mu)g(v) \, dv$$

---

1. In a two-period model the value of the stock in the second period is simply the profit earned in the second period (see chapter 7).

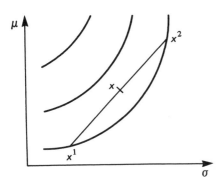

Figure P5.1

with

$$g(v) = \frac{1}{\sqrt{2\pi}} e^{-v^2/2}.$$

The slope of any isoquant is defined by

$$\frac{d\mu}{d\sigma} = -\frac{\int_{-\infty}^{+\infty} vu'g(v)\,dv}{\int_{-\infty}^{+\infty} u'g(v)\,dv}.$$

Since $g(.)$ is symmetric and $u'' < 0$,

$$\int_{-\infty}^{+\infty} vu'g\,dv < 0,$$

and therefore $d\mu/d\sigma > 0$.

To show that a typical isoquant is convex, take two points x^1 and x^2 on an isoquant. Since all the portfolios are normal, $x^1(x^2)$ is distributed normally with mean $\mu^1(\mu^2)$ and standard deviation $\sigma^1(\sigma^2)$. Let x be a point on the chord $x^1\,x^2$ (see figure P5.1):

$$\mu = \lambda\mu^1 + (1 - \lambda)\mu^2,$$

$$\sigma = \lambda\sigma^1 + (1 - \lambda)\sigma^2;$$

$$U(\mu, \sigma) = \int_{-\infty}^{+\infty} u(v(\lambda\sigma^2 + (1 - \lambda)\sigma^2) + \lambda\mu^1 + (1 - \lambda)\mu^2)g(v)\,dv.$$

Since u is concave, for any value of v, we have

$$u(\lambda(v\sigma^1 + \mu^1) + (1 - \lambda)(v\sigma^2 + \mu^2))$$

$$\geqslant \lambda u(v\sigma^1 + \mu^1) + (1 - \lambda)u(v\sigma^2 + \mu^2),$$

which yields $U(\mu, \sigma) \geqslant \lambda U(\mu^1, \sigma^1) + (1 - \lambda)U(\mu^2, \sigma^2)$.

2.   Let $\alpha(1 - \alpha)$ be the quantity of asset 1 (2) purchased. The yield on a portfolio constructed in this way will be

$$\tilde{x} = \alpha\tilde{r}^1 + (1 - \alpha)\tilde{r}^2,$$

$$E\tilde{x} = \alpha\mu^1 + (1 - \alpha)\mu^2, \tag{1}$$

$$\text{Var } \tilde{x} = \alpha^2(\sigma^1)^2 + (1 - \alpha)^2(\sigma^2)^2 + 2\alpha(1 - \alpha)\sigma^1\sigma^2\rho, \tag{2}$$

where $\mu^1(\mu^2)$ is the mean of $\tilde{r}^1(\tilde{r}^2)$, $\sigma^1(\sigma^2)$ is the standard deviation of $\tilde{r}^1(\tilde{r}^2)$, and ρ is the correlation coefficient between $\tilde{r}^1$ and $\tilde{r}^2$.

If short sales are not permitted, we have furthermore $\alpha \in [0, 1]$. From (1) and (2), we can derive a relationship between the mean μ and the variance σ^2 of a portfolio like the one above. Specifically,

$$\sigma^2 = \left(\frac{\mu - \mu^2}{\mu^1 - \mu^2}\right)^2 ((\sigma^1)^2 + (\sigma^2)^2 - 2\rho\sigma^1\sigma^2)$$

$$+ 2\left(\frac{\mu - \mu^2}{\mu^1 - \mu^2}\right)(\sigma^1\sigma^2\rho - (\sigma^2)^2) + (\sigma^2)^2. \tag{3}$$

Since preferences are increasing in the northwest direction, the efficiency frontier (where an efficient investor will necessarily choose to be) consists of the northwest frontier of the curve defined by (3).

We note here three special cases:

(a) $\rho = 1$ (figure P5.2)   The two assets are perfectly correlated. The frontier is the half-line passing through (x^1, x^2); it is restricted to the chord (x^1, x^2) if we do not allow short sales.

(b) $\rho = 0$ (figure P5.3)   For example, if $E\tilde{r}^2 = 1$, $E\tilde{r}^1 = 2$, $\text{Var } \tilde{r}^1 = 4$, and $\text{Var } \tilde{r}^2 = 1$, we obtain the following equation:

$$\sigma^2 = 5(\mu - \tfrac{6}{5})^2 + \tfrac{4}{5},$$

which is a hyperbola represented in figure P5.3 whose upper portion is the efficiency frontier. Note that asset 2 alone does not belong to the efficiency frontier. No agent will hold only asset 2.

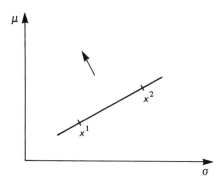

Figure P5.2

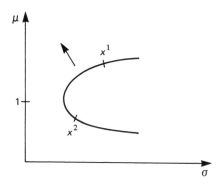

Figure P5.3

(c) $\rho = -1$ (figure P5.4)   Using the above values, we have

$\sigma^2 = 9(\mu - \frac{4}{3})^2.$

The perfect negative correlation between the two assets allows the construction of a riskless portfolio x^3 (with $\alpha = \frac{2}{3}$). In general, the agent chooses the point on the efficiency frontier that maximizes $U(\mu, \sigma)$ (see figure P5.5). Point A on figure P5.5 corresponds to an optimum portfolio with a particular α.

3.   There exists a riskless asset yielding r. The efficiency frontier is obtained by taking the farthest northwest tangent to the efficiency frontier passing through r on the vertical axis (see figure P5.6).

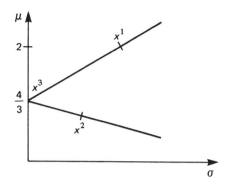

Figure P5.4

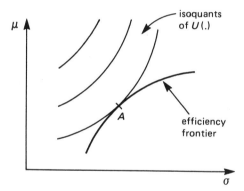

Figure P5.5

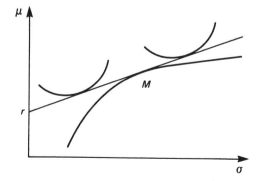

Figure P5.6

Let M be this point of tangency. Point M corresponds to a portfolio of risky assets yielding r^m. Dividing the per dollar investment by allocating λ to the riskless asset and $(1 - \lambda)$ to the portfolio M generates the half-line rM. We then have

$$\tilde{x} = \lambda r + (1 - \lambda)\tilde{r}^m$$

$$E\tilde{x} = \mu = \lambda r + (1 - \lambda)E\tilde{r}^m$$

$$\text{Var } \tilde{x} = \sigma^2 = (1 - \lambda)^2 \text{ Var } \tilde{r}^m.$$

From the above, the equation of the efficiency frontier can be written as

$$\mu = r + \frac{E\tilde{r}^m - r}{\sigma(\tilde{r}^m)} \cdot \sigma.$$

All the agents want to be on this frontier, and therefore their preferences do not influence the nature of the risky portfolio chosen (which is here always M). The portfolio is determined only by the portion of wealth invested in the risky asset as the famous separation theorem states. Since all the agents hold a portfolio of risky assets having the same composition, the equilibrium composition must be equal to the composition of risky assets exchanged on the market.

4. Let a^j be the proportion of a dollar invested in the risky asset j and a^0 be the proportion invested in the riskless asset. Then we must have

$$\sum_{j=1}^{J} a^j + a^0 = 1.$$

The portfolio constructed in this way yields

$$\tilde{r} = \sum_{j=1}^{J} a^j \tilde{r}^j + a^0 r,$$

from which we derive

$$\mu = E\tilde{r} = \sum_{j=1}^{J} a^j E\tilde{r}^j + a^0 r,$$

$$\sigma^2 = \text{Var } \tilde{r} = \sum_{j=1}^{J} \sum_{h=1}^{J} a^j a^h \sigma^{jh}.$$

If we let $\tilde{R} = (\tilde{r}^1, \ldots, \tilde{r}^J)'$, $a = [a^1, \ldots, a^J]'$, and $e = [1, \ldots, 1]'$, the efficient portfolios may be obtained by minimizing the variance for a given expected value (or equivalently by minimizing one-half this variance). Specifically,

$$\operatorname*{Min}_{a,\,a^0} \frac{1}{2}\sigma^2 = \frac{1}{2}a'Va,$$

subject to

$$a'E\tilde{R} + a^0 r = \mu \qquad (\lambda_1), \tag{4}$$

$$a^0 + a'e = 1 \qquad (\lambda_0). \tag{5}$$

Let λ_0 and λ_1 be the Lagrangian multipliers associated with the constraints of this problem. The first-order conditions are

$$Va - \lambda_1 E\tilde{R} + \lambda_0 e = 0 \tag{6}$$

$$-\lambda_1 r + \lambda_0 = 0, \tag{7}$$

from which we derive, using (4) and (5),

$$\alpha = (\mu - r)\frac{V^{-1}(E\tilde{R} - re)}{(E\tilde{R} - re)'V^{-1}(E\tilde{R} - re)} .$$

The proportion of the portfolio invested in risky asset j is $a^j/e'a$ from which it follows that the composition of the portfolio is

$$\frac{a}{e'a} = \frac{V^{-1}(E\tilde{R} - re)}{e'V^{-1}(E\tilde{R} - re)}.$$

This composition is obviously independent of the preferences. Since all the investors have the same risky portfolio, they must hold a portfolio having the market risk.

Furthermore

$$\sigma^2 = a'Va = \frac{(\mu - r)^2}{(E\tilde{R} - re)'V^{-1}(E\tilde{R} - re)},$$

which yields a linear relationship between σ and μ. Therefore the efficiency frontier is a straight line.

Let a^e be the optimal risky portfolio and $\tilde{r}^e$ be its yield. For the stocks belonging to the optimal portfolio, the first-order conditions are written as

$$\sum_{k=1}^{J} \sigma^{jk} a^{ke} - \lambda_1 E\tilde{r}^j + \lambda_0 = 0 \qquad \text{for any } j \text{ in the optimal portfolio}, \tag{8}$$

$$-\lambda_1 r + \lambda_0 = 0. \tag{9}$$

Equation (8) is rewritten as

$$\text{Cov}(\tilde{r}^e, \tilde{r}^j) - \lambda_1(E\tilde{r}^j - r) = 0 \qquad \text{if } a^{je} > 0. \tag{10}$$

Multiplying (10) by a^{je} and summing over j yields

$$\text{Var}\,\tilde{r}^e = \lambda_1 \sum_{j=1}^{J} a^{je}(E\tilde{r}^j - r) = \lambda_1(E\tilde{r}^e - r). \tag{11}$$

By combining (10) and (11), we have

$$E\tilde{r}^j - r = \frac{\text{Cov}(\tilde{r}^e, \tilde{r}^j)}{\text{Var}\,\tilde{r}^e} \cdot (E\tilde{r}^e - r). \tag{12}$$

The expression $E\tilde{r}^j - r$ is the risk premium corresponding to the risky asset j. It depends crucially on the covariance between the yield on this asset and the market return. In particular, if this covariance is negative— that is, the stock is negatively correlated with the market—the premium is negative. In essence, this stock provides insurance against the major risk— that is, the market risk—and therefore it does not require as high an average return to be held in the optimal portfolio. From the preceding question, the yield on each agent's portfolio is identical and equal to the yield on the market portfolio. Therefore we can use the formula obtained in that part to define this yield.

5. Since

$$\tilde{r}^m = \frac{\tilde{d}^m - v^m}{v^m}, \quad \text{Var}\,r^m = \frac{1}{(v^m)^2} \cdot \text{Var}\,\tilde{d}^m.$$

Let θ_0^{ij} be the proportion of the stock of firm j held by investor i, for $j = 1,\ldots,J$, and b_0^i be his initial endowment in the riskless asset. Therefore the initial wealth of agent i is

$$W^i = b_0^i + \sum_{j=1}^{J} \theta_0^{ij} v^j.$$

From question (4), since all the investors have utility functions $U^i(\mu, \sigma)$ that depend only on the mean and variance of their final wealth, any investor i will buy a portion θ^i of the market portfolio having value v^m. Then $(1 - a^{i0})w^i$ will be the proportion of his wealth invested in the market portfolio. His final wealth will be

$$\tilde{x}^i = a^{i0}(1 + r)W^i + (1 - a^{i0})(1 + \tilde{r}^m)W^i$$

$$= a^{i0}(1 + r)W^i + (1 - a^{i0})\frac{\tilde{d}^m}{v^m} \cdot W^i.$$

It follows that

$$E\tilde{x}^i = a^{i0}(1 + r)W^i + (1 - a^{i0})\frac{E\tilde{d}^m}{v^m} \cdot W^i,$$

$$\text{Var } \tilde{x}^i = (1 - a^{i0})^2(W^i)^2 \frac{\text{Var } \tilde{d}^m}{(v^m)^2}.$$

His optimization problem is written as

$$\underset{a^{i0}}{\text{Max}} \{E\tilde{x}^i - \alpha^i \text{Var } \tilde{x}^i\}.$$

The first-order condition is

$$\theta^i = \frac{(1 - a^{i0})W^i}{v^m} = \frac{E\tilde{d}^m - (1 + r)v^m}{2\alpha^i \text{Var } \tilde{d}^m}.$$

Let $A = \sum_{i=1}^{I} 1/\alpha^i$. At the equilibrium we have $\sum_{i=1}^{I} \theta^i = 1$ so that

$$1 = \frac{A(E\tilde{d}^m - (1 + r)v^m)}{2 \text{Var } \tilde{d}^m}.$$

The preceding equation can be rewritten as

$$v^m = \frac{1}{1 + r}\left[E\tilde{d}^m - \frac{2 \text{Var } \tilde{d}^m}{A}\right]. \tag{13}$$

The sum of the market values of the risky assets can be expressed as a function of the exogenous rate of interest. Since the optimal risky portfolio for all the investors at the equilibrium is simply the market portfolio, we can use equation (12) and replace $\tilde{r}^e$ by $\tilde{r}^m$ to obtain J equations, characterizing the prices of the firms' stocks as a function of r.

Therefore from (12) we have

$$E\tilde{r}^j - r = \frac{\text{Cov}(\tilde{r}^m, \tilde{r}^j)}{\text{Var } \tilde{r}^m}(E\tilde{r}^m - r) \qquad j = 1, \ldots, J. \tag{14}$$

However, since $\tilde{r}^m = (\tilde{d}^m - v^m)/v^m$ and $\tilde{r}^j = (\tilde{d}^j - v^j)/v^j$, we have

$$\text{Var}\,\tilde{r}^m = \frac{1}{(v^m)^2}\,\text{Var}\,\tilde{d}^m \quad \text{and} \quad \text{Cov}(\tilde{r}^m, \tilde{r}^j) = \frac{1}{v^j v^m}\,\text{Cov}(\tilde{r}^m, r^j)$$

which, using (14), yields

$$v^j = \frac{1}{(1+r)}\left[E\tilde{d}^j - (E\tilde{d}^m - (1+r)v^m)\frac{\text{Cov}(\tilde{d}^j, \tilde{d}^m)}{\text{Var}\,\tilde{d}^m} \right]. \tag{15}$$

Consequently (15) is a system of $J - 1$ independent linear equations in $v^1, \ldots, v^J$ that combined with (13) determines a vector of equilibrium prices as a function of r and of v^m. This formula shows that the price of a risky asset is equal to the discounted value of its expected gain adjusted by a term that depends on the covariance between the final market value of the stock and the final value of the market portfolio. Finally, notice the possibility of testing this theory empirically since, from (14), all the average returns should be on the line having a y-intercept r and a slope $(Er^m - r)$. Each stock is then identified by its x-coordinate $\text{Cov}(\tilde{r}^m, r^j)/\text{Var}\,\tilde{r}^m$ called its beta.

Problem 6
Radner Equilibrium and Incomplete Markets

Statement of the Problem

Consider an economy with two periods, two goods, and two consumers. In period 0, securities markets are opened. In period 1, there are two possible states of nature $s = 1$ and 2 and spot markets for the goods are organized (see section 6.2). The preferences of consumer i are represented by the following utility function defined over his consumption plans:

$$U^i(x^i_{11}, x^i_{21}, x^i_{12}, x^i_{22}) = \frac{1}{2} \sum_{s=1}^{2} \sum_{l=1}^{2} \alpha^i_l \, \text{Log} \, x^i_{ls}$$

where x^i_{ls} is the quantity consumed of good l in state s by consumer i, $i = 1$ and 2.

We have

$$\alpha^i_l > 0, \quad \alpha^i_1 + \alpha^i_2 = 1 \qquad i = 1, 2, l = 1, 2,$$

and the vectors (α^1_1, α^1_2) and (α^2_1, α^2_2) are linearly independent. In period 0, the consumers have no endowments, but they can purchase and sell stocks. In period 1, they have endowments characterized by

$$w^1_{11} = 1 - \varepsilon \qquad w^1_{12} = \varepsilon$$

$$w^1_{21} = 1 - \varepsilon \qquad w^1_{22} = \varepsilon$$

and

$$w^2_{11} = \varepsilon \qquad w^2_{12} = 1 - \varepsilon$$

$$w^2_{21} = \varepsilon \qquad w^2_{22} = 1 - \varepsilon$$

where w^i_{ls} is the amount of good l in state s held by consumer i.

1. Using a system of complete contingent markets in period 0, determine the Arrow-Debreu equilibrium in which each agent bears no individual risk.

2. In period 0, consider only the two securities characterized by

$$a^1 = \begin{bmatrix} 1 & 1 \\ 0 & 0 \end{bmatrix}, \quad a^2 = \begin{bmatrix} 0 & 0 \\ 1 & 1 \end{bmatrix}.$$

Security 1 permits the unconditional purchase of good 1 (a futures' market), and security 2 permits the unconditional purchase of good 2. Let $p_1 =$

(p_{11}, p_{12}) and $p_2 = (p_{21}, p_{22})$ be the period 2 prices in states 1 and 2, respectively.

Show that if $\varepsilon \neq \frac{1}{2}$, there exists no Radner equilibrium for this structure of a securities' market. Consider in turn the cases where p_1 and p_2 are linearly dependent and then linearly independent. Discuss these results.

3. Now replace the securities in question 2 by two new securities, defined by

$$a^1 = \begin{bmatrix} 1 & 2 \\ 0 & 0 \end{bmatrix}, \quad a^2 = \begin{bmatrix} 0 & 0 \\ 2 & 1 \end{bmatrix}.$$

Show that, with this structure of a securities' market, the allocation in the Arrow-Debreu equilibrium found in the first question can be realized as a Radner equilibrium. Find the conditions on (α_1^i, α_2^i) $i = 1$ and 2 and ε so that there exists another Radner equilibrium in which the securities' markets are inactive. Show that this other equilibrium is not a Pareto optimum in general.

Solution

1. Notice that the utility functions are of the Cobb-Douglas type in the space of four contingent goods, with

$$\tfrac{1}{2}\alpha_1^1 + \tfrac{1}{2}\alpha_2^1 + \tfrac{1}{2}\alpha_1^1 + \tfrac{1}{2}\alpha_2^1 = 1.$$

Let p_{ls} be the price of contingent good l in state s where $l = 1$ and 2 and $s = 1$ and 2. Denote by R^i the income of consumer i, that is,

$$R^i = \sum_{l=1}^{2} \sum_{s=1}^{2} p_{ls} w_{ls}^i \qquad i = 1, 2.$$

Consumer i bears no risk if he has the same vector of consumption in state 1 and in state 2, or formally,

$$x_{11}^i = \frac{1}{2} \alpha_1^i \frac{R^i}{p_{11}} = x_{12}^i = \frac{1}{2} \alpha_1^i \frac{R^i}{p_{12}},$$

from which, it follows that $p_{11} = p_{12}$. Similarly, $p_{21} = p_{22}$.

We can normalize the prices so that $p_{11} = p_{12} = 1$. Now all we need to calculate is a price ratio $p_{22}/p_{11} = p_{22}$. Given this price ratio,

$$R^i = 1 + p_{22} \qquad i = 1, 2.$$

Equality of demand and supply on the market for good 1 in state 1 then yields

$$\tfrac{1}{2}\alpha_1^1[1 + p_{22}] + \tfrac{1}{2}\alpha_1^2[1 + p_{22}] = 1$$

or

$$1 + p_{22} = \frac{2}{\alpha_1^1 + \alpha_1^2}.$$

Then it is obvious that supply equals demand on all markets and that

$$x_{1s}^i = \frac{\alpha_1^i}{\alpha_1^1 + \alpha_1^2} \qquad i = 1, 2, \quad s = 1, 2,$$

$$x_{2s}^i = \frac{\alpha_2^i}{\alpha_2^1 + \alpha_2^2} \qquad i = 1, 2, \quad s = 1, 2.$$

2.   Now we denote by p_{ls} the price of good l once state s is realized, by q_1 and q_2 the prices of securities 1 and 2 in period 0 and by z^{i1} and z^{i2} the purchases of securities 1 and 2 for $i = 1$ and 2. The budget constraints of consumer 1 are written as

$$q_1 z^{11} + q_2 z^{12} = 0, \tag{1}$$

$$p_{11} x_{11}^i + p_{21} x_{21}^i = p_{11}[1 - \varepsilon + z^{i1}] + p_{21}[1 - \varepsilon + z^{i2}], \tag{2}$$

$$p_{12} x_{12}^i + p_{22} x_{22}^i = p_{12}[\varepsilon + z^{i1}] + p_{22}[\varepsilon + z^{i2}], \tag{3}$$

with analogous expressions applying to consumer 2 after replacing ε with $1 - \varepsilon$. Initially, assume that $(p_{11}, p_{21}) = \lambda(p_{12}, p_{22})$ with $\lambda > 0$, that is, the vectors are colinear. Therefore the *monetary* resources procured in states 1 and 2 are proportional because

$$p_{11} z^{i1} + p_{21} z^{i2} = \lambda[p_{12} z^{i1} + p_{22} z^{i2}]$$

$$= \lambda z^{i1}\left[p_{12} - p_{22}\frac{q_1}{q_2}\right]$$

by using (1). Two possibilities arise:

•   either $p_{12} \neq p_{22}(q_1/q_2)$ and by buying an infinite quantity of security 1 if $p_{12} > p_{22}(q_1/q_2)$ (respectively, selling an infinite quantity if $p_{12} < p_{22}(q_1/q_2)$), agent i can assure himself of an infinite income that contradicts the possibility of an equilibrium,

- or $p_{12} = p_{22}(q_1/q_2)$ and the securities prevent any reallocation of resources between the states of nature.

Then we can compute the current prices in each state. In state 1, equality of supply and demand on the market for good 1 yields:

$$\alpha_1^1 (1 - \varepsilon)\left(1 + \frac{p_{21}}{p_{11}}\right) + \alpha_1^2 \varepsilon\left(1 + \frac{p_{21}}{p_{11}}\right) = 1,$$

or

$$1 + \frac{p_{21}}{p_{11}} = \frac{1}{(1 - \varepsilon)\alpha_1^1 + \varepsilon\alpha_1^2}.$$

Similarly, in state 2 we derive

$$1 + \frac{p_{22}}{p_{12}} = \frac{1}{\varepsilon\alpha_1^1 + (1 - \varepsilon)\alpha_1^2}.$$

If $\varepsilon \neq \frac{1}{2}$, colinearity of (p_{11}, p_{21}) and (p_{12}, p_{22}) requires $\alpha_1^1 = \alpha_1^2$, that is, colinearity of (α_1^1, α_2^1) and (α_1^2, α_2^2), which is excluded by assumption. We conclude that we cannot have a Radner equilibrium with colinear prices.

Now suppose that (p_{11}, p_{21}) and (p_{12}, p_{22}) are not colinear. Constraints (2) and (3) can be written as

$$p_{11}x_{11}^1 + p_{21}x_{21}^1 = (p_{11} + p_{21})(1 - \varepsilon) + z^{11}\left[p_{11} - p_{21}\frac{q_1}{q_2}\right], \tag{4}$$

$$p_{12}x_{12}^1 + p_{22}x_{22}^1 = (p_{12} + p_{22})\varepsilon + z^{11}\left[p_{12} - p_{22}\frac{q_1}{q_2}\right], \tag{5}$$

$$p_{11}x_{11}^2 + p_{22}x_{21}^2 = (p_{11} + p_{21})\varepsilon + z^{21}\left[p_{11} - p_{21}\frac{q_1}{q_2}\right], \tag{6}$$

$$p_{12}x_{12}^2 + p_{22}x_{22}^2 = (p_{12} + p_{22})(1 - \varepsilon) + z^{21}\left[p_{12} - p_{22}\frac{q_1}{q_2}\right]. \tag{7}$$

We can normalize the prices in each state of nature so that $p_{11} = 1 = p_{12}$ and normalize as well as in period 0 so that $q_1 = 1$. Also let

$$\Delta_1 = p_{11} - p_{21}\frac{q_1}{q_2} = 1 - \frac{p_{21}}{q_2},$$

$$\Delta_2 = p_{12} - p_{22}\frac{q_1}{q_2} = 1 - \frac{p_{22}}{q_2}.$$

Now Δ_1 and Δ_2 cannot have the same sign; otherwise, the agents would choose an infinite portfolio. Without loss of generality, assume that $\Delta_1 > 0$ and $\Delta_2 < 0$. Multiplying (4) by $k = -\Delta_2/\Delta_1$ and adding this to (5) yields the budget constraint for agent 1 in the following form:

$$kx^1_{11} + kp_{21}x^1_{21} + x^1_{21} + p_{22}x^1_{22} = k(1 + p_{21})(1 - \varepsilon) + (1 + p_{22})\varepsilon,$$

which yields a demand for good 11 and good 12 of

$$x^1_{11} = \alpha^1_1 \frac{k(1 + p_{21})(1 - \varepsilon) + (1 + p_{22})\varepsilon}{k},$$

$$x^1_{12} = \alpha^1_1 [k(1 + p_{21})(1 - \varepsilon) + (1 + p_{22})\varepsilon].$$

Similarly, for agent 2 we obtain

$$x^2_{11} = \alpha^2_1 \frac{k(1 + p_{21})\varepsilon + (1 + p_{22})(1 - \varepsilon)}{k},$$

$$x^2_{12} = \alpha^2_1 [k(1 + p_{21})\varepsilon + (1 + p_{22})(1 - \varepsilon)].$$

By equating demand and supply in the two markets, we conclude that $k = 1$. Similar reasoning for good 2 leads to $k' = 1$ which establishes the colinearity of (p_{11}, p_{21}) and (p_{12}, p_{22}). However, this is excluded by assumption.

3.   With the new securities, the budget constraints for agent 1 are written as

$$q_1 z^{11} + q_2 z^{12} = 0,$$

$$p_{11}x^1_{11} + p_{21}x^1_{21} = p_{11}[1 - \varepsilon + z^{11}] + p_{21}[1 - \varepsilon + 2z^{12}],$$

$$p_{12}x^1_{12} + p_{22}x^1_{22} = p_{12}[\varepsilon + 2z^{11}] + p_{22}[\varepsilon + z^{12}]$$

(with the analogous expressions for agent 2 after replacing ε by $1 - \varepsilon$). Then, by substitution,

$$x^1_{11} + \frac{p_{21}}{p_{11}}x^1_{21} = (1 - \varepsilon)\left(1 + \frac{p_{21}}{p_{11}}\right) + z^{11}\left[1 - 2\frac{q_1}{q_2}p_{21}\right], \qquad (8)$$

$$x^1_{12} + \frac{p_{22}}{p_{12}}x^1_{22} = \varepsilon\left(1 + \frac{p_{22}}{p_{12}}\right) + z^{11}\left[2 - \frac{q_1}{q_2}p_{22}\right]. \qquad (9)$$

To establish an Arrow-Debreu equilibrium, the unique budget constraint obtained by eliminating z^{11} must coincide with that obtained in the Arrow-

Debreu equilibrium. To accomplish this, take the Arrow-Debreu equilibrium prices (p_{ls}), that is,

$$p_{11} = p_{12} = 1,$$

$$p_{21} = p_{22} = \frac{2}{\alpha_1^1 + \alpha_1^2} - 1,$$

and choose q_2/q_1 so that the simple addition of (8) and (9) eliminates z^{11}, that is,

$$\frac{q_2}{q_1} = p_{22} = \frac{2}{\alpha_1^1 + \alpha_1^2} - 1.$$

Thus we obtain

$$x_{11}^1 + \left(\frac{2}{(\alpha_1^1 + \alpha_1^2)} - 1\right)x_{21}^1 + x_{12}^1 + \left(\frac{2}{(\alpha_1^1 + \alpha_1^2)} - 1\right)x_{22}^1 = \frac{2}{\alpha_1^1 + \alpha_1^2}.$$

However, this is precisely the constraint in the Arrow-Debreu equilibrium.

If $z^{11} = 0$, by setting $p_{11} = 1$ and $p_{12} = 1$, consumer i's demands in states 1 and 2 are given by

$$x_{11}^1 = \alpha_1^1(1 - \varepsilon)(1 + p_{21}), \quad x_{12}^1 = \alpha_1^1\varepsilon(1 + p_{22}),$$

$$x_{21}^1 = \alpha_2^1\frac{(1 - \varepsilon)(1 + p_{21})}{p_{21}}, \quad x_{22}^1 = \alpha_2^1\frac{\varepsilon(1 + p_{22})}{p_{22}},$$

and similarly, for consumer 2,

$$x_{11}^2 = \alpha_1^2\varepsilon(1 + p_{21}), \quad x_{12}^1 = \alpha_1^2(1 - \varepsilon)(1 + p_{22}),$$

$$x_{21}^2 = \alpha_2^2\frac{\varepsilon(1 + p_{21})}{p_{21}}, \quad x_{22}^2 = \alpha_2^2\frac{(1 - \varepsilon)(1 + p_{22})}{p_{22}},$$

which yield the prices:

$$1 + p_{21} = \frac{1}{(1 - \varepsilon)\alpha_1^1 + \varepsilon\alpha_1^2},$$

$$1 + p_{22} = \frac{1}{\varepsilon\alpha_1^1 + (1 - \varepsilon)\alpha_1^2}.$$

There will be no exchange in securities' markets if the marginal rate of substitution between one unit of security 1 and one unit of security 2 is the same for both agents. However, for agent 1, the marginal utility of one unit of security 1 yielding one unit of good 1 in state 1 and two units of good 1 in state 2 is

$$\frac{1}{2}\alpha_1^1 \frac{1}{x_{11}^1} + \frac{1}{2}\alpha_1^1 \frac{1}{x_{12}^1} \cdot 2.$$

By similar reasoning for each agent and each security, we have the following condition:

$$\frac{\alpha_1^1/2x_{11}^1 + \alpha_1^1/x_{12}^1}{\alpha_2^1/x_{21}^1 + \alpha_2^1/2x_{22}^1} = \frac{\alpha_1^2/2x_{11}^2 + \alpha_1^2/x_{12}^2}{\alpha_2^2/x_{21}^2 + \alpha_2^2/2x_{22}^2}.$$

However,

$$x_{11}^1 = \frac{\alpha_1^1(1-\varepsilon)}{\alpha_1^1(1-\varepsilon) + \alpha_1^2\varepsilon} \qquad x_{21}^1 = \frac{\alpha_2^1(1-\varepsilon)}{\alpha_2^1(1-\varepsilon) + \alpha_2^2\varepsilon},$$

$$x_{12}^1 = \frac{\alpha_1^1\varepsilon}{\alpha_1^1\varepsilon + \alpha_1^2(1-\varepsilon)} \qquad x_{22}^1 = \frac{\alpha_2^1\varepsilon}{\alpha_2^1\varepsilon + \alpha_2^2(1-\varepsilon)},$$

$$x_{11}^2 = \frac{\alpha_1^2\varepsilon}{\alpha_1^1(1-\varepsilon) + \alpha_1^2\varepsilon} \qquad x_{21}^2 = \frac{\alpha_2^2\varepsilon}{\alpha_2^1(1-\varepsilon) + \alpha_2^2\varepsilon},$$

$$x_{12}^2 = \frac{\alpha_1^2(1-\varepsilon)}{\alpha_1^1\varepsilon + \alpha_1^2(1-\varepsilon)} \qquad x_{22}^2 = \frac{\alpha_2^2(1-\varepsilon)}{\alpha_2^1\varepsilon + \alpha_2^2(1-\varepsilon)}.$$

From this it follows that

$$\frac{(\alpha_1^1(1-\varepsilon) + \alpha_1^2\varepsilon)/2(1-\varepsilon) + (\alpha_1^1\varepsilon + \alpha_1^2(1-\varepsilon))/\varepsilon}{(\alpha_2^1(1-\varepsilon) + \alpha_2^2\varepsilon)/(1-\varepsilon) + (\alpha_2^1\varepsilon + \alpha_2^2(1-\varepsilon))/2\varepsilon}$$

$$= \frac{(\alpha_1^1(1-\varepsilon) + \alpha_1^2\varepsilon)/2\varepsilon + (\alpha_1^1\varepsilon + \alpha_1^2(1-\varepsilon))/(1-\varepsilon)}{(\alpha_2^1(1-\varepsilon) + \alpha_2^2\varepsilon)/\varepsilon + (\alpha_2^1\varepsilon + \alpha_2^2(1-\varepsilon))/2(1-\varepsilon)}.$$

For this equilibrium to be a Pareto optimum, it is necessary that the marginal rates of substitution between the contingent goods be equal. For example, equality of these rates for good 1 in state 1 requires

$$\frac{\alpha_1^1/x_{11}^1}{\alpha_1^1/x_{12}^1} = \frac{\alpha_1^2/x_{11}^2}{\alpha_1^2/x_{12}^2}.$$

so that $\varepsilon^2 = (1-\varepsilon)^2$ or $\varepsilon = \frac{1}{2}$. This is precisely the condition for the absence of risk.

Problem 7
Moral Hazard in Insurance

Statement of the Problem

Consider an economy with one period, one good, and a very large number of identical agents so that frequencies and probabilities are equivalent. Each agent is represented by a strictly increasing concave VNM utility function that depends on the states of nature and by an income (in good 1) of $R = 20$. During the period, each agent has an accident that yields a loss of income $L = 5$ with probability π. The risks of individual accidents are independent.

In the absence of an accident, the VNM utility function of the agent is

$$u_1(x) = x.$$

If an accident occurs, utility is given by

$$u_2(x) = 0.$$

1. Determine the egalitarian Pareto optimum for this economy.

2. An insurance contract is defined here as a unit of reimbursement in state 1 costing q per unit. Each agent can buy any amount of insurance denoted by z.

If he does not have an accident, the agent's budget constraint is

$$x_1 = 20 + z - qz \qquad x_1 \geqslant 0.$$

If he has an accident, his budget constraint is written as

$$x_2 = 20 - 5 - qz \qquad x_2 \geqslant 0.$$

Determine the competitive equilibrium, that is, a price q^* such that the profit on insurance contracts is zero and each agent maximizes his expected utility subject to the available contract constraint defined by q^*. Discuss these results.

3. Now suppose that the agents can influence the probability of avoiding an accident by consuming a quantity x_0 of the good (a preventive good). Then let the probability of not having an accident be equal to

$$1 - \pi(x_0) = 0.9 - 0.8e^{-x_0}.$$

Determine the egalitarian Pareto optimum, and show that the competitive equilibrium is not a Pareto optimum. Explain why.

4. Compute the tax that restores the Pareto optimum by using a general equilibrium argument. Do other solutions exist?

Solution

1. There is a proportion π of agents who have an accident. Therefore average societal income is

$$(1 - \pi)20 + \pi(20 - 5) = 20 - 5\pi.$$

The egalitarian Pareto optimum yields ex ante identical income to all those who can profit from it, specifically, those who do not have an accident. This per capital allocation is $(20 - 5\pi)/(1 - \pi)$, and it generates expected aggregate utility equal to $20 - 5\pi$.

2. The zero-profit constraint for insurance is written as

$$qz = (1 - \pi)z$$

because here payment is made to those who do not have an accident. Indeed, if an agent has an accident, he cannot receive any utility from income. From the zero-profit condition, we have $q^* = 1 - \pi$.

The representative agent solves the following problem:

$$\underset{z}{\text{Max}} \ (1 - \pi)(20 + z - (1 - \pi)z)$$

subject to

$$20 - 5 - (1 - \pi)z \geqslant 0,$$

which yields

$$z = \frac{15}{1 - \pi}.$$

This is the maximum amount of insurance that he can buy. In state 1, his income is then equal to

$$20 + \pi z = 20 + \frac{15\pi}{1 - \pi} = \frac{20 - 5\pi}{1 - \pi}.$$

Therefore the competitive equilibrium is a Pareto optimum.

3. Now average societal income is given by

$$20(0.9 - 0.8e^{-x_0}) + 15(0.1 + 0.8e^{-x_0}) - x_0.$$

At the Pareto optimum, everyone who does not have an accident receives the same income. Therefore we have

$$\frac{20(0.9 - 0.8e^{-x_0}) + 15(0.1 + 0.8e^{-x_0}) - x_0}{0.9 - 0.8e^{-x_0}}$$

x_0 is chosen to maximize expected utility, that is, $19.5 - 4e^{-x_0} - x_0$. Hence $x_0 = \text{Log } 4$.

In the competitive equilibrium the typical agent solves the problem

$$\text{Max } x_1(0.9 - 0.8e^{-x_0})$$

subject to

$$x_0 + x_1 = 20 + z - qz,$$

$$x_0 + x_2 = 15 - qz.$$

Obviously, $x_2 = 0$ so that $x_0 = 15 - qz$ and $x_1 = 5 + z$. Then we have the following problem:

$$\underset{x_0}{\text{Max}} \left(5 + \frac{15 - x_0}{q} \right)(0.9 - 0.8e^{-x_0}).$$

The zero-profit condition for insurance requires that

$$q^* = 0.9 - 0.8e^{-x_0^*}.$$

The derivative of the objective function at $x_0 = \text{Log } 4$ is

$$-\frac{0.1}{q^*} + 0.8\left(5 + \frac{15}{q^*} \right) > 0.$$

Therefore in the competitive equilibrium, $x_0^* > \text{Log } 4$. Consequently the equilibrium cannot be a Pareto optimum.

Let x_0^* be the solution to

$$-1 + \left(5 + \frac{15 - x_0}{0.9 - 0.8e^{-x_0}} \right)0.8e^{-x_0} = 0.$$

Therefore at equilibrium we have

$$q^* = 0.9 - 0.8e^{-x_0^*},$$

$$x_2^* = 0,$$

$$x_1^* = 20 - x_0^* + \frac{(0.1 + 0.8e^{-x_0^*})}{(0.9 - 0.8e^{-x_0^*})}(15 - x_0^*).$$

Collective waste occurs because each agent tries to protect himself against an accident (for example, each agent buys his own fire engine when it would be better for society to provide insurance for all). The private gain from spending x_0 is larger than the social benefit.

4. Assume that we levy a proportional tax t on the purchase of the preventive good and then redistribute the tax revenue to those who do not have an accident, using uniform lump-sum transfers T. The optimization problem for the typical agent is then written as

$$\text{Max } x_1(0.9 - 0.8e^{-x_0})$$

subject to

$$(1 + t)x_0 + x_1 = 20 + z - qz + T,$$

$$(1 + t)x_0 + x_2 = 15 - qz,$$

with

$$T = \frac{tx_0^*}{0.9 - 0.8e^{-x_0^*}}.$$

This problem reduces to

$$\text{Max}_{x_0} \left(5 + T + \frac{15 - (1 + t)x_0}{q}\right)(0.9 - 0.8e^{-x_0}).$$

The first-order condition is

$$-\frac{(1 + t)}{q}(0.9 - 0.8e^{-x_0}) + 0.8e^{-x_0}\left[5 + T + \frac{15 - (1 + t)x_0}{q}\right] = 0.$$

The resulting solution is $x_0 = \text{Log } 4$, with an optimal tax $t^* = (30 - 2 \text{ Log } 4)/7$. To be sure, another solution consists of limiting the market for the self-protective good. This example shows that two inefficiencies—constraint on a market and the presence of an external effect—can be better than one.

Supplementary Reading

Helpman, E., and J.-J. Laffont. 1976. "On Moral Hazard in General Equilibrium Theory." *Journal of Economic Theory* 15:8–23.

Problem 8
Asymmetric Information and Anonymity of the Exchange Process

Statement of the Problem

Consider an exchange economy with two goods, an ordinary good (good 1) with its price normalized to 1 and good 2 having variable quality with its price denoted by p. There are two consumers who behave competitively.[1] Consumer 1 has the following utility function:

$$U^1(x_1^1, x_2^1) = x_1^1 + \int_0^{x_2^1} q(t)\, dt$$

where x_1^1 and x_2^1 are the quantities consumed of goods 1 and 2 and $q(t)$ is the density of the quality of units consumed of good 2.

Consumer 1 has four units of good 2 as his only initial endowment. The quality of these units is uniformly distributed over the interval $[0, 2]$. Consumer 2 is unable to discover the quality of these units of good 2 prior to consuming them. However, consumer 1, who is endowed with good 2, knows the quality of each unit. This *information asymmetry* will be exploited in the marketplace by agent 1 supplying the units of lowest quality first. When he sells n units of good 2, he sells the units whose quality lies between 0 and

$$q(n) = \frac{2n}{4} = \frac{n}{2} \qquad n \in [0, 4].$$

Therefore he keeps the higher-quality units for himself.

1. Determine consumer 1's supply function of good 2.
    Consumer 2 has the following utility function:

$$U^2(x_1^2, x_2^2) = x_1^2 + \frac{3}{2} \int_0^{x_2^2} q(t)\, dt$$

where x_1^2 and x_2^2 are the quantities consumed of goods 1 and 2 and $q(t)$ is the density of the quality of the units of good 2. For agent 2, $q(t)$ is a stochastic process. Consumer 2 is assumed to have three units of good 1 as his initial endowment.

2. By assuming that agent 2 maximizes his expected utility and that he thinks that $q(t)$ is a process with mean μ, determine consumer 2's demand function for good 2.

---

1. For simplification, we treat only two agents here, but this model formalizes an economy with a large number of agents.

3.   Determine the market equilibrium for good 2 and then the levels of utility, both ex ante and ex post, prevailing in the competitive equilibrium.

4.   Now suppose that consumer 2 realizes that the higher the price of good 2, the more of it consumer 1 supplies and as a result the higher is the average quality of the offer of good 2. Let $\mu^a(p)$ be his expectation of the average quality as a function of price. Determine the properties of the competitive equilibrium when $\mu^a(p) = p^2$.

5.   Assume that consumer 2's expectation of the average quality of the offer of good 2 is rational—that is, his expectation is equal to the true average quality of the quantity supplied by consumer 1. Determine the properties of this rational expectations equilibrium. Compare the various equilibria obtained with what could be achieved in the absence of informational asymmetries.

6.   Consider a particular form of false advertising. Consumer 1 makes the following false statement:

The true market price of good 2 is 4, our exceptional sale price is $p = 2$. Hurry while the supply lasts!

Assuming that consumer 2 believes this advertisement, determine the supply and demand at a price $p = 2$. Determine the properties of the equilibrium if supply is then rationed at a price equal to 2. What is the optimal sale price for consumer 1?

Solution

1.   Consumer 1 solves the following problem:

$$\text{Max} \left\{ x_1^1 + \int_{4-x_2^1}^{4} \frac{t}{2}\, dt \right\}$$

subject to

$$x_1^1 + p x_2^1 = 4p,$$

which yields a supply function:

$$4 - x_2^1 = 2p \qquad \text{if } p \leqslant 2,$$
$$\qquad\quad = 4 \qquad \text{if } p > 2.$$

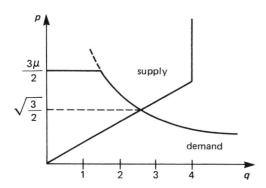

Figure P8.1

2.   Consumer 2 solves the following problem:

$$\text{Max}\left\{x_1^2 + \frac{3}{2}\mu x_2^2\right\}$$

subject to

$$x_1^2 + px_2^2 = 3,$$

which yields

$$x_2^2 = \frac{3}{p} \qquad \text{if } p < \frac{3\mu}{2},$$

$$\in\left[0,\frac{3}{p}\right] \qquad \text{if } p = \frac{3\mu}{2},$$

$$= 0 \qquad \text{if } p > \frac{3\mu}{2}.$$

3.   To determine the market equilibrium for good 2, two cases must be distinguished.

(a) $3\mu/2 \geqslant \sqrt{3/2}$ (figure P8.1)   The intersection occurs on the hyperbolic segment of the demand function so that

$$p^* = \sqrt{\frac{3}{2}} \qquad x_1^{*1} = 3 \qquad x_2^{*1} = 4 - \sqrt{6}$$

$$x_1^{*2} = 0 \qquad x_2^{*2} = \sqrt{6}.$$

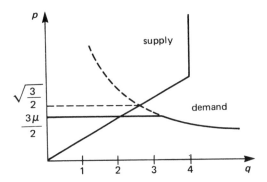

Figure P8.2

The seller's level of utility (ex ante and ex post) is $U^1 = 11/2$. The buyer's ex ante utility level is $U_a^2 = 3\sqrt{3/2}\mu$. Ex post, the true quality for a supply of n will be revealed to be

$$\frac{1}{n}\int_0^n \frac{t}{2}\,dt = \frac{n}{4} = \frac{p}{2},$$

which yields an ex post utility level of $U_p^2 = 9/4 < U_a^2$ because

$$\mu \geqslant \sqrt{2/3}.$$

(b) $3\mu/2 < \sqrt{3/2}$ (figure P8.2)   The intersection occurs on the horizontal section of the demand curve where

$$p^* = \frac{3\mu}{2} \qquad x_1^{*1} = \frac{9\mu^2}{2} \qquad\qquad x_2^{*1} = 4 - 3\mu$$

$$x_1^{*2} = 3 - \frac{9\mu^2}{2} \qquad x_2^{*2} = 3\mu.$$

The seller's utility level (ex ante and ex post) is

$$U^1 = 4 + \frac{9\mu^2}{4}.$$

The buyer's utility levels are

$$U_a^2 = 3,$$

$$U_p^2 = 3 - \frac{9\mu^2}{8}.$$

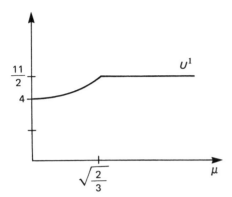

Figure P8.3

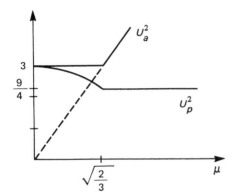

Figure P8.4

We have diagramed the result in figures P8.3 and P8.4.

4.   Let

$P_1 = \{p \colon \frac{3}{2}\mu^a(p) > p\}$,

$P_2 = \{p \colon \frac{3}{2}\mu^a(p) < p\}$.

The buyer's problem is written as

$\mathrm{Max}\,\{x_1^2 + \frac{3}{2}\mu^a(p)x_2^2\}$

subject to

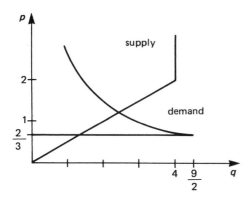

Figure P8.5

$x_1^2 + px_2^2 = 3,$

which yields

$x_2^2 = \dfrac{3}{p}$ if $p \in P_1,$

$\in \left[0, \dfrac{3}{p}\right]$ if $p \notin P_1 \cup P_2, p \geqslant 0,$

$= 0$ if $p \in P_2.$

If $\mu^a(p) = p^2$, we have figure P8.5. We enumerate three equilibria:

(a) $p^* = 0$ $x_2^{*2} = 0$ $U^1 = 4$

                                    $U_a^2 = U_p^2 = 3$

(b) $p^* = \dfrac{2}{3}$ $x_1^{*1} = \dfrac{8}{9}$ $x_2^{*1} = \dfrac{8}{3}$

                 $x_1^{*2} = \dfrac{19}{9}$ $x_2^{*2} = \dfrac{4}{3}$

$U^1 = 4.44$

$U_a^2 = 3$ $U_p^2 = 2.77.$

(c) $p = \sqrt{3/2}$ identical to case a of question 3:

$U^1 = \dfrac{11}{2}$ $U_a^2 = 5.51$ $U_p^2 = \dfrac{9}{4}.$

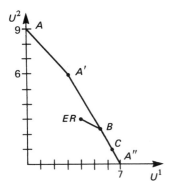

Figure P8.6

5.   If the buyer has rational expectations, his expected average quality is the true average quality, that is, $\mu^a(p) = p/2$. Then there exists a single equilibrium, given by

$$p^* = 0 \qquad x_2^{*2} = 0 \qquad U^1 = 4 \qquad U^2 = 3.$$

From the buyer's perspective, this is the best of the three equilibria obtained in the preceding question.

In the absence of the informational asymmetry, since agent 1 has a marginal rate of substitution between good 2 and 1 that is smaller than the one of agent 2 for an identical quality of good 2, the collective welfare maximum (in a utilitarian sense) allocates the entire quantity of good 2 to agent 2 and makes transfers in good 1. In this way, $U^1 + U^2 = 9$.

In figure P8.6 the frontier of *physically feasible* utilities with complete information, is indicated by $AA'A''$. The point ER corresponds to the rational expectations equilibrium, and the chord ERB is the frontier of ex post feasible utilities when μ varies from 0 to $\sqrt{2/3}$.

Clearly, the informational asymmetry combined with the anonymity of contracts, which itself impedes the use of nonlinear prices, is a hindrance to the realization of mutually advantageous transactions. Moreover, from the utilitarian perspective (ex post), the rational expectations equilibrium is the worst of the equilibria obtained with fixed expectations. The best of these equilibria, equilibrium B, corresponds to expectations such that $\mu \geqslant \sqrt{2/3}$. In this case agent 2 is such an optimist that the spends all his endowment of good 2. Even though he cannot purchase the entire amount of good 2, optimism is beneficial at least according to the utilitarian criterion. This result follows from the fact that in the rational expectations equilibrium, the agents do not internalize the following pecuniary externality. By buying more, an agent increases the price, and as a result the average quality of the good supplied increases.

6.   The consumer believes the advertisement—that is, he interprets the price of 4 to mean a quality of $\mu = 2$ by using his knowledge about the relationship between price and average quality, $\mu(p) = p/2$. Then, at the sale price of 2, he demands $3/2$ (see question 2). At this price of 2, the seller would like to sell 4 so that quantity must be rationed. Specifically,

$$x_1^{*1} = 3 \qquad x_2^{*1} = \frac{5}{2}$$

$$x_1^{*2} = 0 \qquad x_2^{*2} = \frac{3}{2},$$

which yields

$$U^1 = 6.44$$

$$U_a^2 = 4.5 \qquad U_p^2 = 0.84.$$

The seller has succeeded in accentuating his advantage (point C on figure P8.6). Notice that C is still better than ER from the utilitarian perspective. This result is due in part to this particular form of the demand function which yields a constant income of $(3/p) \times p = 3$ to the seller. If he were able to convince the buyer that the quality of the good is μ^*, the seller's maximal price would be $3\mu^*/2$, or here 3. Then we would have

$$x_2^{*2} = 1 \qquad x_2^{*1} = 3$$

$$x_1^{*2} = 0 \qquad x_1^{*1} = 3$$

$$U^1 = 6.75$$

$$U_a^2 = 3 \qquad U_p^2 = \frac{3}{8}.$$

   This problem shows that nonrational expectations can be beneficial ex post for society. However, we should not conclude from this that manipulating expectations is desirable. We must pursue the analysis further by considering the existence of revelation mechanisms that respect the decentralization of information and that permit an improvement, in the Pareto sense, on the rational expectations equilibrium (see chapter 9, or Belloc 1986).

Supplementary Readings

Akerlof, G. A. 1970. "The Market for Lemons: Quality Uncertainty and the Market Mechanism." *Quarterly Journal of Economics* 84:488–500.

Belloc, B. 1986. "Some Normative Aspects of Akerlof's Problem." *Economic Letters* 20:107–110.

Laffont, J.-J. 1975. "Optimism and Experts against Adverse Selection in a Competitive Economy." *Journal of Economic Theory* 10:284–300.

Problem 9
Transmission of Information by Prices

Statement of the Problem

Consider an economy with two goods and a large number of consumers represented by the continuum $[0, 1]$. Consumer $i \in [0, 1]$ has the following utility function:

$$U^i(x_1^i, x_2^i, \theta, \eta^i) = x_1^i + [\theta + \alpha^i \eta^i] x_2^i - \tfrac{1}{2}(x_2^i)^2$$

where x_l^i is the consumption of good l, $l = 1$ and 2. The initial endowments of good 1 and 2 are given by

$$w_1^i > 0, \quad w_2^i > 0.$$

We distinguish three dates

ex ante	interim	ex post
0	1	2

At date zero (ex ante), the stochastic variable $\tilde{\theta}$ is drawn and takes its value θ that is unobservable. At date 1 (interim), each consumer observes an unbiased private signal of θ, given by $\tilde{\eta}^i = \theta + \tilde{\varepsilon}^i$. At date 2 (ex post), all consumers observe θ. Consumption takes place at date 2.

The stochastic variables $\tilde{\theta}$, $(\tilde{\varepsilon}^i)$ are independent. By convention, we assume that

$$\int_0^1 \varepsilon^i \, di = 0 \qquad \int_0^1 (\varepsilon^i)^2 \, di = s^2$$

for all realizations of these processes—that is, we assume that the law of large numbers applies to these processes. Finally, we assume that the process generating the (α^i) is independent of the other processes and that

$$\int_0^1 \alpha^i \, di = 1 \qquad \int_0^1 (\alpha^i - 1)^2 \, di = \sigma_\alpha^2 \qquad \alpha^i \in [0, 2].$$

It follows that

$$\int_0^1 \alpha^i \varepsilon^i \, di = 0.$$

We denote

$$\bar{w}_1 = \int_0^1 w_1^i \, di \qquad \bar{w}_2 = \int_0^1 w_2^i \, di.$$

1. At date 1, consider the intervention of a central planner who implements a revelation mechanism that allows him to discover the decentralized information (η^i).

Consider only anonymous mechanisms of the form

$$x_1^i(\eta^i, \theta), \quad x_2^i(\eta^i, \theta)$$

that specify agent i's consumption if he reports η^i and if the average of the others' reports is θ. Explain why the differential mechanisms that lead agent i to reveal his true η^i are characterized by the following equations (when agent i believes that the others are telling the truth):

$$\frac{\partial x_1^i}{\partial \eta^i}(\eta^i, \theta) + [(\theta + \alpha^i \eta^i) - x_2^i(\eta^i, \theta)] \frac{\partial x_2^i}{\partial \eta^i}(\eta^i, \theta) = 0, \tag{1}$$

$$\frac{\partial x_2^i}{\partial \eta^i}(\eta^i, \theta) \geq 0. \tag{2}$$

Furthermore impose the following physical constraints:

$$\int_0^1 x_1^i(\eta^i, \theta) \, di = \bar{w}_1, \tag{3}$$

$$\int_0^1 x_2^i(\eta^i, \theta) \, di = \bar{w}_2. \tag{4}$$

Determine the competitive equilibrium of the economy when all the consumers are completely informed (that is, consumer i knows η^i and θ). Show that the allocation defined by this equilibrium satisfies (1), (2), (3), and (4). Interpret this result.

2. Now assume that, at date 1, markets for goods 1 and 2 are opened. Determine the rational expectations equilibrium that transmits θ to all the consumers. Why is this equilibrium Pareto optimal?

3. Now consider the case in which there exist two relevant stochastic variables θ_1 and θ_2. Let the utility functions be given by

$$U^i(x_1^i, x_2^i, \theta_1, \theta_2, \eta_1^i, \eta_2^i) = x_1^i + [\theta_1 + \eta_1^i + (\theta_2 + \eta_2^i)\alpha^i] x_2^i - \tfrac{1}{2}(x_2^i)^2.$$

The assumptions are analogous to those made above, in particular,

$$\tilde{\eta}_1^i = \theta_1 + \tilde{\varepsilon}_1^i,$$

$$\tilde{\eta}_2^i = \theta_2 + \tilde{\varepsilon}_2^i.$$

$\tilde{\theta}_1, \tilde{\theta}_2, (\tilde{\varepsilon}_1^i), (\tilde{\varepsilon}_1^i)$ are all independent. Moreover, to permit explicit computations,[1] we assume that

$$\tilde{\theta}_1 \to \mathcal{N}(1, \sigma^2)* \qquad \tilde{\theta}_2 \to \mathcal{N}(1, \sigma^2)$$

$$(\varepsilon_1^i) \to \mathcal{N}(0, s^2) \qquad (\varepsilon_2^i) \to \mathcal{N}(0, s^2) \qquad \forall i.$$

We are looking for price functions of the form

$$p(\theta_1, \theta_2) = \lambda\theta_1 + \mu\theta_2 + \delta$$

that are rational expectations equilibria.

(a)   Determine the joint probability distribution of

$$(\theta_1, \theta_2, p = \lambda\theta_1 + \mu\theta_2 + \delta, \eta_1^i, \eta_2^i).$$

Derive from this, the mean of the conditional distribution of

θ_1, θ_2 given p, η_1^i, η_2^i.

Hint: Let $(\tilde{x}_1, \tilde{x}_2)$ be a vector that is distributed normally with mean μ and variance Σ where

$$\mu = \begin{bmatrix} \mu_1 \\ \mu_2 \end{bmatrix}, \quad \Sigma = \begin{bmatrix} \Sigma_{11} & \Sigma_{12} \\ \Sigma_{21} & \Sigma_{22} \end{bmatrix}$$

and suppose that x_1 and x_2 are also vectors. Then the conditional distribution of $x_1 | x_2$ has as its mean

$$\mu_1 + \Sigma_{12}[\Sigma_{22}]^{-1}[x_2 - \mu_2].$$

(b)   Determine

$$E[U^i(x_1^i, x_2^i, \tilde{\theta}_1, \tilde{\theta}_2, \eta_1^i, \eta_2^i)|p, \eta_1^i, \eta_2^i]$$

that is, the expected utility function when the agent's information consists of $p(\theta_1, \theta_2)$, η_1^i, η_2^i. Use this expected utility function to determine the demand functions. Equate supply and demand on the market for good 2 and, by using $p(\theta_1, \theta_2) = \lambda\theta_1 + \mu\theta_2 + \delta$, obtain an identity in (θ_1, θ_2) that facilitates the computation of λ, μ, δ, to characterize the rational expectations equilibrium. Derive the corresponding allocation. Is it an ex post Pareto optimum?

---

1. $\tilde{x} \to \mathcal{N}(\mu, \sigma^2)$ indicates that the stochastic variable $\tilde{x}$ is distributed normally, with mean μ and variance σ^2.

Solution

1. Faced with the mechanism $x_1^i(\eta^i, \theta)$, $x_2^i(\eta^i, \theta)$, agent i maximizes the following with respect to η^i:

$$x_1^i(\eta^i, \theta) + (\theta + \alpha^i \hat{\eta}^i) x_2^i(\eta^i, \theta) - \tfrac{1}{2}[x^i(\eta^i, \theta)]^2.$$

In this problem we have denoted the true signal observed by agent i as $\hat{\eta}^i$ and assumed that the mean of the signals reported by the other agents is its true value θ. A necessary condition for the true signal to be an optimal response is

$$\frac{\partial x_1^i}{\partial \eta^i}(\eta^i, \theta) + [\theta + \alpha^i \eta^i - x_2^i(\eta^i, \theta)] \frac{\partial x_2^i}{\partial \eta^i}(\eta^i, \theta) = 0. \tag{1}$$

The necessary local second-order condition (concavity at $\eta^i = \hat{\eta}^i$) is written as

$$\frac{\partial x_2^i}{\partial \eta^i}(\eta^i, \theta) \geqslant 0. \tag{2}$$

Then agent i's problem is concave in η^i and (1) and (2) characterize the differential mechanisms that lead agent i to reveal his true signal. For these mechanisms to be feasible, we must have

$$\int_0^1 x_1^i(\eta^i, \theta) \, di = \bar{w}_1, \tag{3}$$

$$\int_0^1 x_2^i(\eta^i, \theta) \, di = \bar{w}_2. \tag{4}$$

To determine the competitive equilibrium of the complete-information economy, we normalize the price of good 1 to be 1 and denote by p the price of good 2. The demand functions of consumer i are obtained by solving the following:

$$\text{Max} \, \{x_1^i + (\theta + \alpha^i \eta^i) x_2^i - \tfrac{1}{2}(x_2^i)^2\}$$

subject to

$$x_1^i + p x_2^i = w_1^i + p w_2^i,$$

which yields

$$x_2^i = \theta + \alpha^i \eta^i - p$$

$$x_1^i = w_1^i + pw_2^i - p(\theta + \alpha^i \eta^i - p).$$

Equality of supply and demand on the market for good 2 yields

$$p = 2\theta - \bar{w}_2$$

from which it follows that

$$x_2^i = \alpha^i \eta^i - \theta + \bar{w}_2, \tag{5}$$

$$x_1^i = w_1^i + (2\theta - \bar{w}_2)(w_2^i - x_2^i). \tag{6}$$

We verify immediately that (5) and (6) satisfy (1), (2), (3), and (4). Therefore the allocation defined by (5) and (6) can be interpreted as being derived from the following incentive mechanism:

Give me your signal; then the mechanism will calculate the mean of the signals, compute the price $p = 2\theta - \bar{w}_2$ and allocate to each agent i the vector of goods that maximizes his utility function (characterized by the parameters given in the responses) subject to his budget constraint.

We have shown that if agent i believes that the others are telling the truth, he will also tell the truth.

2. Competitive markets are opened at date 1. Assume that the price transmits the information θ—that is, it is monotonic in θ. Then each agent has all the information that he needs to behave like he would in the competitive equilibrium of a complete-information economy. From the preceding question, we know that the price function is then given by

$$p(\theta) = 2\theta - \bar{w}_2,$$

which is indeed monotonic in θ. Therefore the fully revealing rational-expectations equilibrium coincides with the competitive equilibrium of the complete-information economy. Since all the agents are completely informed ex post, this allocation is ex post Pareto optimal. Moreover we have shown that it is incentive compatible in a certain sense.

3. We look for affine price functions that are rational expectations equilibria. The joint distribution of

$$(\tilde{\theta}_1, \tilde{\theta}_2, p = \lambda \tilde{\theta}_1 + \mu \tilde{\theta}_2 + \delta, \tilde{\eta}_1^i, \tilde{\eta}_2^i)$$

is distributed normally with mean $[1, 1, \lambda + \mu + \delta, 1, 1]$ and covariance

matrix equal to

$$\Sigma = \begin{bmatrix} \sigma^2 & 0 & \lambda\sigma^2 & \sigma^2 & 0 \\ 0 & \sigma^2 & \mu\sigma^2 & 0 & \sigma^2 \\ \lambda\sigma^2 & \mu\sigma^2 & (\lambda^2+\mu^2)\sigma^2 & \lambda\sigma^2 & \mu\sigma^2 \\ \sigma^2 & 0 & \lambda\sigma^2 & \sigma^2+s^2 & 0 \\ 0 & \sigma^2 & \mu\sigma^2 & 0 & \sigma^2+s^2 \end{bmatrix} = \begin{bmatrix} \Sigma_{11} & \Sigma_{12} \\ \Sigma_{21} & \Sigma_{22} \end{bmatrix}.$$

The mean of the conditional distribution of (θ_1, θ_2), given p, η_1^i, η_2^i, is

$$\begin{bmatrix} 1 \\ 1 \end{bmatrix} + \Sigma_{12}(\Sigma_{22})^{-1} \begin{bmatrix} p - \lambda - \mu - \delta \\ \eta_1^i - 1 \\ \eta_2^i - 1 \end{bmatrix}. \tag{7}$$

The demand functions for agent i, who observes p, η_1^i, η_2^i, are determined from the following problem:

Max $E[U^i(x_1^i, x_2^i, \theta_1, \theta_2, \eta_1^i, \eta_2^i)|p, \eta_1^i, \eta_2^i]$

subject to

$$x_1^i + px_2^i = w_1^i + pw_2^i$$

$$x_2^i = \eta_1^i + \alpha^i\eta_2^i + E[(\theta_1 + \alpha^i\theta_2)|p, \eta_1^i, \eta_2^i] - p.$$

Using (7), we obtain

$$x_2^i = \eta_1^i + 1 + \alpha^i(\eta_2^i + 1) + \frac{(\lambda + \alpha^i\mu)}{\mu^2 + \lambda^2}(p - \lambda - \mu - \delta).$$

$$+ \frac{1}{(\lambda^2+\mu^2)(\sigma^2+s^2)}[\mu\sigma^2(\mu - \lambda\alpha^i)(\eta_1^i - 1) + \lambda\sigma^2(\lambda\alpha^i - \mu)(\eta_2^i - 1)] - p.$$

By equating supply and demand,

$$\int_0^1 x_2^i \, di = \bar{w}_2,$$

and by using $p = \lambda\theta_1 + \mu\theta_2 + \delta$, we obtain the following identity:

$$\theta_1 + \theta_2 + 2 + \frac{(\lambda + \mu)}{(\lambda^2 + \mu^2)}(\lambda\theta_1 + \mu\theta_2 - \lambda - \mu) + \frac{1}{(\lambda^2 + \mu^2)(\sigma^2 + s^2)}$$

$$\cdot [\mu\sigma^2(\mu - \lambda)(\theta_1 - 1) + \lambda\sigma^2(\lambda - \mu)(\theta_2 - 1)] - \lambda\theta_1 - \mu\theta_2 - \delta = \bar{w}_2.$$

A function $p(\theta_1, \theta_2) = \lambda\theta_1 + \mu\theta_2 + \delta$ is therefore a rational-expectations equilibrium if and only if

$$1 + \frac{\lambda(\lambda + \mu)}{\lambda^2 + \mu^2} + \frac{\mu\sigma^2(\mu - \lambda)}{(\lambda^2 + \mu^2)(\sigma^2 + s^2)} - \lambda = 0 \tag{8}$$

$$1 + \frac{\mu(\lambda + \mu)}{\lambda^2 + \mu^2} + \frac{\lambda\sigma^2(\lambda - \mu)}{(\lambda^2 + \mu^2)(\sigma^2 + s^2)} - \mu = 0 \tag{9}$$

$$2 - \frac{(\lambda + \mu)^2}{\lambda^2 + \mu^2} - \frac{(\lambda - \mu)^2\sigma^2}{(\lambda^2 + \mu^2)(\sigma^2 + s^2)} - \delta = \bar{w}_2. \tag{10}$$

The only solution of (8), (9), and (10) is

$$\lambda = \mu = 2$$

$$\delta = -\bar{w}_2.$$

Therefore $p = 2(\theta_1 + \theta_2) - \bar{w}_2$, and the corresponding allocation is

$$x_2^i = \eta_1^i \left[1 + \frac{\sigma^2}{\sigma^2 + s^2} \left(\frac{1 - \alpha^i}{2} \right) \right] + \eta_2^i \left[\alpha^i + \frac{\sigma^2}{\sigma^2 + s^2} \left(\frac{\alpha^i - 1}{2} \right) \right]$$

$$+ \theta_1 \left(\frac{\alpha^i - 3}{2} \right) + \theta_2 \left(\frac{\alpha^i - 3}{2} \right) + \bar{w}_2, \tag{11}$$

$$x_1^i = w_1^i + (2\theta_1 + 2\theta_2 - \bar{w}_2)(w_2^i - x_2^i).$$

Since the utility functions are quasi linear (the marginal utility of good 1 is constant), all the ex post Pareto-optimal (interior) allocations involve consuming the same quantity of good 2. However, by an argument analogous to that in the preceding question, the allocation in the competitive equilibrium of the complete-information economy (which is ex post Pareto optimal) yields

$$x_2^i = \eta_1^i + \alpha^i\eta_2^i - \theta_1 + \theta_2(2 - \alpha^i) + \bar{w}_2. \tag{12}$$

Since (11) differs from (12), the rational expectations equilibrium is not ex post Pareto optimal.

Supplementary Reading

Laffont, J.-J. 1985. "On the Welfare Analysis of Rational Expectations Equilibria with Asymmetric Information." *Econometrica* 53:1–30.

Problem 10
Rational Expectations Equilibrium and Incomplete Markets

Statement of the Problem

Consider an economy with two goods and two competitive consumers. Consumer 1 has preferences represented by the following Cobb-Douglas function:

$$(x_1^1)^\beta (x_2^1)^{1-\beta}$$

and stochastic endowments of good 1 denoted by $\tilde{w}_1^1 > 0$. Consumer 2 likes only good 1. He has a deterministic endowment of good 1 given by w_1^2. Moreover he owns a firm that produces good 2, using good 1 according to the following technology:

$$y_2 = y_1^\gamma \qquad y_1 > 0, 0 < \gamma < 1.$$

The firm is a competitive one.

After the realization of the state of nature that specifies the value taken by the stochastic variable $\tilde{w}_1^1$, competitive markets for goods 1 and 2 are opened. Good 1 is taken to be the numéraire and p the price of good 2. Ex ante, this is a stochastic variable $\tilde{p}$. In the assumed organizational framework the firm must decide upon its production program (y_1, y_2) ex ante. The firm chooses (y_1, y_2) by maximizing the expected value of its profits, given by

$$(E\tilde{p})y_2 - y_1$$

subject to its technical constraints.

1. Determine the rational expectations equilibrium of this economy, that is, the function $p(w_1^1)$ such that if this function is anticipated by the firm, it will make production plans that lead to an ex post price $p(w_1^1)$ if $\tilde{w}_1^1 = w_1^1$.

2. Assume that consumer 2 is risk-neutral. Organize a system of complete ex ante contingent markets by retaining the constraint that the firm's production plan cannot be contingent. Determine the equilibrium prices and the equilibrium allocation; compare these with question 1.

   A numerical example: two states of nature each occurring with probability of $\frac{1}{2}$ and $\beta = \gamma = \frac{1}{2}$, $w_1^1 = 1$, $w_2^1 = 3$, $w_1^2 = 1$. Show that the contingent-market equilibrium is Pareto superior to the rational expectations equilibrium.

Solution

1. The firm maximizes

$$E\tilde{p}y_1^\gamma - y_1,$$

which yields $\gamma y_1^{\gamma-1} = 1/E\tilde{p}$ and $y_2 = (\gamma E\tilde{p})^{\gamma/(1-\gamma)}$. Ex post, consumer i's demands are determined by

$$\text{Max}\,(x_1^i)^\beta (x_2^i)^{1-\beta}$$

subject to

$$x_1^1 + px_2^1 = w_1^1,$$

which yields

$$x_1^1 = \beta w_1^1, \quad x_2^1 = \frac{(1-\beta)w_1^1}{p}.$$

The ex post Walrasian equilibrium is obtained by equating supply and demand on the market for good 2 in the following manner:

$$(\gamma E\tilde{p})^{\gamma/(1-\gamma)} = \frac{(1-\beta)w_1^1}{p} \qquad \forall w_1^1,$$

or

$$p(\gamma E\tilde{p})^{\gamma/(1-\gamma)} = (1-\beta)w_1^1 \qquad \forall w_1^1. \tag{1}$$

If the firm has rational expectations, $E\tilde{p}$ is identical to the expectation of the true price obtained in (1). By taking the expectation in (1), we have

$$\gamma^{\gamma/(1-\gamma)}(E\tilde{p})^{1/(1-\gamma)} = (1-\beta)E\tilde{w}_1^1$$

or

$$(E\tilde{p}) = ((1-\beta)E\tilde{w}_1^1)^{1-\gamma}\gamma^{-\gamma},$$

and by substituting into (1), we calculate

$$p = (1-\beta)^{1-\gamma}\gamma^{-\gamma}w_1^1 \cdot (E\tilde{w}_1^1)^{-\gamma}.$$

2. Now we assume that there exists ex ante a system of contingent prices for the different possible values of the stochastic variable $\tilde{w}_1^1$, which we denote $w_1^1, \ldots, w_1^S$. Let q_s and p_s be the prices of goods 1 and 2 contingent

on state s, and let π_s be the probability of state s expected by all the agents. Consumer 2, who is risk-neutral, solves

$$\text{Max} \sum_{s=1}^{S} \pi_s x_{1s}^2$$

subject to

$$\sum_{s=1}^{S} q_s x_{1s}^2 = \left(\sum_{s=1}^{S} q_s \right) w_1^2 + \text{profit,}$$

which yields

$$q_s = \pi_s \qquad \text{(by the appropriate normalization).} \tag{2}$$

Consumer 1 solves

$$\text{Max} \sum_{s=1}^{S} \pi_s (x_{1s}^1)^\beta (x_{2s}^1)^{1-\beta}$$

subject to

$$\sum_{s=1}^{S} q_s x_{1s}^1 + \sum_{s=1}^{S} p_s x_{2s}^1 = \sum_{s=1}^{S} q_s w_{1s}^1,$$

which yields

$$p_s x_{2s}^1 = \frac{1-\beta}{\beta} \cdot q_s x_{1s}^1. \tag{3}$$

By substituting (3) into the objective function, the problem reduces to

$$\text{Max} \sum_{s=1}^{S} \pi_s \left(\frac{1-\beta}{\beta} \frac{q_s}{p_s} \right)^{1-\beta} x_{1s}^1$$

subject to

$$\sum_{s=1}^{S} \frac{q_s}{\beta} \cdot x_{1s}^1 = \sum_{s=1}^{S} q_s w_{1s}^1,$$

which yields

$$\frac{q_s}{\beta} = \lambda \pi_s \left(\frac{1-\beta}{\beta} \right)^{1-\beta} \left(\frac{q_s}{p_s} \right)^{1-\beta}$$

where λ is a coefficient of positive proportionality, or by using (2), we compute

$$p_s = \lambda^{1/(1-\beta)} \pi_s \left(\frac{1-\beta}{\beta} \right) \beta^{1/(1-\beta)} = \lambda^{1/(1-\beta)} B \pi_s = \tilde{\lambda} B \pi_s \tag{5}$$

with

$$\tilde{\lambda} = \lambda^{1/(1-\beta)}$$

and

$$B = \left(\frac{1-\beta}{\beta} \right) \beta^{1/(1-\beta)}.$$

The firm is constrained to choose the same quantities in all the states of nature, so that it solves

$$\text{Max} \left(\sum_{s=1}^{S} \pi_s p_s \right) y_1^{\gamma} - \left(\sum_{s=1}^{S} \pi_s q_s \right) y_1,$$

which yields

$$y_2 = \left(\gamma \frac{\sum_{s=1}^{S} \pi_s p_s}{\sum_{s=1}^{S} \pi_s q_s} \right)^{\gamma/(1-\gamma)} = (\tilde{\lambda} \gamma B)^{\gamma/(1-\gamma)}.$$

Up to a scalar multiple $\tilde{\lambda}$, prices are determined by (2) and (5). Equality of supply and demand on the market for good 2 and (3) yield

$$\tilde{\lambda} B \cdot (\gamma \tilde{\lambda} B)^{\gamma/(1-\gamma)} = \left(\frac{1-\beta}{\beta} \right) x_{1s}^1,$$

and $\tilde{\lambda}$ is determined by using the budget constraint of consumer 1, that is, equation (4):

$$\tilde{\lambda}^{1/(1-\gamma)} = \frac{(1-\beta) E \tilde{w}_1^1}{\gamma^{\gamma/(1-\gamma)} B^{1/(1-\gamma)}}.$$

The quantity consumed of good 1 by consumer 2 is

$$x_{1s}^2 = w_{1s}^1 - y_1 - x_{1s}^1 + w_1^2.$$

Contrary to the situation in the first question, here consumer 1, who is risk-averse, is completely insured, and his marginal rate of substitution is independent of the state as the following indicates:

$$\frac{\beta \pi_s x_{2s}^1}{(1-\beta) \pi_s x_{1s}^1} = \frac{\beta}{(1-\beta)} \cdot \frac{(1-\beta)}{\beta} \cdot \frac{q_s}{p_s} = \frac{1}{\lambda B}.$$

Problem 11
Futures' Markets and Efficiency

Statement of the Problem

Consider an economy with $T + 1$ periods and a single good. At each date $t = 0, 1, \ldots, T - 1$, there exists a futures' market that delivers the good unconditionally at date T. At date T a spot market also exists. At each date t a certain number of stochastic events occur. We study the behavior of a producer who has the following quadratic utility function:

$$u(W) = -(W - v_0)^2$$

where W is his final wealth, which is his wealth at date T whose expectation at date 0 is v_0. An improvement in his information over time is formalized by a sequence Ω_t of partitions of the set of states of nature Ω leading at date T to the knowledge of the state of nature θ. At date t an element of the partition Ω_t is denoted by ω_t. Let $\mu(.)$ be its prior probability on Ω and $\mu(.|\omega_t)$ be its probability conditional on event ω_t. Finally, the producer knows that at date T he will supply an amount $z(\theta)$ of the good, which, evaluated at the spot market price $p(\theta)$, will yield revenue equal to $v(\theta) = p(\theta) \cdot z(\theta)$.

We study the producer's optimal strategy in futures' markets. An exchange strategy for the producer in futures' markets is a sequence $x = (x_0, x_1, \ldots, x_{T-1})$ where x_t is a mapping of Ω_t into $\mathbf{R}$ that defines the *total* accumulated aggregate sales (positive or negative) to which the producer is already committed at date T for each ω_t. Let $p_t(\omega_t)$ be the price on the futures market if event ω_t occurs at date t.

1. Explain why the wealth of the producer at the final date is given by

$$W(\theta, x) = v(\theta) + \sum_{t=0}^{T-1} [p_t(\omega_t) - p_{t+1}(\omega_{t+1})] x_t(\omega_t).$$

If the prices on futures' markets are determined by the arbitrage of risk-neutral agents who have the same information that the producer considers, show that

$$E_0[W(\theta, x)|\omega_0] = E_0(v(\theta)|\omega_0) \equiv v_0.$$

What would the producer's utility level be at date 0 (and at date T) if we had a system of complete Arrow-Debreu markets at date 0? Using the formula $\operatorname{Var} x = E(\operatorname{Var}(x|y)) + \operatorname{Var}(Ex|y)$, show that

$$E[u(W(\theta, x))|\omega_0] = -\text{Var}[W(\theta, x)|\omega_0]$$

$$= \sum_{t=0}^{T-1} \sum_{\omega_t \in \Omega_t} \mu(\omega_t) \text{Var}[(EW(\theta, x)|\omega_{t+1}|\omega_t]$$

$$= \sum_{t=0}^{T-1} \sum_{\omega_t \in \Omega_t} \mu(\omega_t) \text{Var}[w_{t+1}(\theta, x)|\omega_t]$$

by setting

$$w_{t+1}(\theta, x) = E[W(\theta, x)|\omega_{t+1}].$$

Show that

$$w_{t+1}(\theta, x) \equiv E[W(\theta, x)|\omega_{t+1}]$$

$$= E[v(\theta)|\omega_{t+1}] - p_{t+1}(\omega_{t+1})x_t(\omega_t) + a(\omega_t)$$

where $a(\omega_t)$ depends only on ω_t. Conclude from this that $\text{Var}[w_{t+1}(\theta, x)|\omega_t]$ depends only on $x_t(\omega_t)$.

2.   Using the results of the preceding section, show that the producer's optimal strategy is

$$x_t^*(\omega_t) = \frac{\text{Cov}_t(p_{t+1}, v_{t+1}|\omega_t)}{\text{Var}(p_{t+1}|\omega_t)} \qquad \omega_t \in \Omega_t, t = 0, \ldots, T-1,$$

where $v_{t+1} = E_t(v(\theta)|\omega_t)$. From this, derive the producer's utility level at date 0 for the optimal strategy.

3.   Determine the necessary and sufficient conditions for the producer to attain the same utility level as in the system of complete Arrow-Debreu markets.

4.   When $p(.)$ and $z(.)$ are independent, show that the producer's utility is bounded above by $-E[p(.)|\omega_0]^2 \cdot \text{Var}(z(\theta)|\omega_0)$. What do you conclude from this?

Solution

1.   At date 0 the agent sells (or buys if this quantity is negative) $x_0(\omega_0)$ units of the good for delivery at date T at a price $p_0(\omega_0)$. When date 1 arrives, we assume that he repurchases (or sells if negative) $x_0(\omega_0)$ units of

the good at the date 1 price, that is, $p_1(\omega_1)$, and sells at this price $x_1(\omega_1)$ units of the good for delivery at date T. Therefore, at date 1, his financial situation is characterized by

$$p_0(\omega_0)x_0(\omega_0) + p_1(\omega_1)[x_1(\omega_1) - x_0(\omega_0)].$$

By repeating these operations up to date $T - 1$, his financial situation at date T can be expressed by

$$p_0(\omega_0)x_0(\omega_0) + p_1(\omega_1)[x_1(\omega_1) - x_0(\omega_0)] + \cdots$$
$$+ p_{T-1}(\omega_{T-1})[x_{T-1}(\omega_{T-1}) - x_{T-2}(\omega_{T-2})]$$
$$- p_T(\omega_T)x_{T-1}(\omega_{T-1})$$
$$= \sum_{t=0}^{T-1} [p_t(\omega_t) - p_{t+1}(\omega_{t+1})]x_t(\omega_t),$$

which must be added to his revenue $p(\theta)z(\theta) = v(\theta)$ to obtain his final wealth $W(\theta, x)$.

Arbitrage among risk-neutral agents leads to the following prices

$$p_t(\omega_t) = E_t[p(\theta)|\omega_t] \qquad \forall t, \forall \omega_t.$$

Therefore

$$p_t(\omega_t) - p_{t+1}(\omega_{t+1}) = E_t[p(\theta)|\omega_t] - E_{t+1}[p(\theta)|\omega_{t+1}].$$

Consequently

$$E_0[(p_t(\omega_t) - p_{t+1}(\omega_{t+1}))|\omega_0] = E_0\{[E_t(p(\theta)|\omega_t) - E_{t+1}(p(\theta)|\omega_{t+1}]|\omega_0\}$$
$$= E_0[p(\theta)|\omega_0] - E_0[p(\theta)|\omega_0] = 0.$$

From this we derive

$$E_0[W(\theta, x)|\omega_0] = E_0[v(\theta)|\omega_0] = v_0.$$

If a system of complete markets exists with risk-neutral agents participating in exchange, the producer can insure himself completely at actuarially fair prices. Therefore his utility evaluated at date 0 is $u(v_0) = 0$. By applying the formula given in the statement of the problem, we have

$$\text{Var}[W(\theta, x)|\omega_0] = \text{Var}\, E[W(\theta, x)|\omega_1] + E[\text{Var}\, W(\theta, x)|\omega_1].$$

By definition,

$$E[\text{Var } W(\theta, x)|\omega_1] = \sum_{\omega_1 \in \Omega_1} \mu(\omega_1) \text{Var } [W(\theta, x)|\omega_1]$$

$$\text{Var } [EW(\theta, x)|\omega_1] = \text{Var } w_1(\theta, x).$$

By applying the formula again, we have

$$\text{Var } [W(\theta, x)|\omega_1] = \text{Var } w_2(\theta, x) + \sum_{\omega_2 \in \Omega_2} \mu(\omega_2|\omega_1) \text{Var } [W(\theta, x)|\omega_2].$$

From this we derive

$$\text{Var } [W(\theta, x)|\omega_0] = \text{Var } w_1(\theta, x) + \sum_{\omega_1 \in \Omega_1} \mu(\omega_1) \text{Var } [w_2(\theta, x)|\omega_1]$$

$$+ \sum_{\omega_1 \in \Omega_1} \mu(\omega_1) \left[\sum_{\omega_2 \in \Omega_2} \mu(\omega_2|\omega_1) \text{Var } [W(\theta, x)|\omega_2] \right]$$

$$= \text{Var } w_1(\theta, x) + \sum_{\omega_1 \in \Omega_1} \mu(\omega_1) \text{Var } [w_2(\theta, x)|\omega_1]$$

$$+ \sum_{\omega_2 \in \Omega_2} \mu(\omega_2) \text{Var } [W(\theta, x)|\omega_2].$$

By applying the formula iteratively and by observing that $\text{Var } [W(\theta, x)|\omega_T] = 0$, we obtain

$$\text{Var } (W(\theta, x)|\omega_0) = \sum_{t=0}^{T-1} \sum_{\omega_t \in \Omega_t} \mu(\omega_t) \text{Var } [w_{t+1}(\theta, x)|\omega_t]. \tag{1}$$

Moreover

$$w_{t+1}(\theta, x) \equiv E[W(\theta, x)|\omega_{t+1}]$$

$$= E[v(\theta)|\omega_{t+1}] + \sum_{j=0}^{t-1} [p_j(\omega_j) - p_{j+1}(\omega_{j+1})]x_j(\omega_j) + p_t(\omega_t)x_t(\omega_t)$$

$$- p_{t+1}(\omega_{t+1}) \cdot x_t(\omega_t) + E\left[\sum_{j=t+1}^{T-1} [p_j(\omega_j) - p_{j+1}(\omega_{j+1})]x_j(\omega_j)|\omega_{t+1} \right].$$

However,

$$E[[p_j(\omega_j) - p_{j+1}(\omega_{j+1})]x_j(\omega_j)|\omega_{t+1}] = 0 \qquad \text{if } j \geqslant t + 1,$$

by arbitrage. Therefore

$$w_{t+1}(\theta, x) \equiv E[v(\theta)|\omega_{t+1}] - p_{t+1}(\omega_{t+1}) \cdot x_t(\omega_t) + a(\omega_t)$$

where $a(\omega_t)$ depends only on ω_t.

2. From the preceding section $w_{t+1}(\theta, x)$ depends only on $x_t(\omega_t)$ so that the optimal strategy can be derived by minimizing each term of $\mathrm{Var}\,(W(\theta, x)|\omega_0)$ given by (1):

$$
\begin{aligned}
\mathrm{Var}\,[w_{t+1}(\theta, x)|\omega_t] &= \mathrm{Var}\,[v_{t+1} - p_{t+1}(\omega_{t+1})x_t(\omega_t)|\omega_t] \\
&= E[[v_{t+1} - v_t - (p_{t+1} - p_t)x_t]^2|\omega_t] \\
&= \mathrm{Var}\,(v_{t+1}|\omega_t) - 2\,\mathrm{Cov}\,(p_{t+1}, v_{t+1}|\omega_t)x_t(\omega_t) \\
&\quad + \mathrm{Var}\,(p_{t+1}|\omega_t)x_t(\omega_t)^2.
\end{aligned}
\tag{2}
$$

From (2) it follows that

$$
x_t^*(\omega_t) = \frac{\mathrm{Cov}\,(p_{t+1}, v_{t+1}|\omega_t)}{\mathrm{Var}\,(p_{t+1}|\omega_t)} \qquad \forall \omega_t \in \Omega_t,\ \forall t = 0, \dots, T-1.
$$

By substituting this optimal strategy in (2), we obtain

$$
\mathrm{Var}\,(w_{t+1}|\omega_t) = \mathrm{Var}\,(v_{t+1}|\omega_t) - \frac{\mathrm{Cov}\,(p_{t+1}, v_{t+1}|\omega_t)^2}{\mathrm{Var}\,(p_{t+1}|\omega_t)},
$$

which yields

$$
\begin{aligned}
-\mathrm{Var}\,(W(\theta, x)|\omega_0) &= -\sum_{t=0}^{T-1} E\,\mathrm{Var}\,(v_{t+1}|\omega_t) + \sum_{t=0}^{T-1} E\left(\frac{\mathrm{Cov}\,(p_{t+1}, v_{t+1}|\omega_t)^2}{\mathrm{Var}\,(p_{t+1}|\omega_t)}\right) \\
&= -\mathrm{Var}\,v(\theta) + \sum_{t=0}^{T-1} E\left(\frac{\mathrm{Cov}\,(p_{t+1}, v_{t+1}|\omega_t)^2}{\mathrm{Var}\,(p_{t+1}|\omega_t)}\right).
\end{aligned}
\tag{3}
$$

3. The producer's utility level can be rewritten as

$$
-\sum_{t=0}^{T-1} E\left[\mathrm{Var}\,(v_{t+1}|\omega_t)\left[1 - \frac{\mathrm{Cov}\,(p_{t+1}, v_{t+1}|\omega_t)^2}{\mathrm{Var}\,(v_{t+1}|\omega_t)\cdot\mathrm{Var}\,(p_{t+1}|\omega_t)}\right]\right].
$$

It coincides with the level obtained when there is complete insurance—that is, it equals zero if and only if

$$
\frac{\mathrm{Cov}\,(p_{t+1}, v_{t+1}|\omega_t)^2}{\mathrm{Var}\,(v_{t+1}|\omega_t)\cdot\mathrm{Var}\,(p_{t+1}|\omega_t)} = 1 \qquad \forall t,
$$

in other words, if p_{t+1} and v_{t+1} conditional on ω_t are perfectly correlated. For example, if the producer faces no uncertainty about the quantities ($z_t = \bar{z}\ \forall t$), $v_{t+1} = \bar{z}p_{t+1}$ and the above condition is satisfied.

The above condition is also satisfied if the vector (p_{t+1}, v_{t+1}) can take only two values conditional on ω_t. Then we say that the information is binomial. Therefore, if the information arrives rather slowly in relation to the frequency of trading on the futures' market, it is possible to insure oneself completely by trading only on the futures' market.

4. If $p(\theta)$ and $z(\theta)$ are independent, by letting

$$z_t = E(z(\theta)|\omega_t) \qquad \forall t,$$

$$\operatorname{Var}(v_{t+1}|\omega_t) = z_t^2 \cdot \operatorname{Var}(p_{t+1}|\omega_t) + E(p_{t+1}^2|\omega_t)\operatorname{Var}(z_{t+1}|\omega_t).$$

The equation follows from applying the formula $\operatorname{Var} XY = EX^2 \operatorname{Var} Y + EY^2 \operatorname{Var} X$ when X and Y are independent. Moreover we have

$$\operatorname{Cov}(p_{t+1}, v_{t+1}) = z_t \cdot \operatorname{Var}(p_{t+1}|\omega_t).$$

Therefore

$$EU = -\sum_{t=0}^{T-1}\left\{E\left(\operatorname{Var}(v_{t+1}|\omega_t) - \frac{\operatorname{Cov}(p_{t+1}, v_{t+1}|\omega_t)^2}{\operatorname{Var}(p_{t+1}|\omega_t)}\right)\right\}$$

$$= -\sum_{t=0}^{T-1} E(E(p_{t+1}^2|\omega_t) \cdot \operatorname{Var}(z_{t+1}|\omega_t))$$

$$= -\sum_{t=0}^{T-1} E(p_{t+1}^2|\omega_0)E\operatorname{Var}(z_{t+1}|\omega_t).$$

However,

$$p_1 = E(p(\theta)|\omega_1),$$

$$p_0 = E(p(\theta)|\omega_0),$$

which yields $E(p_1|\omega_0) = p_0$. By Jensen's inequality,

$$p_0^2 \leqslant E(p_1^2|\omega_0).$$

Now, by continuing iteratively, we have

$$p_0^2 \leqslant E(p_{t+1}^2|\omega_0).$$

Consequently we have

$$EU \leqslant -p_0^2 \cdot \operatorname{Var}(z(\theta)|\omega_0).$$

Therefore it appears that regardless of the frequency of trading, if $p(.)$ and $v(.)$ are independent, expected utility cannot approach the level of perfect insurance.

Supplementary Readings

Nermuth, M. 1983. "On the Inefficiency of Incomplete Markets." W. P. University of Vienna.

Kreps, D. 1982. "Multiperiod Securities and the Efficient Allocation of Risk." In J. McCall (ed.), *The Economics of Information and Uncertainty*. NBER.

Problem 12
Incentive Contracts between Firms and the Government

Statement of the Problem

The government wants to arrange the production of a public good by a firm having the following cost function:

$$c = (\beta - e)q$$

where q is the quantity of the public good produced, β is a parameter, and e is the level of effort supplied by the firm's manager. If t is the payment from the government to the firm, the manager's utility level is

$$t - c - \psi(e)$$

where $\psi(e)$ is the manager's disutility of effort with

$$\psi' > 0, \quad \psi'' > 0, \quad \text{and} \quad \psi''' > 0.$$

Let $\bar{u}$ the manager's reservation utility level below which he refuses to work for the government. Let $S(q)$ be the gross consumer surplus associated with a quantity q of the public good. The opportunity cost of public expenditure is given by $1 + \lambda$ (with $\lambda > 0$ because of the indirect taxes used to finance the public good). Net consumer surplus is therefore

$$S(q) - (1 + \lambda)t.$$

1. By assuming that the government uses the utilitarian criterion (in other words, it maximizes the sum of the utilities of the consumers and the manager) and that it has complete information on all the variables, determine the government's optimal policy. (Assume that $1 + \lambda < -S'' \cdot \psi''$.)

2. Now assume that the government does not know β and cannot observe e. The government has a uniform prior probability distribution on β over the interval $[\underline{\beta}, \bar{\beta}]$ with $\bar{\beta} - \underline{\beta} = 1$, and it observes the cost ex post. Solve for e as a function of c, q, β, and substitute this into $\psi(.)$. Show that we are faced again with a pure adverse selection problem where the payment is t, the actions are q, and $\bar{c} = c/q$.

Characterize the revelation mechanisms that lead the manager to reveal the true value of his parameter β, and determine the optimal mechanism for an utilitarian government. (We shall use the manager's utility level as a state variable in the appropriately defined optimal control problem.)

Show that we can write the payment in the following form:

$$(1 - k(\beta))(c - c^a(\beta)) + G(\beta)$$

where $c^a(\beta)$ is the reported cost. Discuss this result.

3.   If we have a stochastic error term $\tilde{\varepsilon}$ with zero mean added to the cost, show that the formula obtained in question 2 which is linear in $c - c^a(\beta))$ is still appropriate to achieve the optimal policy.

4.   Consider another firm, firm 0, with the parameter $\beta_0 \in (\underline{\beta}, \bar{\beta})$. Assume that this parameter is known to the government and that the firm's cost function is given by $c = (\beta_0 - e)q$. Assume that the new firm's manager has the same disutility of effort ψ as the manager in firm β considered above. Reconsider the conditions in question 2.

Now the revelation mechanism consists of a payment $t(\beta)$, a quantity $q(\beta)$, an average cost $\bar{c}(\beta)$, and a value $\beta^*(\beta)$ above which firm β is rejected and the contract is given to firm 0. Determine the optimal mechanism and determine which firm it favors (the relationship between $\beta^*(\beta)$ and β_0) compared with the complete information case. Discuss these results.

Solution

1.   The objective function of a utilitarian government is

$$S(q) - (1 + \lambda)t + t - c - \psi(e) = S(q) - c - \psi(e) - \lambda t.$$

The government maximizes this function with respect to e, q, and t subject to the manager's individual rationality constraint which is written as

$$t - c - \psi(e) \geqslant 0.$$

The first-order conditions for this problem are

$$S'(q) = (1 + \lambda)(\beta - e), \tag{1}$$

$$\psi'(e) = q, \tag{2}$$

$$t = c + \psi(e). \tag{3}$$

It is necessary to satisfy the manager's individual rationality constraint with equality because the payment made to the manager is socially costly $(\lambda > 0)$. We must equate the marginal utility of the project to its marginal cost, including the financial costs (equation 1), and we must equate the manager's marginal disutility of effort to his marginal utility (equation 2).

2. $e = \beta - \bar{c}$ with $\bar{c} = c/q$. The manager's objective function is written as

$$t - \bar{c}q - \psi(\beta - \bar{c}).$$

Therefore we have an adverse selection problem, with a payment t and *two* action variables q and $\bar{c}$. We consider the revelation mechanism characterized by

$$t(.), \quad q(.), \quad \text{and } \bar{c}(.).$$

To induce truthful revelation, we must have

$$\frac{dt}{d\beta} = \frac{d}{d\beta}(\bar{c}(\beta)q(\beta)) - \psi'(\beta - \bar{c})\frac{d\bar{c}}{d\beta}. \tag{4}$$

From chapter 10, sufficient conditions are then

$$\psi''\frac{d\bar{c}}{d\beta} \geqslant 0 \quad \text{or} \quad \frac{d\bar{c}}{d\beta} \geqslant 0.$$

We will neglect this second-order condition for now, but we will verify later on that it is indeed satisfied. The profit of manager β is

$$\pi(\beta) = t(\beta) - \bar{c}(\beta)q(\beta) - \psi(\beta - \bar{c}(\beta)).$$

By using (4), we have

$$\dot{\pi}(\beta) = -\psi'(\beta - \bar{c}(\beta)) < 0.$$

Therefore the individual rationality constraint ($\pi(\beta) \geqslant 0$) needs to be imposed only at $\bar{\beta}$. Moreover the government's objective function can be written as

$$S(q) - (1 + \lambda)(\bar{c}q + \psi(\beta - \bar{c})) - \lambda\pi.$$

Therefore the government's optimization problem is

$$\text{Max} \int_{\underline{\beta}}^{\bar{\beta}} [S(q(\beta)) - (1 + \beta)(\bar{c}(\beta)q(\beta) + \psi(\beta - \bar{c}(\beta))) - \lambda\pi(\beta)] \, d\beta$$

subject to

$$\dot{\pi}(\beta) = -\psi'(\beta - \bar{c}(\beta)) \qquad (\mu),$$

$$\pi(\bar{\beta}) = \bar{u}.$$

The Hamiltonian for this problem is

$$H = S(q(\beta)) - (1 + \lambda)(\bar{c}(\beta)q(\beta) + \psi(\beta - \bar{c}(\beta)) - \lambda\pi(\beta))$$
$$- \mu(\beta)\psi'(\beta - \bar{c}(\beta)).$$

Pontryagin's principle yields

$$\dot{\mu}(\beta) = -\frac{\partial H}{\partial \pi} = \lambda, \tag{5}$$

$$S'(q) = (1 + \lambda)\bar{c}, \tag{6}$$

$$\psi'(\beta - \bar{c}) = q - \frac{\mu}{1 + \lambda}\psi''(\beta - \bar{c}), \tag{7}$$

$$\mu(\underline{\beta}) = 0 \qquad \text{(transversality condition)}. \tag{8}$$

By integrating (5) and using (8), we have $\mu(\beta) = \lambda(\beta - \underline{\beta})$, and the equations that determine q and $\bar{c}$ are written as

$$S'(q) = (1 + \lambda)\bar{c},$$

$$\psi'(\beta - \bar{c}) = q - \frac{\lambda(\beta - \underline{\beta})}{1 + \lambda}\psi''(\beta - \bar{c}).$$

As figure P12.1 indicates, the level of production is lower with incomplete information (for the same value of β) and the average cost is higher. In essence, the firm now receives additional profit (monopoly rent), and to attenuate this cost, the government reduces the level of output.

The payment is determined by solving (4), which may be rewritten as

$$\frac{dt}{d\beta} = \frac{d}{d\beta}c(\beta) - \frac{\psi'(\beta - \bar{c}(\beta))}{q(\beta)}\frac{dc(\beta)}{d\beta} + \frac{\psi'(\beta - \bar{c}(\beta))\bar{c}(\beta)}{q(\beta)}\frac{dq}{d\beta}.$$

The solution of this differential equation is

$$t(\beta) = [1 - k(\beta)]c(\beta) + F(\beta),$$

with

$$k(\beta) = \frac{\psi'(e(\beta))}{q(\beta)}$$

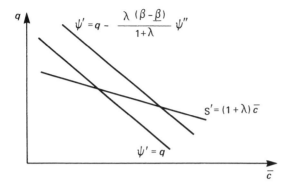

Figure P12.1

and

$$F(\beta) = \int \left\{ \frac{\psi'(\beta - \overline{c}(\beta))\overline{c}(\beta)}{q(\beta)} \frac{dq}{d\beta}(\beta) + c(\beta)\frac{d}{d\beta}\left(\frac{\psi'(e(\beta))}{q(\beta)}\right) \right\} d\beta.$$

The boundary condition is

$$t(\overline{\beta}) = c(\overline{\beta}) + \psi(\overline{\beta} - \overline{c}(\overline{\beta})) + \overline{u}.$$

By definition, let

$$c^a(\beta) = \overline{c}(\beta)q(\beta);$$

therefore

$$t(\beta) = (1 - k(\beta))(c(\beta) - c^a(\beta)) + G(\beta),$$

with

$$G(\beta) = F(\beta) + (1 - k(\beta))c^a(\beta).$$

3. If $\tilde{c} = (\beta - e)q + \tilde{\varepsilon}$ where $\tilde{\varepsilon}$ has zero mean, the payment,

$$\tilde{t}(\beta) = (1 - k(\beta))(\tilde{c}(\beta)) - c^a(\beta)) + G(\beta)$$

where $c^a(\beta)$ should be interpreted as the reported expected average cost, induces the manager to reveal his true β. Indeed, since he is risk-neutral, his expected utility is equivalent to the utility considered in the preceding question.

The formula obtained indicates that the divergence between ex post observed cost and reported cost is shared between the government and the manager, using the coefficient $1 - k(\beta)$. If $\beta = \underline{\beta}$, $\psi'(\beta - \overline{c}(\beta)) = q$ so that $1 - k = 0$ since $k(\beta) = 1$. Consequently we have a fixed price contract. Here the idea is to encourage the better manager to perform at a higher level of effort by making him bear all the cost of not doing so. If $k = 0$, we have a cost plus contract in which the manager is fully reimbursed for all his costs. For some $\beta > \underline{\beta}$, we have an *incentive* contract with $1 - k$ between 0 and 1.

4. If the contract is awarded to firm 0, the government can impose on the manager the complete-information effort level that we derive in question 1 because the firm's cost is observable and its parameter β_0 is known. Therefore we have

$$S'(q_0) = (1 + \lambda)(\beta_0 - e_0),$$

$$\psi'(e_0) = q_0.$$

Here social welfare according to the utilitarian criterion is

$$S(q_0) - (1 + \lambda)(c_0 + \psi(e_0))$$

with

$$c_0 = (\beta_0 - e_0)q_0.$$

Let $\beta^*(\beta)$, $q(\beta)$, $c(\beta)$, and $t(\beta)$ characterize the revelation mechanism. If $\beta < \beta^*(\beta)$, the first-order condition for firm β is the same as in question 2. If $\beta > \beta^*(\beta)$, the firm is indifferent among all the responses because it does not receive the contract. The manager's utility level must be continuous in β to ensure global incentive compability so that

$$\pi(\beta^*(\beta)) = \overline{u}.$$

Therefore we have the same incentive conditions as in question 2, with $\beta^*(\beta)$ replacing $\overline{\beta}$. Expected social welfare is then

$$\int_{\underline{\beta}}^{\beta^*(\beta)} [S(q(\beta)) - (1 + \lambda)(\overline{c}(\beta)q(\beta) + \psi(\beta - \overline{c}(\beta))) - \lambda\pi(\beta)] \, d\beta$$

$$+ [\overline{\beta} - \beta^*(\beta)][S(q_0) - (1 + \lambda)(\overline{c}_0q_0 + \psi(e_0))]. \tag{9}$$

The government maximizes (9) subject to the following constraint:

$$\dot{\pi}(\beta) = -\psi'(\beta - \overline{c}(\beta)).$$

To conditions (5), (6), (7), and (8), add the following condition obtained from

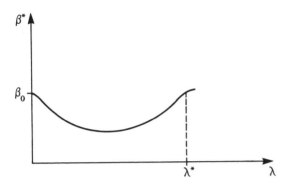

Figure P12.2

maximizing (9) with respect to β^* subject to the above constraint:

$$S(q(\beta^*)) - (1 + \lambda)(\bar{c}(\beta^*)q(\beta^*) + \psi(\beta^* - \bar{c}(\beta^*))) - \lambda\pi(\beta^*)$$

$$= S(q_0) - (1 + \lambda)(\bar{c}_0 q_0 + \psi(e_0)). \tag{10}$$

If $\lambda = 0$, we have $\beta^* = \beta_0$. By differentiating (10) with respect to β^* and λ and by using the first-order conditions, we obtain

$$-\left[\psi'(\beta^* - \bar{c}(\beta^*)) + \lambda(\beta^* - \beta)\psi''(\beta^* - \bar{c}(\beta^*))\frac{d\bar{c}}{d\beta}\right]d\beta^*$$

$$= d\lambda[\pi(\beta^*) + \bar{c}(\beta^*)q(\beta^*) + \psi(\beta^* - \bar{c}(\beta^*)) - (\bar{c}_0 q_0 + \psi(e_0))]. \tag{11}$$

At $\lambda = 0$,

$$\frac{d\beta^*}{d\lambda} = -\frac{\pi(\beta_0)}{\psi'(e_0)} < 0.$$

In the neighborhood of $\lambda = 0$, $d\beta^*/d\lambda < 0$.

By *reductio ad absurdum* we show that β^* cannot again become equal to β_0.

If such were the case, for example, at λ^*, we would require that $d\beta^*/d\lambda \geqslant 0$ (see figure P12.2). However, at such a point, the total cost $c + \psi$ is necessarily higher because of incomplete information. Therefore from (11), $d\beta^*/d\lambda < 0$, which establishes the contradiction.

Consequently, in this arrangement, we favor firm 0 since it performs better when marginal costs are identical because it does not suffer from adverse selection problems.

Supplementary Readings

Guesnerie, R., and J.-J. Laffont. 1984. "Control of Public Firms under Incomplete Information." *Journal of Public Economics* 25:329–369.

Laffont, J.-J., and J. Tirole. 1986. "Using Cost Observation to Regulate Firms." *Journal of Political Economy* 94:614–641.

EXERCISES WITHOUT SOLUTIONS

Exercise 1
Input Choice under Uncertainty

Consider a producer having a production function $\tilde{y} = a\tilde{x}$, where a is the level of input and $\tilde{x}$ is a stochastic variable. The input is purchased (before knowing the value of $\tilde{x}$) at a price w, and the output is sold at a price p. The producer has a VNM utility function u, with $u' > 0$ and $u'' < 0$.

1. If the coefficient of absolute risk aversion of u is decreasing in income, show that the demand for the input is a decreasing function of the price of the input.

2. Now assume that the producer has a very large initial income so that bankruptcy problems may be ignored. Show that the optimal level of a is positive if and only if $E\tilde{x} > w/p$. Assume that the coefficient of relative risk aversion of $u(.)$ is decreasing and greater than 1. Then show that an increase in the riskiness of $\tilde{x}$ in the Rothschild-Stiglitz sense increases the demand for the input.

Exercise 2
The Choice of a Risky Portfolio

Consider an agent who has an initial wealth w. He can invest a part A (and a proportion a) in a risky asset, yielding a stochastic return given by $\tilde{r}$. Assume that the remainder of this wealth is held as money earning no return.

1. When his VNM utility function is

$$u(R) = -\alpha R^2 + \beta R \qquad \alpha > 0, \beta > 0,$$

where R in his final wealth, determine the coefficients of risk aversion for this function. By assuming here, and in what follows, that the maximum is an interior one, show that the optimal value of A decreases with w, increases with β, and decreases with α.

2. When the VNM function is $u(R) = -e^{-\gamma R}$, determine the coefficients of risk aversion and show that the optimal value of A is independent of w and decreases with γ. When $\tilde{r}$ is distributed normally with mean μ and variance σ^2, show that the optimal value of A is increasing in μ and decreasing in both γ and σ^2.

3. When the VNM function is $u(I) = kI^k$ for $0 < k < 1$ or $u(I) = \text{Log}\,I$, determine the coefficients of risk aversion and show that the optimal level of a is independent of w.

Exercise 3
Risk Aversion and a Measure of Risk

Consider a firm that produces a single good, using labor according to the technology $f(l)$. The wage w and the price p are determined competitively. At the moment when the firm chooses l, assume that w is known but that the price is unknown and represented by the stochastic variable $\tilde{p}$. The entrepreneur determines l by maximizing:

$$Eu(\tilde{p}f(l) - wl)$$

where $u(.)$ is the VNM utility function of the firm ($u' > 0$ and $u'' < 0$). Let l_u be the solution to this problem. Define the certainty equivalence price p_u as the solution to

$$u(p_u f(l(p_u)) - wl(p_u)) = Eu(\tilde{p}f(l_u) - wl_u)$$

where $l(p_u)$ maximizes $p_u f(l) - wl$.

1. Show that $p_u < E\tilde{p}$. If some utility function u_1 has an absolute aversion to risk greater than that of some other utility function u_2 at every point, show that

$$p_{u_1} < p_{u_2}.$$

2. If $\tilde{p}$ is subjected to an increase in riskiness in the Rothschild-Stiglitz sense, show that p_u decreases.

Exercise 4
The Demand for Information

An investor having initial wealth w can invest either in money (a safe asset returning the principal only with certainty), or in a risky asset yielding a stochastic per dollar total return $\tilde{r}$ that is equal to either r_1 or r_2, with $r_1 < 1 < r_2$. To determine his portfolio, the investor maximizes his expected income. In the absence of information, his expectations are represented by his prior distribution, which has the following probabilities:

$\pi_1 = \Pr(\tilde{r} = r_1), \quad \pi_2 = \Pr(\tilde{r} = r_2).$

We assume that $r_1 \pi_1 + r_2 \pi_2 > 1$.

It is possible to purchase information of varying dependability. The information structure in which θ is characterized by the conditional probability distribution $f^\theta(y|r)$ (that is, the signal y_i forecasts the return r_i) can be summarized by the matrix

$$\begin{bmatrix} \phi(\theta) & 1 - \phi(\theta) \\ 1 - \phi(\theta) & \phi(\theta) \end{bmatrix}; \quad \tfrac{1}{2} \leqslant \phi(\theta) \leqslant 1.$$

$\theta = 0$ corresponds to information with zero content so that $\phi(\theta) = \tfrac{1}{2}$. Moreover $\phi'(\theta) > 0$, and $\lim_{\theta \to \infty} \phi(\theta) = 1$. Assume that the cost of obtaining information θ is $p\theta$, with $p > 0$.

1. For each value of θ, determine the posterior distribution on $\tilde{r}$ denoted $v^\theta(r|y_i)$ for $i = 1$ and 2. For each value of the signal, determine the optimal risky investment and the expected value of final wealth $V(\theta, p, y_i)$. Then determine the value of information θ, net of the cost $p\theta$, denoted $V(\theta)$.

2. Show that $V'(0) < 0$. Find the conditions under which $\theta = 0$ is optimal.

3. If the optimal level of θ is positive, show that the following must hold:

$$\frac{\partial \theta}{\partial p} < 0 \quad \text{and} \quad \frac{\partial \theta}{\partial w} > 0.$$

Exercise 5
General Equilibrium under Uncertainty

Consider an economy with one good and I consumers. The VNM utility function of consumer i is written as

$$-e^{-a^i x^i} \qquad i = 1, \ldots, I,$$

where x^i is his consumption. There are two possible states of nature and consumer i has endowments w_s^i in state s where $s = 1$ and 2 and $i = 1, \ldots, I$. All the consumers consider the occurrence of state s to have the same probability π_s for $s = 1$ and 2.

1. Compute the Arrow-Debreu equilibrium with a system of complete contingent goods. Normalize the prices so that $p_1 + p_2 = 1$.

2. How are the equilibrium prices affected by an increase in the coefficient of absolute risk aversion for consumer i?

3. Verify that $p_2/p_1 < \pi_2/\pi_1$ if $w_2 = \sum_i w_2^i > w_1 = \sum_i w_1^i$. Now assume that I is very large so that we may neglect, in a first approximation, the effects on the prices of the following changes: if the coefficient of absolute risk aversion of consumer i increases, show that the expected value of his consumption given by $\bar{x}^i = \pi_1 x_1^i + \pi_2 x_2^i$ decreases but that the distribution of $x_1^i - \bar{x}^i$, $x_2^i - \bar{x}^i$ becomes less risky in the Rothschild-Stiglitz sense.

Exercise 6
Evaluation of Assets in a Stationary Environment

Consider an economy with one good and a single consumer who represents a large number of identical agents. The representative consumer maximizes:

$$E \sum_{t=0}^{\infty} \beta^t U(c_t)$$

where c_t is his consumption at date t and β is a discount factor. The good can be produced by J production units, the output of each being exogenous at date t and given by

$$y_t^j \qquad j = 1, \ldots, J.$$

The distribution of the vector $y_t = (y_t^1, \ldots, y_t^J)$ is stationary and characterized by the distribution function $F(y_t)$,

$$F(y_t) = \Pr(\tilde{y}_t \leqslant y_t).$$

Ownership shares of the production units are exchanged in a stock market. Let v_t^j be the price of firm j's stock at date t, and let $z_t = (z_t^1, \ldots, z_t^J)$ be the vector of stock shares held by the consumer.

Since the problem is a stationary one, we look for a stationary equilibrium. Here a Radner equilibrium is a price function $v(y)$ and a valuation function $U(z, y)$ such that

(i) $U(z, y) = \text{Max}_{x, \theta} \{u(x) + \beta \int U(\theta, y') \, dF(y')\}$

subject to

$$x + v(y)\theta \leqslant yz + v(y)z \qquad x \geqslant 0,$$

(ii)   for any y, $U(\mathbf{1}, y)$ is attained by $\theta = \sum_j y^j$ and $\theta = \mathbf{1}$ (with $\mathbf{1} = [1, \ldots, 1]'$)

1.   Why do you think that this definition is appropriate?

2.   Assume the existence of a unique equilibrium and make all the appropriate differentiability assumptions. By using the envelope theorem, show that

$$\frac{\partial U(z, y)}{\partial z_i^j} = u'(x)[y^j + p^j(y)].$$

Conclude from this that, at the equilibrium, we have the following stochastic Euler equation:

$$u'\left(\sum_i y^i\right)p^j(y) = \beta \int u'\left(\sum_i y'^i\right)(y'^j + p^j(y'))\,dF(y') \qquad \forall y.$$

3.   Consider the particular case of a linear utility function.

4.   Consider the particular case of a single asset. Show that

$$p'(y) = p(y)\left(\frac{-U''(y)}{U'(y)}\right).$$

Interpret this result.

5.   Show that it is not the differences in prices $v_{t+1}^j - v_t^j$ but rather the expression

$$w_{t+1}^j = \beta u'\left(\sum_j y_{t+1}^j\right)(y_{t+1}^j + v_{t+1}^j) - u'(\sum y_t^j)v_t^i$$

that exhibits the martingale property, namely,

$$E[w_{t+1}^j \mid \text{the information at date } t] = 0.$$

Discuss this result.

Supplementary Reading

Lucas, R. 1978. "Asset Prices in an Exchange Economy." *Econometrica* 46:1429–1446.

Index